Sir Thomas Beecham

The Man and the Music

Sir Thomas Beecham

The Man and the Music

ALAN BLACKWOOD

EBURY PRESS
London

First published 1994

1 3 5 7 9 10 8 6 4 2

Editor: Elisabeth Ingles
Jacket design: David Fordham

First published in the United Kingdom in 1994 by
Barrie & Jenkins Limited, an imprint of Ebury Press,
Random House, 20 Vauxhall Bridge Road, London SW1V 2SA

Random House Australia (Pty) Limited
20 Alfred Street, Milsons Point, Sydney,
New South Wales 2061, Australia

Random House New Zealand Limited
18 Poland Road, Glenfield
Auckland 10, New Zealand

Random House South Africa (Pty) Limited
PO Box 337, Bergvlei, South Africa

Random House UK Limited Reg. No 954009

A CIP catalogue record for this book
is available from the British Library

ISBN 0 09 178434 4

Printed in Great Britain by Clays Ltd, St Ives plc

Editor's note

A word of explanation about the titles of operas, ballets and other works may be helpful to the reader. Throughout Beecham's career it was quite usual for him to give operas in English, and their English titles are billed in programmes and prospectuses alongside works in the original. For the sake of consistency, however, and as a help to the reader who wishes to consult reference books, we have decided to give all titles in the original if they are French, German, Italian or Spanish. We have followed *The New Grove* in this, and in using English translations for works in Russian, Czech and other less familiar languages. A translation, where necessary, is given in parentheses at the first or most important reference to the piece; thereafter the original title is used.

A distinction is made between such works as Rimsky-Korsakov's *The Golden Cockerel*, written and first performed in Russia, and Stravinsky's *Le Sacre du Printemps*, created for a French-based company and first given in Paris. Role names are given as they appear in the original libretto, unless they are discussed in a non-operatic context (as Sophocles' Electra).

Introduction

Sir Thomas Beecham, conductor, founder of orchestras, concert and opera impresario, died in 1961. Those who knew him are a dwindling band. Even those who saw him conduct must now be mostly in their fifties, or older. All the stories about him, the witty or outrageous things he is supposed to have said and done, are beginning to fade. What remains is infinitely more important.

He was the last great musical amateur, using that word in its traditional sense of somebody with the money and the opportunity to indulge his love of music. He went through a fortune doing it. He was, by the same token, the last great outsider. No one today, in any sphere of activity, could go their own way as he did, creating so much that was entirely in his own image. Toscanini called him a *pagliaccio*, a clown. The two men were poles apart. Toscanini, risen from the orchestral ranks, was the dedicated martinet, the man who said of orchestras, 'they won't play well for you unless they hate you'. No wonder he could not understand the flamboyant Beecham, the maverick entrepreneur as much as the unconventional and sometimes quixotic musician. Indeed, the world has grown too small, or too closely-knit, or perhaps too tame, for people of Beecham's stamp.

For sixty years this supremely gifted amateur, with the intellect, energy and flair of twenty other men, was at the centre of British musical life. Looking beyond the British Isles, he drew into his orbit many of his greatest contemporaries, in music and the allied arts. He resurrected Mozart and blew the dust off Handel. He was among the first to champion Berlioz. He promoted Richard Strauss and Stravinsky when they were still shockingly modern. He cherished the music of another outsider, Delius. He was a pioneer of recording and of broadcasting. He travelled the world. His career probably impinged upon more aspects of this century's music – not to mention its social history and its politics – than that of any other single person.

Thomas Beecham was born, it could be said, with the proverbial silver spoon in his mouth, in St Helens, Lancashire (now Mersey-side), on 29 April 1879. His grandfather, also Thomas, had, some thirty-five years earlier, opened a chemist's shop in Wigan and patented the famous little pill that was to make the family fortune. His father Joseph was already a very rich man. When Thomas junior was six years old, the family moved from St Helens to nearby Huyton, to a grandly appointed house and garden, complete with conservatory, called Ewanville. Thanks to Joseph's own liking for music, the house had two pianos, a two-manual organ (in the billiards room), and a Swiss-made Orchestrion, the last word in mechanical instruments, with a repertory of Beethoven, Mozart, Rossini, Verdi and Wagner.

The child Thomas started piano lessons at six, making his first public appearance at a local concert two years later, playing from memory pieces he heard on the Orchestrion. At about the same time, so it is reported, he could recite almost the whole of *Macbeth* – even stronger evidence of an already prodigious memory. He also learnt chess, studying and remembering, move by move, many famous games. Education at a local boarding school (where on one occasion he played percussion with a visiting contingent of the Hallé Orchestra) was punctuated by frequent trips in the family landau to neighbouring Liverpool, to concerts and opera perfor-mances by the visiting Carl Rosa Company. Pietro Mascagni's *Cavalleria Rusticana*, then a contemporary work, was the piece that really bowled over the twelve-year-old Thomas. He bought the vocal score and soon learnt to play it by heart at the piano. The only kind of music he could not stand, apparently, was that of brass bands, an aversion (surprising perhaps in a north-countryman) he never overcame.

With his teens, thanks to his generally indulgent father, Thomas's horizons broadened ever more rapidly. He went on holidays to France, Switzerland and Scandinavia (few young people in the 1890s even got to the seaside). He accompanied his father on a business trip to New York, Boston and Niagara. He spent a year and a half at Oxford, playing sport, studying intermittently, going off again, this time to Germany and Italy, in search of more music and adventure. He returned to Huyton on the assumption that he would, sooner or later, settle down and enter the family business. He did take a nominal position in the firm, while giving most of his energies to music. He founded the St Helens Orchestral Society, comprising around fifty players, with a nucleus of professionals from Liverpool and Manchester, bolstered by competent locals. For their first concert, Thomas directed them in Mendelssohn's D minor piano concerto and *Ruy Blas* overture, Rossini's *Guillaume Tell* overture, and one of Grieg's *Peer Gynt* suites, a comparatively modern piece. He shared the conducting at a second, combined concert with the local choral society, when he gave an account of Beethoven's First Symphony.

These events, notable enough in themselves, were very soon eclipsed by the installation of his father as mayor of St Helens. Joseph had taken the bold step of engaging, for an inaugural concert in the Town Hall, the Hallé Orchestra of Manchester with their prestigious German conductor Dr Hans Richter, who twenty-three years before had directed the first complete *Ring* cycle at Bayreuth. Then Richter bowed out. Thomas instantly offered to take his place, claiming that he already knew the planned programme by heart. Joseph agreed, and, what was more surprising, persuaded the orchestra to fall in with the idea. The concert duly took place, after one rehearsal, on 6 December 1899. Wagner's *Die Meistersinger* overture opened it. Beethoven's Fifth Symphony and the march from Tchaikovsky's recently composed 'Pathétique' Symphony followed, as well as some operatic arias sung by a highly regarded young American soprano, Lillian Blauvelt, who had missed the rehearsal but whom Thomas accompanied without apparent mishap. Even allowing for the fact that the orchestra knew most of the music, it was a remarkable triumph for the young man.

Some of his comments, made afterwards to a local newspaper reporter, are just as interesting. Asked about his training and experience, he mentioned, among other things, his debt to Dr John Varley Roberts, organist and choirmaster at Magdalen College, Oxford, who had given him some private and informal instruction. 'Then,' he said, 'I have travelled a good deal on the Continent, heard all the best orchestras, mixed with the members and the conductors personally and picked up hints from them. In that way you hear good things. Mixing with conductors and experienced and eminent artists is of great value to one.' He also said, 'I have drifted into conducting because I am fond of it.' To another question he replied, 'I was going to take a musical degree last year, but I was not so well at the time. I may take one, but I am not in a hurry. I can try any time I choose to go up for an examination. A degree is useful but, of course, nothing very wonderful.'

So Thomas Beecham junior, with that studied insouciance that was already a part of him, summed up his already astonishing if rather haphazard and self-indulgent musical life. He was twenty years old, and in a few days' time the bells would ring in the twentieth century.

CHAPTER ONE

Das Land ohne Musik – 'The Land Without Music': that was how musically-minded Germans once viewed the British Isles. What they really meant was that Britain had no music of its own. It was all imported, and most of it from them. It must be admitted that from the time of Handel's arrival in London from Germany in 1710, through the period of Haydn's two triumphant visits, Weber's success at Covent Garden, to Queen Victoria's and Prince Albert's lionisation of Mendelssohn and beyond, this was broadly true. During a period of close on two hundred years, from the death of Purcell in 1695, there is hardly one British composer whom most of us can readily call to mind (Thomas Arne, perhaps William Boyce). Towards the end of the nineteenth century, Hubert Parry, Charles Villiers Stanford and Arthur Sullivan (the last two Anglo-Irish) were doing something to restore the balance, but by training and inclination they were still strongly Teutonic. Likewise, German or Austrian conductors and pianists dominated British concert life. Hans Richter in Manchester was one example among many. Aspiring young native-born musicians often assumed German-sounding names to help their careers (unless they were singers, in which case an Italian one might be more useful).

By the start of the new century, however, such a musical scenario was complicated by politics. The German Empire under Bismarck was the new industrial giant of Europe. It was also carving out a colonial empire in Africa. The two older colonial powers, Britain and France, somewhat to the surprise of both, were being drawn together in the face of this threat. Most Britons still felt closer to the German people. Alas, the latter were also deemed to be arrogant, and they were swamping the market with manufactured goods which should, by rights, have been British-made. They were also building dreadnoughts, an unthinkable challenge to the Royal Navy and the Empire. The French, of course, had already had a nasty taste of German military prowess in 1871, with the Franco-Prussian War. So Edward VII was dispatched to Paris, and with champagne and cigars the *entente cordiale* was born.

The young Thomas Beecham, very presciently, echoed something of all this. Some of his wittiest remarks reflect his lifetime antipathy towards a large part of the German-speaking musical repertory. Bach was 'too much counterpoint, and what is worse, Protestant counterpoint!' The last movement of Beethoven's Choral Symphony was composed 'by a kind of Mr Gladstone of music'. In one movement of a Bruckner symphony he detected 'six pregnancies and at least four miscarriages'. Such comments may have been made with a twinkle in his eye, but Beecham was seldom merely flippant. What he clearly disliked was, as he saw or heard it, the element of metaphysics or of moral edification in much Teutonic music. Beethoven 'was the first cause of disruption of music's natural style and speech'. For him, 'music should release us from the tyranny of conscious thought'. It should, 'first and last, sound well, should allure and enchant the ear, never mind the inner significance'.

This opposition, almost from the start of his career, to the staple Anglo-Saxon diet of the Three Bs (Bach, Beethoven, Brahms) did not automatically put him in the same camp as Cecil Sharp, the young Ralph Vaughan Williams and Gustav Holst, who, in the early years of this century, were leading the revival of English folk and other indigenous music. Two things, Beecham said, he would never do: commit incest and go morris dancing! He did, admittedly, take an early interest in English Tudor music, helping his friend the choral conductor and musical historian Charles Kennedy Scott form the Oriana Madrigal Society, writing some scholarly notes on pieces by John Wilbye, William Byrd, Thomas Tomkins, Orlando Gibbons, Thomas Weelkes, Thomas Morley and others, even singing bass in some of their early performances. (Some years later Beecham met the celebrated French scholar and teacher Nadia Boulanger, who kept alive his interest in madrigals, especially those of Claudio Monteverdi.) But while Scott was truly committed to English music, later joining the composer Rutland Boughton in his efforts to create a centre for English opera at Glastonbury, Beecham's tastes were much more Latin and Gallic than English and nationalist, inclining to French elegance and charm, Italian warmth and lyricism. ('I would give the whole of Bach's Brandenburg Concertos for Massenet's *Manon*,' he said on one occasion, 'and would think I had vastly profited by the exchange.') The newer Russian school, brazen and exotic, also appealed to him. These inclinations, almost uncannily reflecting the change in the political weather, set him apart from many of his contemporaries.

In 1900, though, he was not yet sure what musical path to follow. Despite his precocious triumph with the Hallé Orchestra, he toyed with the idea of further piano studies. He thought, too, about composition. He had shown some very early composition sketches to Dr Roberts while still at Oxford. More recently he had been encouraged in this direction by Frederic Austin, a young composition teacher in Liverpool, who was later to work closely with him as a singer and also a manager. A family crisis erupted at this point. His mother, Josephine, a delicate and hypersensitive woman, had developed some nervous disorder, and his father had placed her in a mental home. Thomas bitterly objected and immediately left Ewanville for London. Sooner or later he must have made the move in any case.

The world's largest city, as it then was, the hub of empire, was still pretty much as portrayed in the famous Victorian painting by John O'Connor looking down Pentonville Road to the smoky gothic outline of St Pancras station. Smoke there certainly was, from millions of chimneys, from the great railway stations and yards, from workshops and gasworks, from the cranes and derricks loading and unloading the ships along the miles of docks stretching down the estuary from Tower Bridge, from all the ships and tugs themselves. Smoke was what made London notorious for its fogs and smogs, captured in evocative paintings by Claude Monet. Soot encrusted its stone monuments in a gloomy magnificence. By contrast, the sun of imperial splendour was at its very zenith, the scarlet and the gold, the plumed hats, the gleam of breastplates, captured this time in sound by Elgar's *Cockaigne* overture. But through the swagger of the music comes also the faint snatch of a Salvation Army band, the organisation born in that same city, among the mean and miserable streets where Jack the Ripper had so recently stalked.

Beecham already had in London someone to whom he could turn, Dr Charles Welles, an American friend of the family, now in the diplomatic service and living in Kensington. (Thomas was to marry his daughter Utica three years later.) Meanwhile, with composition in mind, he first approached Charles Stanford, then the doyen among British composers. Stanford was professor of composition at the Royal College of Music, across the road from the Royal Albert Hall, and the teacher of, among others, Vaughan Williams and Arthur Bliss. He referred Beecham to a colleague, the organist and composer Dr Charles Wood, and for two years the young man studied some of the elements of composition with him. At the same time, he completed an opera, *Marmion*, to his own libretto, based on a novel by Sir Walter Scott. This, in itself, was a considerable achievement. It is of special interest because, although he may not have appreciated this at the time, it added to Beecham's training and experience as a conductor. In the vain hope of getting it staged, he took his score along one day to the offices of the Imperial Grand Opera Company, housed in the Old Vic Theatre in the Waterloo Road. In his memoirs, *A Mingled Chime*, Beecham gives an amusing account of what followed. He waited for a long time outside the manager's office, where auditions were being held. Finally, he says, he heard shouting from within, and the manager, Kelston Trueman ('portly and choleric'), came rushing out to ask if anyone could play on the piano, from memory, excerpts from Gounod's *Faust*. A lady auditioning for the role of Marguerite had failed to bring her music. Beecham saved the day, then raised the matter of his own opera. 'Good God!' cried the flabbergasted Trueman, 'what an idea!' But he instantly hired the young composer of *Marmion* as accompanist and assistant conductor for the forthcoming season.

The Imperial Grand Opera Company was not quite as grand as its name. The star of the season was Blanche Marchesi, a well-known French soprano. Beecham recalls another singer, Marie Duma, as giving the best performance of Leonora in *Il Trovatore* that he ever heard. Otherwise, he gives us a picture of the less glamorous side to London's theatrical life around the turn of the century, as the company moved from theatre to theatre, from Stratford in the east, with its sprawling railway works, across the river to New Cross, not far from the Surrey Commercial Docks, on to what were then the more genteel purlieus of Brixton, Clapham and back over the river to Fulham. The chorus and orchestra were sad, old and weary, the latter, as he puts it, with reference to the pubs en route, only too willing 'to take a bar's rest'. So too were costumes and scenery, patched up, painted over, pressed into service for almost every production. 'Sometimes', he said of their gaslit performances of *Faust* and *Carmen*, before rows of empty seats, 'I would feel a touch of astonishment that we had an audience at all for the motley kind of entertainment we were offering, and at others an uncomfortable twinge of conscience, as if I were an accomplice in some rather discreditable racket.'

Beecham married Utica in 1903, and with composition still in mind set off with his bride to the continent, not, as nearly all his compatriots would have done, to Berlin, Leipzig or Vienna but, in line with his already well-formed musical tastes, to France. In Paris, as in London, he went straight to the top, to André Messager, composer of such charming and popular operettas and ballets as

Véronique and *Les Deux Pigeons*. Messager was also eminent as a conductor and had recently been involved with a real musical landmark, directing the première of Debussy's opera *Pelléas et Mélisande*. Messager, like Stanford in London, passed him on, this time to Moritz Moszkowski, German-Polish composer of the popular *Spanish Dances* for piano duet and a piano concerto in E major with a finale every bit as catchy as the better known Scherzo from Henry Litolff's *Concerto-Symphonique* No. 4. At his own suggestion, Beecham orchestrated short pieces in the style of different composers, a clever if unorthodox way of learning orchestration, and one which seems to have given Moszkowski much amusement. From Paris he proceeded in the summer of 1904 to Italy, to seek advice from the librettist Luigi Illica and no less a figure than Giacomo Puccini, on his ideas for an opera based on the life of the Elizabethan playwright Christopher Marlowe. Illica, apparently, introduced him in a letter to Puccini as 'Signor Tom Beecham, a little Englishman with a nervous facial twitch and a chronic sniff'. The composer, then in the throes of revising *Madama Butterfly* after its initial flop, took very little notice of Beecham, while showing more interest in his lovely young wife. It seems, however, that Illica did provide Beecham with some sort of draft libretto, and the audacious 'little Englishman' then retired with Utica to a spot by Lake Lucerne to work on his score, and, incidentally, teach himself the trombone, sitting in a boat in the middle of the lake. *Christopher Marlowe* fizzled out. The manuscripts of both that and of *Marmion* were lost, and, as Beecham said in *A Mingled Chime*, he prayed that they might never be found again.

During this time Utica gave birth to their first son, Adrian, and on her parents' advice stayed in Italy through the winter of that year while Beecham returned to London. Conducting, after all, was to be his vocation. London's concert life around the turn of the century may not have been quite the cornucopia it is today, but it was as lively as that of anywhere in the world. The Royal Philharmonic Society's annual concerts went back to the time of Beethoven. There had also been, until recently, the German-born Sir George Henschel's own season of concerts, and the popular concerts of Sir August Manns (also German by birth) in the Crystal Palace, the huge iron and glass structure moved from Hyde Park to Sydenham in south London soon after the Great Exhibition of 1851. These had ended; but other things were happening in their place. In 1893, the Queen's Hall opened its doors for the first time. This new concert hall was situated just north of Oxford Circus, across the road from All Souls, Langham Place (and subsequently from Broadcasting House). The main auditorium, grand and ornate with its mirrors and potted palms, seated close on 2500, and it remained London's premier concert hall up to the night it was bombed, 11 May 1941. In 1895 the Queen's Hall manager, Robert Newman, with his resident conductor Henry Wood, set the seal on its success with the launching of their famous Promenade Concerts (though these were not the first to be so named). A number of other, smaller concert or recital rooms kept it company. The Steinway Hall in Wigmore Street had opened in grand style in 1878 with a concert given by Hans von Bülow. Alas, it was badly damaged during the Second World War and then demolished. In 1901 it was joined by the rival Bechstein Hall just down the road, adjoining that company's showrooms, which was noted for an excellent acoustic and gorgeous *art nouveau* decor. During the First World War this changed management and altered its Germanic name to the Wigmore Hall; as such it still flourishes, a favourite venue for artists making their London début. There was also the Aeolian Hall in New Bond Street, opened in 1904 and boasting an organ. This was later taken over by the BBC and used by them for various purposes until 1975.

A few words about the Queen's Hall Orchestra itself will give us an interesting, behind-the-scenes picture of London's musical life at this time. Its members were basically freelance. They were paid according to their attendance, so much for rehearsals, so much for an actual concert. This left them free to take other engagements, for example, to play at the many private functions, dances and balls, receptions, recitals and soirées, that enlivened Edwardian London society. Indeed, if some more lucrative work of that sort clashed with an orchestral rehearsal, even a concert, they might try to find somebody to stand in for them. Thus at concerts it was not unusual to find some members of the orchestra who had not rehearsed the music, while others were not there at all. Being without the security of full-time employment, they saw nothing wrong with this. Wood, on the other hand, was keen to introduce new, often difficult music into his programmes, requiring plenty of rehearsal with everybody present. So he announced one day that the deputy system, as it was called, must end, whereupon a large number of his players walked out. Very soon afterwards they formed themselves into their own self-governing London Symphony Orchestra, giving their first concert, conducted by the ubiquitous Hans Richter, at the Queen's Hall in June 1904.

These new concert halls and new orchestras provided the background to Beecham's London conducting début (leaving aside his efforts with the Imperial Grand Opera Company), and the real start to his career. He began in the way he meant to carry on, by hiring about forty members of the Queen's Hall Orchestra and the Bechstein Hall. His programme was quite extraordinary for the time – indeed, for almost any time. During his stay in Paris, seeing Messager and Moszkowski, he had attended a performance of André Grétry's best-known opera, *Richard Coeur de Lion* (first produced in 1784), and was enchanted by it. It confirmed him in his taste for both French and Italian music, and for music of the classical eighteenth and early nineteenth centuries. He then spent much of his remaining time in Paris browsing round second-hand bookshops and in the Bibliothèque Nationale, digging out more music by Grétry himself and many of his French and Italian contemporaries: Luigi Boccherini, François-Adrien Boieldieu, Luigi Cherubini, Domenico Cimarosa, Nicolas Dalayrac, Nicolò Isouard, Etienne Méhul, Pierre-Alexandre Monsigny, Giovanni Paisiello, Niccolò Zingarelli. So it was that he chose the music of some of these relatively obscure composers, rather than more popular pieces, for his début. He also included one modern piece, Cyril Scott's *The Ballad of Fair Helen of Kirkconnel* for baritone and orchestra (featuring Beecham's friend from Liverpool, Frederic Austin). Scott, born the same year as Beecham, became known as 'the English Debussy', on account of his harmonies and generally impressionistic musical style, and was a big name in British music through the first half of this century. Scott, incidentally, also took a fashionable interest in the occult, publishing a number of books on the subject, including *Music, Its Secret Influence*. Later in life he cut a remarkable figure, like a character out of *The Tales of Hoffmann*, with his long white hair, black cloak, black fedora hat and cane. He died in 1970.

The concert took place in December 1905. The unknown young conductor and his esoteric programme did not cause much of a stir. One lukewarm notice in *The Times* said the Queen's Hall players were insubordinate to Mr Beecham, meaning, presumably, that they didn't take much notice of him. Still, he was on his way.

CHAPTER TWO

When Beecham was a young man, conductors were still a comparatively recent breed, which had sprung up during the early years of
the nineteenth century in response to the growing complexity,
expressive range and larger orchestras of romantic music, and the
need for a single person to impress his interpretation upon a work.
At first, conducting was still in the hands of the composers themselves, where previously they had led performances of their own
music from the harpsichord or the first desk of the violins. Weber,
Mendelssohn, Ludwig Spohr (reputedly the first to use a proper
baton), Berlioz, Verdi and Wagner all engaged in it. The idea of the
virtuoso conductor, of someone specialising in the art or technique
of conducting, began with Hans von Bülow, the apostle first of
Wagner (directing the premières of *Tristan und Isolde* and *Die
Meistersinger von Nürnberg*) and then of Brahms. The first generation of conductors to follow him were still in their prime when
Beecham made his professional début.

It did not need the critic of *The Times* to tell him that he still had
much to learn. In *A Mingled Chime* he readily confesses that he
failed, on that first occasion in the Bechstein Hall, to draw from the
players the effects he wanted. In search of further enlightenment,
he went on a kind of crash course of concert-going, hoping to learn
something from other more professional conductors. This seems to
have depressed him even more. Questions of interpretation apart,
he was, like Henry Wood, dissatisfied with standards of orchestral
playing. The brass, he noted, were too strident and obtrusive one
minute, then failed to deliver just when they were needed. The
strings were either too shrill or too flaccid. Overall there was
seldom the balance, the crispness, the euphonious blend of sound
he heard in his inner ear. He wondered, at first, if the fault lay with
him, since audiences and critics alike seemed, on the whole, well
satisfied with what they heard. Like many true artists in their
formative period, he knew what he wanted, but not yet how to
achieve it.

Then he had the break all artists need, no matter how great their natural talents. It came about, indirectly, through the activities of the Sunday Orchestral Society, an instrumental group which was giving a short season of Sunday afternoon chamber concerts at the Coronet, a little theatre in Notting Hill, west London. The concerts failed commercially, but the group, which included such excellent players as the clarinettist Charles Draper and the horn-player Aubrey Brain (later principal horn of the BBC Symphony Orchestra and father of Dennis), liked playing together and formed a committee in the hope that they might organise other events. They had also heard of Mr Thomas Beecham, heir to a family fortune and aspiring conductor. So it was that Charles Draper was deputed to take the train out to Beecham's new home, at Borehamwood in Hertfordshire. The two men went for a walk across the fields to talk things over, found, according to the story, not one but three horseshoes, and taking this as a happy omen, decided then and there to plan a new concert series, backed by Beecham.

So the Sunday Orchestral Society was reborn as the New Symphony Orchestra, though at the outset with fewer than forty players, with young Mr Beecham at the helm. Now, with a group of generally excellent and sympathetic musicians at his disposal, he could start working towards the kind of standards and style he had in mind, and begin also to shape his own conducting manner and technique. 'All you have to do,' he replied in that lordly manner of his years later, when asked how he achieved such beautiful orchestral tone, 'is select the finest players . . . and you let them play.' Beecham certainly was at the opposite end of the spectrum from those conductors who work over every detail of a score at rehearsal, so that the actual performance is more or less a formality. He could leave many options open at rehearsal, often playing through a whole piece with hardly any comment, trusting to his flair and sense of occasion to bring it alive in performance. On the other hand, he would sometimes take infinite trouble shaping a particular phrase at rehearsal, then at the actual performance would allow his players the time and freedom to render the passage as though it were quite spontaneous. In other words, he did not drill them. He sensed what they could do. This ability to lift players out of themselves – something that we shall return to later in this narrative – could also apply to the music. Critics sometimes said that Beecham was the finest conductor of second-rate music, meaning that he could astonish and delight everybody by giving a generally underrated or neglected piece an unexpected beauty or charm. Of course, behind all the flamboyance of his rostrum manner, those quick and elegant flicks of the wrist, the wild punches into the air, the sudden glances from his darting eyes, sometimes the impulsive shout, lay sheer, unremitting hard work. He often sat up all night, working over his scores, marking them bar by bar with his meticulous blue-pencilled dynamics (including the famous 'hairpins' indicating gradations of volume), or marking up string parts with the bowing best suited to his phrasing.

With his New Symphony Orchestra Beecham again booked the Bechstein Hall, this time for a series of four concerts between November 1906 and January 1907. He was in exalted company. Programmes for the winter of 1906–7 include the names of Ferruccio Busoni, the great intellectual among pianists, with his editions ranging from Bach to Liszt and his own compositions of an awesome size and complexity; Camille Saint-Saëns, most versatile and by that time most venerable French composer of his age; the Spanish violin virtuoso Pablo Sarasate; the Hungarian violinist Joseph Joachim and the German clarinettist Richard Mühlfeld, both close associates of Brahms; the eccentric Russian pianist Vladimir de Pachmann; the French baritone Victor Maurel, who created for Verdi the roles of Iago and Falstaff. The eye is attracted by other names, such as the pianist Gertrude Peppercorn and the Nora Clench string quartet, who may have been quite brilliant in their day. And there among them all, the famous and the forgotten, on the cover to the programmes of the New Symphony Orchestra, is a photograph of the twenty-seven-year-old Mr Thomas Beecham, dark hair neatly parted, gazing out from the past, so it would seem, a little plaintively. In fact, he was clearly not asking for any favours. Undeterred by his début, or by any doubts raised by his new business manager, Leslie Hibberd, he filled his programmes with more music from the eighteenth century, ranging from Mozart's Clarinet Concerto and Haydn's 'Drum Roll' Symphony (No. 103 in E flat) to more pieces by those lesser-known French and Italian composers already mentioned. Another rarity was a symphony in D major by Carl Philipp Emanuel Bach, now considered the most original of J. S. Bach's sons, but not given much attention in 1906.

Beecham put a good case for his choice of programmes, in that relaxed and orotund way of his that could conceal a burning enthusiasm. In the programme prospectus he wrote:

> Though these concerts are devoted mainly to the works of eighteenth-century masters – rarely and in many cases never performed – they are not in any sense meant to be historical

or 'antiquarian'. If it is remembered that it was no uncommon thing for a composer of the period to turn out in the course of his career some fifty or sixty operas (without taking into consideration other branches of composition) and that the number of these composers is almost bewilderingly numerous, it may be safely affirmed that there is a considerable quantity of fine and interesting music which, for no fault of its own, has dropped out of the ordinary orchestral repertoire. One of the chief causes for this has been the disappearance of the original publishing house, with the resultant difficulty and sometimes impossibility of procuring scores and parts. Consequently, with plenty of good modern works near at hand and easy of access, the attention of both performer and public has been diverted from these productions of an earlier age. This is a matter for genuine regret, and it is the aim of the giver of these concerts to show that they possess all the elements of freshness, charm, and originality that characterize this springtime period of modern orchestral writing, and that they amply justify their revival.

He was years ahead of his time, though, as we shall see later, he had little sympathy with the much broader movement for the revival of old music and its 'authentic' performance, which has so changed musical practice and taste during the last thirty years.

Some of the press notices were encouraging. 'Mr Beecham', wrote the critic of the *Morning Post*, 'proved himself an excellent conductor, sensitive and alert.' The C. P. E. Bach symphony was 'played with great precision and go under Mr Beecham's vigilant guidance'. The same critic added, 'One cannot but feel grateful to those who strike out on a path of their own.' Such initiative, as Mr Hibberd no doubt feared, was not rewarded at the box office, and the final concert was cancelled. Undismayed, Beecham set about increasing the strength of the New Symphony Orchestra to around eighty musicians. The great builder of orchestras was flexing his muscles. He was also showing a flair for publicity. He wrote frequent letters to the press and published provocative articles, and more pictures of him appeared in newspapers, magazines and on posters, with his dark, still youthful good looks, a mesmeric gaze, and a beard. This was a great time for beards, notably on the rostrum, ranging from Richter's facial sporran to Artur Nikisch's more dashing trim *à la* d'Artagnan. Beecham favoured the latter. In fact, he looked quite like Nikisch, another of that illustrious band of German-speaking conductors (though born in Hungary), and to some extent, took his appearance as a model.

His first series of three concerts with the augmented New Symphony Orchestra took place in the Queen's Hall in the late autumn of 1907. He was clearly out to challenge the Queen's Hall and London Symphony orchestras, and the primacy of Richter, Nikisch and Wood. They were remarkable events in several respects. There was, to begin with, Beecham's adventurous programme building. French music was again strongly featured, though this time more up to date. There were two works by Vincent d'Indy, pupil of César Franck, founder of the Paris *Schola Cantorum* for the revival and study of old church music, but a supporter also of Wagner and Debussy. These were his 'symphonic legend' *La Forêt enchantée*, and the second of three *Wallenstein* 'symphonic overtures'. Edouard Lalo, another influence on d'Indy, was represented by his Symphony in G minor. Apart from French works there were Smetana's *Šárka*, a movement from his cycle of symphonic poems *Má Vlast* ('My Country'); Beecham's erstwhile teacher Charles Wood's *Symphonic Variations on an Irish Air*; and Mahler's Fourth Symphony, with Blanche Marchesi (of Imperial Grand Opera Company days) singing the soprano part in the last movement. Beecham conducted very little Mahler over the years: he was not in sympathy with what he regarded as Mahler's emotional over-indulgence. But even those who may feel the same way usually have a soft spot for the child-like radiance of the Fourth Symphony. In any case, in 1907 it was still a tricky and substantial modern work for Beecham to tackle.

At these concerts he also presided over two notable débuts. The fifteen-year-old Hungarian-born Joseph (billed as Joska) Szigeti, soon to become one of this century's leading violinists, played both the Tchaikovsky Concerto and J. S. Bach's in E major. Myra Hess, two years older, played Beethoven's fourth and Saint-Saëns's fourth piano concertos. Despite her German-sounding name, Myra Hess was born in London and earned great fame and affection during the Second World War with her recitals at the National Gallery. She also made a well-known piano arrangement of the chorale with counter-melody from Bach's Church Cantata No. 147, known in English as 'Jesu, Joy of Man's Desiring'.

Szigeti and Myra Hess both had good press notices. Beecham himself was again praised for his enterprising programmes. The concerts could be deemed a success. The most significant event, however, took place off stage. At the end of the first concert, Beecham was visited in his dressing-room by a composer of whom he knew little or nothing up to that moment. Indeed, the composer was better known in Germany than in England, thanks largely to the efforts of a provincial opera house conductor, Fritz Cassirer, who had recently presented his opera *A Village Romeo and Juliet* in Berlin. He and Cassirer had come to London primarily to hear the Queen's Hall and London Symphony orchestras, and were pleasantly surprised to find a third excellent orchestra on the scene. They now wondered whether the New Symphony Orchestra might play for them. Beecham, on his side, was impressed by his visitor. 'His features', he recalled of that first meeting, 'had that mingled cast of asceticism and shrewdness one mentally associates with high-ranking ecclesiastics. I was also struck by a general air of fastidiousness and sober elegance, rarely observed in artists of any kind.' He spoke 'with decision and emphasis and a slight North-country accent'.

The composer was Frederick Delius, then aged forty-five and not yet, by a long way, the pathetic figure, blind, paralysed, wasted by disease, that people remember him as today. He was an egocentric man, by all accounts, even for an artist, caring little for anybody else's music, and while appearing disarmingly casual for much of the time could quickly fly into a rage. There were, though, no rages on that occasion. The meeting went well. Delius and Cassirer hired the New Symphony Orchestra for a concert of their own in the Queen's Hall. Beecham sat in on rehearsals and attended the concert on 22 November 1907, conducted by Cassirer, at which *Appalachia*, 'Variations on an old slave melody', for baritone, chorus and orchestra (inspired by the composer's early years in America), was performed. In *A Mingled Chime* Beecham says that the piece was generally well received without creating much excitement. His own reaction, by contrast, was strong and immediate. Two things about the music instantly gripped him. One was what he called the 'remotely alien' sound of it, something quite strange and new to English music. Coupled with this, in Beecham's opinion, was the composer's highly personal and original orchestration. Thus he determined to get hold of as much of Delius's music as he could and start performing it with his orchestra as soon as possible.

Beecham acknowledges the music as English, but also calls it 'remotely alien'. English music-lovers, with such pieces in mind as *On Hearing the First Cuckoo in Spring* and *Brigg Fair*, instantly associate Delius with the gentle melancholy of their own countryside. In so far as such pieces do have anything specifically English about them, they represent only one small part of his output. Delius was born in Bradford, but by descent he was part Dutch, part German. As a young man, desperate to escape from Yorkshire and the woollen trade, he went to Florida to manage an orange grove.

Failing at this, he made his way up the eastern seaboard of the United States, then returned to Europe, married the painter Jelka Rosen and settled with her in the village of Grez-sur-Loing, some way south of Paris, on the fringes of the Fontainebleau forest. His English links are therefore fairly tenuous. Comparisons are sometimes made between his music and Debussy's impressionism. There are some quite striking similarities between certain passages of Delius and of Wagner, notably from *Tristan und Isolde* and *Parsifal*. His harmonies and instrumental timbres, it may also be said, owe something to the black plantation and Creole songs and dances he heard in America, something to the textures of his friend Grieg. Otherwise, as Beecham immediately understood, the music is on its own, almost impossible to identify with any other school or movement, echoing the pantheism, the worship of nature, alternately ecstatic and profoundly melancholic, that informed his life.

For all his worldly disdain and diffidence, and the rarefied qualities of the music, Delius was not the totally isolated figure (Beecham apart) he is sometimes made out to be. Fritz Cassirer, himself now almost forgotten, we have already mentioned. Other much more famous contemporaries who knew something of his work included Mahler, Alban Berg, Bartók, and the celebrated French scholar and teacher Nadia Boulanger. Among conductors, Carl Schuricht, Otto Klemperer, Jascha Horenstein, Ernest Ansermet, Rudolf Kempe and Eugene Ormandy either performed works by Delius or expressed an interest in his music. In the land of his birth, a sterling band of at least half a dozen luminaries from Sir Henry Wood onwards have all espoused his cause (for a list of outstanding interpreters see page 214). The great black American jazz composer and bandleader Duke Ellington, incidentally, said that *In A Summer Garden* was one of his favourite pieces. No one, however, would deny that Beecham was the man who, from the end of 1907 to the very end of his life, made the cause of Delius his own, and made sure that that extraordinary body of music was not forgotten.

CHAPTER THREE

In his later years Sir Thomas Beecham was a paternal and conservative figure. In 1908, and for many years to come, Mr Thomas Beecham was a pioneer, a champion of the new, the unfamiliar, and sometimes the downright odd. Between the covers of the prospectus for his new concert season at the Queen's Hall – the best in contemporary design, with *art nouveau* lettering and logo centred between wide margins, black on dark beige – the programmes met the progressive's highest hopes or filled the traditionalist with dismay. There was a scattering of established classics, and of those lesser-known classical masters whom Beecham had made his own. He also shared the platform with other young prodigies, as he had done in previous seasons. A brilliant fifteen-year-old German-Hungarian pianist, Ernst Lengyel, hailed at the time as 'the Hungarian Mozart', was the soloist in Mozart's C minor concerto (K491). The *Observer* dismissed this concerto as 'a five-finger exercise' – some comment on current attitudes towards Mozart, which Beecham would strive mightily to change. The Russian teenage virtuoso Mischa Elman played the Mendelssohn Violin Concerto (his teacher Leopold Auer had earlier declared the Tchaikovsky Concerto to be unplayable). But the music was predominantly new or, at any rate, unfamiliar to most listeners. There were orchestrated versions of Debussy's *Petite Suite* and Hugo Wolf's *Italienische Serenade*. There were pieces by Gabriel Fauré, who was still very active, by César Franck and the contemporary German composer Max von Schillings, who was also chorus-master at the Bayreuth Festival.

There was much more new music from the home front. After being in the doldrums for so long, British music was a living force again, though the *Observer*'s outspoken critic G. H. Clutsam, whom we shall meet again as a composer, had his reservations.

The few and furtive attempts we have made at rehabilitation have been induced by exterior influences. A quantity of respectable music was conceived in the sunlight of Mendelssohn, and

later a larger quantity in the grey shadow of Brahms. To expect
the song of the people to serve as a fount of style is too naive a
proposition to be seriously considered.

Beecham may well have agreed with this rather jaundiced view. He
said many rude things of his own about the state of music in his
homeland; and he was certainly not drawn to the revival of English
musical traditions as such. He was, nevertheless, in his early years,
a good friend to the new and the rising generation of British
composers. He picked a winner in Vaughan Williams by giving his
Norfolk Rhapsody a hearing. Others whom he promoted have not
lasted so well, or are all but forgotten, though some were big
enough names in their day. He conducted two song cycles by
Granville Bantock, *Sappho* and *Ferishtah's Fancies* (settings of
poems by Robert Browning); also Balfour Gardiner's *Fantasy for
Orchestra* and *Shepherd Fennel's Dance*. Bantock, a keen amateur
magician, was already a prominent figure in British musical life, as
composer and educationalist, principally in Birmingham, and another enthusiast for new music. He was one of the first in Britain
to take up the cause of Sibelius, well ahead of Beecham himself.
Gardiner later abandoned music for pig farming, breaking off one
holiday to care for a favourite sow, a mark of that charming
eccentricity once associated with certain types of Englishman, almost as though they were acting a part. W. H. Bell, a rising figure
in English musical circles in the early years of this century before he
emigrated to South Africa, was represented in Beecham's concerts
by his tone-poems *Love Among the Ruins* and *The Shepherd*.
Beecham also included Norman O'Neill's concert overture *In
Springtime*. O'Neill was a teacher at the Royal Academy of Music
and Treasurer of the Royal Philharmonic Society.
    Then there was Joseph Holbrooke, intense and aesthetic in ap-
pearance, a composer much in the public eye at that time. Holbrooke, immensely energetic and self-opinionated, was certainly no
apostle of the pastoral English tradition. The arch-romanticism of
Liszt, the mammoth orchestral canvases of Mahler and Richard
Strauss, largely shaped his style. He also shared the fashionable
interest, already noted, in the occult and the macabre, and was
especially keen on the writings of Edgar Allan Poe (something he
had in common with Debussy and Baudelaire). His symphonic
poems *The Raven* and *The Bells* (the subject also of a choral
symphony by Rachmaninov) were both inspired by Poe. A Wagner-
ian-style trilogy of operas, *The Children of Don*, *Dylan* and *Bron-
wen*, was based on an ancient Welsh epic. There was also his

'illuminated dramatic symphony with choral epilogue', *Apollo and the Seaman*. The première of this, directed by Beecham in the Queen's Hall in January 1908, was one of the most remarkable events in the annals of British concert life.

The music of *Apollo and the Seaman* was intended to accompany the words and pictures of a lengthy allegorical poem by a minor poet, Herbert Trench. These were to be projected as lantern slides on to a large screen. Holbrooke scored the music for a massive orchestra (plus chorus) which, among other novelties, called for a bass sarrusophone, an instrument of French design, similar in pitch to a double bassoon. Beecham and Holbrooke went specially to Paris to seek out a sarrusophone player. For the performance, a big screen across the front of the platform separated orchestra and chorus from the audience. On the evening of the première, the latter waited with growing apprehension, while the auditorium, following the composer's directions, was plunged into darkness and the lowest pedal note on the organ pulsated softly and eerily about them. They had to wait longer than planned, because Beecham had missed his train from Borehamwood and was late. When he did finally scramble onto the rostrum, the percussionist, with evident relief, gave his cymbals a mighty clash, as the first image of Apollo was thrown onto the screen. The audience jumped out of their skins, then showed their relief by bursting into spontaneous laughter and applause, which was not at all what the composer intended. The aged sarrusophonist, apparently, was so overwhelmed by the occasion, also perhaps by pre-concert hospitality, that he fluffed a couple of entries and took no further part in the proceedings.

The event attracted almost an entire column in *The Times*. What the reviewer said about the whole question of combining music with words and pictures is of interest. He argued that the music was almost bound to suffer because,

> in England today, we are so accustomed to the sound of music, of one sort or another, going on while we try to write letters, to dine, to talk, or to see a play, that it is difficult to get free from the mental habit of ignoring it altogether. [This in 1908!] Music in what may be called its ancillary aspect is only too thoroughly understood among us, and in any union of music with another art it is the other art which is apt to receive our attention. It is probable that the bulk of the audience took last night's entertainment as a poem with musical illustration, rather than as a symphony explained by the poetical commentary that was to be read during its progress.

Setting aside such aesthetic problems, *The Times*'s critic called Holbrooke 'a modern of the moderns. No one will expect him to write music that is conventionally beautiful. That he will revel in discords is as certain as that his work will be scored for a very large orchestra.' From that point on, the review becomes noticeably cooler. Clearly, it was the oddity of the work that attracted so much coverage. So this extraordinary piece, under Beecham's auspices, had its hour upon the stage (though there was a repeat performance) before fading into the realm of memory and anecdote.

All this, however, was secondary to Beecham's new dedication to Delius, who was, technically at any rate, also a part of the renaissance of British music. In February 1908 he and the New Symphony Orchestra performed the relatively early *Paris: the Song of a Great City*, and played this again in April. The work, described as a 'Nocturne', also a kind of symphonic poem, celebrates Paris as the composer knew it in the 1890s, with its Moulin Rouge and *demimonde*, so vividly portrayed by the artist Henri de Toulouse-Lautrec. It may have been then that Delius contracted the syphilis that eventually destroyed him. In March came the recently completed *Brigg Fair: an English Rhapsody*, a set of fairly free variations on a Lincolnshire folk song, apparently introduced to Delius by the Australian pianist and folk-music enthusiast Percy Grainger, who had joined the composer's circle of friends at Grez-sur-Loing. Thus, as its title acknowledges, *Brigg Fair* does have genuine English roots, and is also, in many people's opinion, one of the composer's finest works. The early *Over the Hills and Far Away* was given by Beecham in May.

Notwithstanding G. H. Clutsam's overall gloomy view of contemporary British music, he wrote most perceptively about these Delius performances and about the character of the music (still very new and strange to most people). 'Mr Delius', he said, 'insists that he is Mr Delius, and rack your recollection as you may, you admit you have not had the pleasure of meeting him before.' Writing in a poetic vein of *Paris: the Song of a Great City*, he said,

> The characteristic, recurring dance movement, retaining a conventional rhythm, reflected the vulgarity of middle-night Paris, and one particularly fine mood was reached in a poignant episode typical of the gloom and sorrow of an underworld in the city of light, whose shadows no glare or glitter could ever dispel.

The critic of *The Times* drew the fairly obvious comparison between *Paris* and Elgar's *Cockaigne* overture, the two works being composed within two years of each other. They are, indeed, a kind of musical 'Tale of Two Cities'. The same critic compared *Brigg Fair*, now thought of as quintessential Delius, with the 'Forest Murmurs' interlude in Wagner's *Siegfried*. 'It seems', he wrote, 'to represent English country life as a remarkably sophisticated and decadent thing.' There was more praise for Beecham himself. 'Mr Beecham's own powers', said the *Observer*,

> have grown with those of his orchestra. With all his complacent mannerisms, the affectation of dispensing with the baton for certain works, for no perceptible reason, and the occasional Sousa-like swing of the body [a reference to the American band-master and composer John Philip Sousa], there is always in evidence a potent musical personality. He squeezes every little bit of effect out of his scores without any conspicuous effort.

With specific regard to Delius, *The Times* declared, 'Mr Beecham is very assiduous in playing the works of this clever composer, and rightly so, in view of the misrepresentations which bar the way to a just appreciation of them.'

Reference to such 'misrepresentations' invites a closer look at Delius's own approach and attitudes to his work. Just as much, if not more than, Clutsam and Beecham, he fulminated against the state of music in England, the stuffy respectability and the hypocrisy of English society, the domination of English musical life by the Germans. Yet his anger and his resentment did not spur him to any great effort on behalf of his own music. Most composers of the time peppered their scores with instructions and indications of every kind, in their desire to have it performed exactly as they conceived it. Not so with Delius: his autograph scores were often little more than bare notation. Beecham was always asking for guidance on such matters as tempo, dynamics and phrasing. 'Take it just as you think, my dear fellow,' the composer would reply airily. Consequently Beecham, who was wont to take a cavalier attitude towards any composer's music, was only too happy to take Delius at his word, and his extensive editing or re-editing of the scores extends, sometimes, even to the notes themselves. Delius seems never to have objected. 'Perfect, Thomas, perfect!' he would declare after a performance. 'Splendid, Thomas! That's how I want my music to be played!' Writing to the composer Ethel Smyth in 1909, he said of Beecham, 'I am very glad you met Mr Beecham. He is quite a remarkable man and musician and really understands and likes modern music ... He is wonderfully gifted and destined to play, perhaps, the most important part in the development of modern music in England. My prophecy! Don't forget it!' Ethel Smyth, as we shall see, soon had good cause of her own to be grateful to the young conductor.

Beecham struck up a personal friendship with Delius almost from the start. He paid the first of many visits to the house at Grez-sur-Loing as early as the winter of 1907. The following summer he accompanied the composer to Norway. While the garden and surrounding countryside at Grez were the inspiration for some of Delius's more intimate and impressionistic pieces, the majestic mountains and fiords of Norway inspired a number of his more visionary works. The two of them were supposed to be going on a walking holiday, though it proved to be rather an ordeal for Beecham, if Delius is to be believed. 'We left Skaare in Stryn on Wednesday midday,' he wrote home to Jelka,

> and walked up to the Sundalhut, a dirty little place and nothing to eat. We had to sleep on some dry twigs, with only a dirty cover over us. Of course we were eaten up by fleas, and neither of us slept at all. Next day we left for our big walk over the Jostedal glacier, to Mysahytten. There we could only get a cup of coffee and a few pieces of bread and butter. It had rained all night and our hut was swimming. It was a frightfully tough walk up to the glacier ... five hours almost as steep as a house! Beecham seemed quite done up and faint and I thought we should have to turn back; he pulled together, however, very pluckily; I carried his knapsack and the guide carried mine. The walk over the glacier was grandiose, nothing but snow in sight, and snow-covered peaks. After we crossed the glacier we descended gradually to Mysahyttenhut, which was a frightful distance. We were fourteen hours walking with only a couple of sandwiches each. Beecham could scarcely walk any more. We had to wade a stream which took me almost up to my waist. The man carried Beecham across.

Delius must still have been as strong as an ox.

CHAPTER FOUR

Beecham's progress as a conductor was being matched by his activities as an impresario. Ethel Smyth, who was soon to play a big part in his professional life, marvelled at the originality and daring of his programme planning and also at the excellence of the New Symphony Orchestra. How he managed it fascinated her just as much. 'The money,' she exclaimed, almost aghast, 'that someone must have dropped over these concerts, each one emptier than the last, owing to the programmes being devoted to the music of totally unknown composers!' The money was not always 'dropped' quite so providentially as that. Beecham may have had a family fortune behind him, but he did not always have access to the money when he wanted it. He was proving a very clever businessman, juggling with his debts. Over the years he would become quite legendary for this kind of financial legerdemain.

It was at this time also that he formed a new orchestra. He paid his players in the New Symphony Orchestra above the going rate (which led to some of them being blacklisted by the managements of the Queen's Hall and London Symphony orchestras). So, when they persisted with the bad old deputy system, it was he who walked out on them. As far as he was concerned, that was the end of the New Symphony Orchestra, though they did survive without him, becoming, in 1920, the Royal Albert Hall Orchestra. He, meanwhile, with much flair and gusto, set about the formation of another new orchestra, even more strongly stamped in his image.

He could not have found a better assistant in this enterprise than Verdi Fawcett, one of a large Victorian musical family all christened (the males anyway) in honour of a composer. Fawcett had played in the second violins of the New Symphony Orchestra. He was jovial, gregarious, popular, knew the musical scene inside out and kept his ear close to the ground – an orchestral factotum or 'fixer' in the best sense of the word. Beecham and Fawcett combed the country for new talent, seeking it out in pit orchestras, music halls, palm courts, music societies, colleges and schools. In two months they had assembled a new orchestra. The strings, in particular, were outstanding for their strength of talent. Among the first violins, and soon to be the orchestra's leader, was Albert Sammons, recruited from a band playing at the Waldorf Hotel in London, with a great future ahead of him as a virtuoso soloist. The viola players included Lionel Tertis, doyen of his instrument, for whom William Walton was to write his Viola Concerto; and Eric Coates, with a brilliant career ahead of him as a composer of such popular light orchestral classics as the *Knightsbridge March* and *By a Sleepy Lagoon*, both used in long-running BBC radio programmes, and the *Dambusters' March*. The double-basses had Eugene Cruft, future principal in both the BBC Symphony and Covent Garden orchestras. The average age of the players was a remarkably young twenty-five, with Beecham himself coming up to his thirtieth birthday. They were, in a real sense, Beecham's own creation. They were the Beecham Symphony Orchestra.

They made their début at the Queen's Hall on 22 February 1909. The concert opened with Berlioz's *Carnaval Romain* overture, the perfect orchestral showpiece, with which Beecham was to launch the London Philharmonic Orchestra twenty-three years later. Berlioz was another of Beecham's special causes among composers, and in some ways very different from the others. Known in his own day as 'Mad Hector of the Flaming Locks', Berlioz was the personification of the wild young romantic artist, in his music marrying highly idiosyncratic melodies and harmonies to a dazzling orchestration. In contrast to the elegance and charm of many of Beecham's other favourites, Berlioz must have appealed to the more wilful and rebellious side of his own nature. At any rate, much of the credit for that composer's high standing today, not least in his own country, can go to Beecham. On this occasion, he not only opened with Berlioz, but concluded with his grand and extrovert setting of the *Te Deum*. In between came *Storm*, a part-song by Roland Rogers (a composer now almost sunk without trace), Vaughan Williams's orchestral landscape *In the Fen Country*, and *Sea Drift*, Delius's beautiful and poignantly sad setting for baritone, chorus and orchestra of the American poet Walt Whitman's touching lament for an abandoned seabird (the première of which Henry Wood, to his credit, had earlier given in England). This time Delius was present, to take a bow.

The press gave orchestra and conductor a very warm welcome. 'I have previously had the pleasure of pointing out,' wrote Clutsam in the *Observer*, 'that in Mr Beecham we have a musical factor that is seriously to be reckoned with. Primarily it is evident that the artistic spirit rather than the commercial is Mr Beecham's first consideration.' *The Times*, heading its music column 'The Beecham Orchestra', declared,

> The exact circumstances of the severance between Mr Beecham and the New Symphony Orchestra scarcely concern the public, but the net result is that the distinguished conductor has formed a new band under the above title; and from its initial performance last night of the *Carnaval Romain* of Berlioz, it is clear that it should do great things. The tone is remarkably fine, and the players know how to obey the beat of the conductor. Everyman seems to have but one aim, to do justice to the music and to Mr Beecham's vigorous interpretation of it.

There was praise, too, for the North Staffordshire Choir, Beecham's own favourite ensemble, and for their choirmaster, James Whewall, a taciturn north-countryman who was also a spiritualist. Turning to the new music in the programme, *The Times* critic liked the Vaughan Williams piece. 'Though the theme is fragrant of the soil, it appears to be only in the style of folk music, not an actual specimen.' That is to say, like all the best 'nationalist' composers, Vaughan Williams had absorbed his country's folk idiom into his own style instead of simply dressing up existing folk tunes. Clutsam was not so sure about *Sea Drift*, speaking of Delius's 'usual atmospheric vagueness' and suggesting he might take a leaf out of Vaughan Williams's book regarding orchestration – an interesting comment in the light of the reputation Vaughan Williams has since earned for rather heavy scoring.

Someone else very impressed by Beecham was the sixteen-year-old Eugene Goossens, then studying at the Royal College of Music, and destined to work closely with him in a few years' time:

> Everything about Beecham was refreshingly unconventional. His deportment, appearance, programmes, and, in particular, his individual style marked him as a personality unlike any the London public had up to that time encountered. There was an electrifying something about his performances that evening, which, inexperienced though I was in the subtleties of interpretation, fascinated me. His stick technique, of an unusual kind, aroused much comment. So did his mannerisms, but certain exaggerations were discounted because of the superlative performance of the orchestra and the dynamic personality of the new star.

During the rest of that season with his new orchestra, Beecham introduced another work by d'Indy, *Jour d'Eté à la Montagne*

('Summer Day on the Mountain', described by one critic as 'mod-
ernised Berlioz'); otherwise, as far as new music was concerned, he
performed sterling service on behalf of British composers. There
were more new pieces by W. H. Bell, an all-Holbrooke programme,
including his dramatic choral symphony *Homage to Poe*, excerpts
from Smyth's opera *The Wreckers* (the complete production of
which is described in the next chapter), the concert overture *Grey
Galloway* by J. B. McEwen, and the tone poem *Into the Twilight*
by the young Arnold Bax. Viewed in the broader context of the
revival of British music at the beginning of the century, the pieces
by McEwen and Bax belong to what has been called the Celtic
Revival, with their evocations of Cornwall, Ireland and Scotland,
as distinct from the English pastoral tradition of Vaughan Williams, George Butterworth, some of the music of Frank Bridge and
John Ireland, and Delius. In his day Sir Arnold Bax, Master of the
King's Musick, was as big a name as any of the aforementioned.
His richly orchestrated tone poems *Tintagel* and *The Garden of
Fand*, and some, at least, of his seven symphonies, were in the
repertory of every major British orchestra; and after a long period
out of favour, they are being heard again.

The performance of *Into the Twilight*, it is worth noting, provides an example of Beecham's devil-may-care approach to some
works and of his unflappability. Bax recalled that the rehearsal on
the morning of the concert was a disaster, because of all the wrong
notes copied into the orchestral parts. He managed to correct these
just in time for that evening's performance. 'But,' he wrote, 'any
other conductor than the nonchalant Beecham would have declined
to take the chance after the chaos of the morning, and I do not
know what impish perversity prompted him to leave the piece in
the programme.' In the circumstances, the *Observer*'s dismissal of
it as 'a tragic tangle of crudities' probably says more about the
performance than about the music.

That first season of the Beecham Symphony Orchestra ended on
7 June 1909 with the first complete British performance of Delius's
most ambitious concert work, *A Mass of Life*, for soprano, contralto, tenor, bass, chorus and orchestra. This was the work of his that
attracted the most cosmopolitan interest. The Austrian composer
and conductor Franz Schreker had already given a performance of
it in Vienna, which had made a strong impression on Bartók and
Kódaly. Mahler admired the score, and might well have followed
suit but for his illness and death in 1911. Such widespread interest
can be attributed, in part, to the literary work that inspired it, the
German philosopher Friedrich Nietzsche's *Also Sprach Zarathus-*

tra ('Thus Spake Zoroaster', also the inspiration for Richard Strauss's symphonic poem of that name, written in 1896, whose rising fifths and octaves and emphatic drum beats were to feature in the 1968 film *2001, A Space Odyssey*). Delius and Fritz Cassirer (to whom it is dedicated) selected the passages which are the basis of the work's eleven movements. It is not a 'mass' in any Christian sense of the term. The German *Messe*, also meaning 'festival', 'fair' or 'feast', best sums up its pantheistic celebration of nature and of free will, close to the composer's own heart. Nonetheless, some early critics had already spoken of what they considered the generally pessimistic, even nihilistic tone of the work. 'Mr Delius's music', said one, 'is bizarre and cacophonous to a degree almost unapproached. It is his manifest duty to cheer up!' Another complained of a 'Mess of Life!'

It was no doubt a mark both of Beecham's special sympathy for the music and his growing mastery as a conductor that this performance attracted much more positive and constructive comment. *The Times* certainly greeted it as a major event. Its critic wrote:

> The general characteristics of Mr Delius's music are now fairly familiar, from 'Appalachia' and 'Sea Drift', as well as works for orchestra alone. Most of them appear again in the 'Mass of Life', from the masterly orchestration to the arresting and angular harmonic progressions. But the largeness of the scheme requires a larger musical plan than any of the former works, and its subject calls for a depth of thought, the lack of which could not be made up for by any amount of technical facility and orchestral effectiveness. Mr Delius has responded to these demands in a remarkable way, and the sincerity of expression is the first quality which is felt.

Beecham, once more directing his favourite North Staffordshire Choir, was also praised for tackling such a difficult and demanding modern score. 'There was', concluded the lengthy review, 'a fairly large and appreciative audience, and Mr Delius was called to the platform and heartily applauded.' The contrast between this critic's recent cool reception of *Sea Drift* and his enthusiasm for *A Mass of Life* is, it may be added, fairly typical of the equivocation towards Delius's music which has marked it ever since. What has amounted, at times, to a craze for some of his pieces has been counterbalanced by the almost total neglect of others; and his music, as a whole, has swung dramatically in and out of fashion.

Beecham did not confine himself to London. Soon after their first season in the capital, he took his orchestra on tour to Edinburgh, Glasgow, Cardiff, Liverpool, Dublin and many points in between. These were the colourful days of rail travel, when each British railway company boasted its own distinctive feature, the black and gold of the London and North Western, Midland red, the dark green, chocolate and cream of the aristocratic Great Western, the Great Northern's Stirling 'Singles' still a recent memory as they pounded up the line from King's Cross. No traveller in those days was without his or her Bradshaw. Beecham and his orchestra must soon have been familiar with its contents. They also enlivened their journeys by letting off fireworks, notably at Crewe Junction, hub of the rail network for much of northern England. That once famous station must often have echoed to the unsolicited crackles and bangs of Beecham's 'Fireworks Orchestra'.

Perhaps it was as a seasoned railway traveller that Beecham chose to compare Elgar's music with various railway stations. Sir Edward Elgar was, by then, approaching the height of his fame and adulation. Born in Worcester, he had lived in comparative obscurity until he was over forty years old, when his oratorio *The Dream of Gerontius* and his orchestral 'Enigma' Variations finally won him recognition, not just in his own country, but in Germany also, no doubt because of their Brahmsian provenance. Elgar was thenceforth hailed as the greatest English composer since Purcell. He certainly is a very English composer in the way his feeling for the English countryside, especially the Malvern Hills close to his birthplace, colours much of his music. At the same time, he wrote mainly in German symphonic forms and identified himself with the 'Nobilmente' (one of his favourite words) and pomp of the Edwardian age. It must have been this latter aspect of his music that Beecham said was like the original Euston station, with its imposing Doric arch and grand and dignified waiting room, redolent of a London club.

The work that drew Beecham and Elgar together – not with the happiest results – was the Symphony No. 1 in A flat. Elgar, taking his lead from Brahms, clearly regarded the writing of a symphony as the greatest test of a serious composer, and waited until his full maturity before producing one. Its première was given in 1908 by Richter and the Hallé Orchestra, and promptly hailed, in Richter's own words, as 'the greatest symphony of modern times'. Beecham, less reverently, compared it with another London terminus, Sir George Gilbert Scott's St Pancras, a weighty and florid gothic edifice. But, as a major new work by a composer of Elgar's stature, he decided to add it to the repertory of his 'Fireworks Orchestra'. He decided also to chip away at its own musical masonry, cutting out whole sections of the score. Indeed, with successive performances, his cuts became more and more savage, until they caused quite a scandal. One person they upset was Havergal Brian, a peripheral but interesting figure in British music, the composer of no less than thirty-two symphonies on his own account, many of them of Mahlerian proportions, who died in 1972 aged ninety-six. 'The first movement', Brian wrote to the editor of the *Musical Times* of one of Beecham's renderings, 'was cut down by one half; part of the exposition and the whole of the development were cut out, and some minutes were sacrificed in the succeeding movements. Those who know the symphony will be astonished to hear that the actual time occupied in its performance was only thirty-eight minutes! [The full playing time is close on an hour.] It was an insult to the composer!' (Several years later, when Beecham conducted Brian's *Festal Dance*, the composer called him 'brilliant' and said that the salvation of English music appeared to have passed into his, Beecham's, hands.) But, to return briefly to the matter under review, the editor of the *Musical Times* added his own postscript. 'The mutilation of Elgar's Symphony calls for severe censure . . . How is English music to be held in respect if it is to be so badly treated by a native conductor?' Elgar himself, every inch an Edwardian gentleman, distanced himself from all the fuss. In truth, after so many years of neglect, he was probably happier with mangled performances of his music than no performance at all.

Charles Reid, in his book *Thomas Beecham: an Independent Biography*, suggests that Beecham's commitment to Delius led him to undervalue Elgar, and possibly to resent the composer then being lionised by almost everybody else in England. Beecham himself, when subsequently tackled on the subject, always denied any prejudice against Elgar. Writing in *A Mingled Chime* he quite willingly concedes that, by and large, Elgar's mature works, in such forms as the symphony and oratorio, are superior to anything produced by his English predecessors and contemporaries. The writing, he says, is clear and varied in style, the grasp of the material close and keen, the orchestration often quite admirable. But, adds Beecham, the composer could sometimes stray dangerously close to the commonplace and the vulgar.

CHAPTER FIVE

Opera has never been a part of the social fabric of British life as it has been in Italy, France and Germany. Dr Samuel Johnson, in his bluff and hearty way, called it 'an exotic and irrational entertainment', a sentiment which probably still holds good for most British people. For the conductor, however, British or otherwise, opera has long been the key to success. Every conductor of world rank, from Hans von Bülow to Pierre Boulez, has made his mark in the opera house. By the age of thirty Beecham had already created two fine orchestras, and he was a major new force in British music. In later years he was to establish two more concert orchestras, this time of world repute. In between came his own years in the opera house (leaving aside his more youthful apprenticeship with the Imperial Grand Opera Company). They alone entitle him to a place among the greatest of his kind.

Despite Dr Johnson's sentiments, and the large measure of agreement they may have found among the bulldog breed, Victorian and Edwardian London was well served for opera. Covent Garden, then as now, was the premier international opera house. The earlier theatre had burnt down in 1856, and the present one (in fact the third on the same site) was rebuilt in record time to the designs of Edward Barry, son of the architect Sir Charles Barry who built the Houses of Parliament.

It opened in 1858 with a production of Meyerbeer's spectacular *Les Huguenots*. It continued for some years as the home of the Royal Italian Opera, which performed almost everything in that language, regardless of origin. After a rather bad patch artistically and financially, the building's lease was taken up by the impresario Sir Augustus Harris, who had previously staged some opera at the neighbouring Drury Lane Theatre. He removed the word 'Italian' from the company's name, presenting operas in their native language and featuring many of the greatest singers of the age. Dame Nellie Melba made her Covent Garden début under his auspices. A complete *Ring* cycle (though not the first in London), sung in

German and directed by Mahler, was another of his triumphs. When Harris died in 1896, a management board called the Grand Opera Syndicate took over. Beecham was to become involved with them.

During this period, opera was also regularly staged at the Theatre Royal, Drury Lane (as we have just noted), at Her (later His) Majesty's Theatre in the Haymarket, and more intermittently at the Lyceum off the Strand. For a briefer period there was the Opera Comique, the name of another theatre in the Strand, not a company, though in 1870 it gave refuge to the Comédie-Française while Paris was under siege during the Franco-Prussian War. The same theatre then staged the premières of some of the early Gilbert and Sullivan operettas, before the impresario Richard D'Oyly Carte opened the new Savoy Theatre in 1881. Just over ten years later, in response to the growing debate about the promotion of British or English national opera, D'Oyly Carte also opened the Royal English Opera House in Cambridge Circus with the first production of Sullivan's grand opera *Ivanhoe*, a timely reminder that the composer had a career quite separate from his collaboration with W. S. Gilbert. *Ivanhoe* itself had a good run; but no suitable follow-up was found – a sad comment on the dearth of good British operas ever since the solitary example of Purcell's *Dido and Aeneas* – and the theatre soon changed to the Palace Theatre of Varieties. Lilian Baylis, who had dreams of her own about native opera, and who went on to establish the Sadler's Wells Opera, meanwhile brought opera to the Old Vic Theatre in 1898 with a production of the Irish-born Michael Balfe's *The Bohemian Girl* (which Beecham revived again at Covent Garden many years later). To add to this quite lively scene, in 1905 the American impresario team of the Shubert Brothers opened the Strand Theatre (originally called the Waldorf) with a season of Italian opera. There were also some enterprising touring companies. One was the Moody-Manners Opera Company, named after its founders, the English soprano Fanny Moody (the first English Tatiana in Tchaikovsky's *Eugene Onegin*) and her husband, the Irish bass Charles Manners (the first Private Willis in Gilbert and Sullivan's *Iolanthe*). Another was the much longer-lived Carl Rosa Company, founded by the German violinist Karl Rose, which presented operas mainly in English (staging the British premières of Massenet's *Manon* and Puccini's *La Bohème* among other works) and which had so thrilled young Master Thomas Beecham on some of those family outings from Ewanville to Liverpool in 1891. By 1909, Mr Thomas Beecham was surveying the operatic scene and mulling over ideas of his own. The person who set him going in this new field of operations in the summer of that year was Ethel Smyth.

This formidable lady prompts a few words about women composers. In the twelfth century a German abbess, Hildegarde of Bingen, was one of the leading scholars, poets, mystics and musician-composers of the Middle Ages. For the period of the next six or seven hundred years, most people would be hard pressed to come up with the name of a single female composer. With the nineteenth century came such figures as Fanny Mendelssohn and Clara Schumann, who might have achieved more fame if they had not been so docile and ready to live in the shadow of their brother and husband respectively. In France, Cécile Chaminade, who lived well into this century, was a more determined figure, composing opera, ballets and various concert works, though she is remembered only by a handful of 'salon' piano pieces today. Ethel Smyth was made of even sterner stuff; and the distinguished line of British women composers through this century may fairly be said to start with her.

She was born in 1858 (the same year as the opening of the new Covent Garden Theatre), into an upper-class English family with a military background. This may have helped to shape her own strong and assertive personality. Her musical career went hand in hand with her militant support for the Suffragette Movement and her close personal friendship with the movement's leader, Emmeline Pankhurst. Beecham gives an amusing account in *A Mingled Chime* of a visit he paid to her in Holloway prison, where she was serving time for throwing a brick through a window of the Home Secretary's house. There he found her leaning out of her cell waving a toothbrush, as she led fellow inmates in the singing of her campaign song 'March of the Women'. This side of her life, plus her penchant for male attire, cigars and her parade-ground manner, were parodied years later on BBC radio by the author and scriptwriter Henry Reed's fictional adventures of the composer Dame Hilda Bracket. None of this, however, detracts from Ethel Smyth's own standing as a serious composer. She studied in Germany, and in her travels met Clara Schumann, Brahms, Joachim, Tchaikovsky, Dvořák, Grieg and Mahler. Her own music is purposeful, sometimes harmonically quite daring, if also somewhat derivative. Her most famous work is her opera *The Wreckers*, which *The New Grove Dictionary of Music and Musicians* describes, somewhat obliquely, as 'uneasily indebted to Wagner and Sullivan'. It is a story of doomed love set against the background of the gangs who once lured ships on to the rocks along the Cornish coast and plundered them. It had a chequered history. The libretto was by her companion and lover of many years, the dramatist Henry Brewster. This was originally written in French (entitled *Les Naufrageurs*) in the hope – vainly as it turned out – of attracting André Messager during his time as artistic director at Covent Garden from 1901 to 1906. After many set-backs, the première of the opera finally took place in Leipzig in 1906 (this time in German under the title of *Strandrecht*), though in a shortened form. Two years later, Nikisch conducted excerpts from it at a Queen's Hall concert.

Smyth and Beecham were initially brought together by a friend of the composer's family, the American millionairess and art patron Mary Dodge, who offered to back a new production of *The Wreckers* at His Majesty's Theatre. She also proposed Beecham as conductor, with his own orchestra. Smyth instantly welcomed him as a new champion of her music. Beecham for his part was delighted at this first real step on the operatic ladder, and agreed to conduct for nothing. In later years, he reminisced humorously but fondly about their work together. It was indeed a remarkable association, given his well-known antipathy towards female musicians in general, and her own passionate views about female emancipation. It must have been the attraction of opposites. In any case, they soon had each other's measure. He found out that she was the exact opposite of someone like Delius; a very dogged and persistent lady who knew her own mind on everything and would browbeat anyone who let her. She soon learnt that she could not browbeat Beecham. From all accounts, he gave her a tough time. She had to contend with his notorious unpunctuality, his maddening ability to disappear as if by magic when he knew someone was after him, his other maddening habit of ignoring letters. During work on *The Wreckers* he kept leaving London to attend rehearsals of Delius's *A Mass of Life* in Hanley. He did not care when the two principal singers could not make a rehearsal because of fog, and carried on blithely without them. She protested, to little avail, at his cavalier reading of her score. She was not the only one to complain about this. During another rehearsal the leading tenor, John Coates, asked him, 'Is this the place where I am supposed to be drowned by the waves or by the orchestra?' Then and later Beecham was often criticised for driving the orchestra hard at the expense of the singers. This may have been partly a desire to best the singers, especially the prima donnas, and partly inexperience. In this case Beecham blamed the composer. 'We had a hell of a time with the damned thing, making it go,' he wrote afterwards to Delius. 'The woman has some good notions but she is hopelessly narrow and amateurish.'

Leaving all that aside, it seems clear that Beecham revealed his great talent for pulling things off on the day, in this instance the opening matinee performance of *The Wreckers* in June 1909. 'It may be said at once', wrote the critic of *The Times*,

> that yesterday's performance at His Majesty's Theatre under Mr Beecham was a great success. The dramatic story, the strong passionate music that gripped the attention from the opening strains of the Revival Hymn, the enthusiasm of the singers, and the careful stage management of the crowds all combined to leave a vivid impression on the mind of the audience and must have startled the sceptic in his unshakeable belief that English music is still in the cradle and the English temperament incapable of being dramatic.

Ethel Smyth could not have asked for more from the critics. But she still wanted more for her opera, and by pulling some influential strings, arranged an extra royal gala performance. This is worth mentioning because of the far-reaching consequences for Beecham himself. He was at the time still estranged from his father, following the family quarrel about his mother's custody in a mental home of nearly ten years earlier. Despite this, father Joseph had been following his son's career with growing interest and pride, sometimes sneaking into rehearsals or performances and sneaking away again. With his love of pomp and ceremony, this gala performance was something he could not resist. This time Thomas spotted him. During the rehearsal for the performance, he whispered to Ethel Smyth, 'Don't look now, but the man standing behind that pillar at the back of the stalls is my father.' After the performance, Thomas was presented to the King. A few days later, and of far more importance to his career as we shall soon see, he met his father. There was, apparently, no outward show of emotion. Joseph said, 'You know, you annoyed me.' Thomas replied, 'And you annoyed me!' And with that they were reconciled.

During this year also (the year that Louis Blériot flew across the Channel), Beecham's second son, Thomas (Thomas III to distinguish him from both his great-grandfather and his father) was born to Utica. Such a happy event, however, was little more than a footnote to the increasingly hectic pace of his life. This was not exclusively concerned with music. The dashing young conductor was quickly snapped up by the *beau monde*. Taking its name and its example from the monarch whom the Oxford historian A. J. P. Taylor described as 'trailing cigar smoke and scandal', Edwardian society had broken free from the constraints of Victorian England. It saw the final, golden years of music hall, of Marie Lloyd and Vesta Tilley, parading themselves in feathers and furs or cheekily dressed in drag, investing their songs with all sorts of innuendo, before the change to the more 'respectable' Variety, and before the cinema and then the radio eclipsed them both. Beecham's own manner, appearance and personality fitted into this scenario perfectly; and in many ways he cut an Edwardian figure for the rest of his life. In 1909 his name was soon being linked with that of Mrs Maud Christian Foster, the first of a succession of wealthy American women, besides Utica, with whom he became involved in one way or another. Mrs Foster's husband was a property dealer, while she painted pictures and learnt to sing. By an unhappy irony – unhappy at any rate for Utica – Beecham met Mrs Foster while she was painting a portrait of his father-in-law, Dr Welles. He was soon a regular guest at her home in smart, elegant Redcliffe Square, strategically placed between fashionable South Kensington and the more Bohemian reaches of Chelsea. She offered to help his career through her many contacts in Europe and America, and she referred to him as 'The Boy' (calling to mind Noël Coward's song 'Mad About The Boy'). It seems that outwardly Beecham behaved towards her with that languid detachment he could so easily assume, and which was a part of his attraction. Clandestine letters and notes between them, though, suggested a quickening of the pulse beneath a cool exterior. When one of these was intercepted, Mr Foster decided there were grounds for divorce.

In those days divorce was still a weighty matter, often involving the full majesty of the law. It was largely the preserve of the rich and famous, and attracted much publicity on this account. Mr Foster's action against his wife and Beecham (cited as co-respondent) was no exception. The hearing introduced evidence about a seedy private detective, and a secret code allegedly used by Mrs Foster and Beecham, using such names as 'Beastie', 'Ortrud' and 'Brangäne'. The latter two, of course, are Wagnerian characters, Brangäne being pounced upon by Mr Foster's counsel as the character in *Tristan und Isolde* who acts as the lovers' go-between. Beecham, Utica and Mrs Foster all took the stand. The evidence was circumstantial, as it nearly always is in such actions, but the jury found the case proved. Mr Foster was granted his divorce and Beecham was faced with the costs. The episode had little real bearing upon his career. But the operatic ring to it all – the interception of secret missives, the Wagnerian allusions – are like an offstage commentary on the progress of that career. For while the case was brewing, he was taking London's operatic world by storm.

CHAPTER SIX

The year 1910 was a great one for headlines in the British press. King Edward VII died, bringing to an end the brief but glittering Edwardian period. So did Florence Nightingale, aged ninety-one. There were two general elections called by the prime minister Herbert Asquith over such issues as taxation, national insurance and the powers of the House of Lords. With the aid of wireless telegraphy, Dr Hawley Crippen, most famous name in British criminal history, was arrested at sea for murder, tried and hanged. Captain Robert Falcon Scott set out on his tragic bid to reach the South Pole. And Thomas Beecham, financially backed by his father, launched into an orgy of opera, generating the kind of sensational-ism and gossip now reserved for pop stars and royalty.

There was much being said and written about opera at that time, not least about the promotion of British opera and of native-born singers in preference to foreign ones, and about the pros and cons of singing opera in its original language or in English translation. Beecham had contributed to all this. Now he saw himself as throw-ing down some sort of gauntlet. With his own orchestra, augmented to around a hundred players, plus a chorus of eighty, he presented three opera seasons, two at Covent Garden, separated by one at His Majesty's Theatre. His repertory for these three seasons embraced more than thirty operas (new productions or revivals), totalling nearly two hundred performances, with Beecham himself taking the lion's share of the conducting. Add to these basic facts, astounding enough in themselves, all the crises that are part of any operatic enterprise, and his work for this single year can be seen as a truly herculean achievement.

'The question as to the amount of interest in opera that exists, whether latent or otherwise, in this country is an open one,' he wrote in his introduction to the prospectus for the opening season.

Here, as elsewhere, certain singers of established reputation never fail to attract large audiences, but crowds such as nightly fill the countless opera houses on the Continent are drawn from a far more serious section of art-lovers. Does there, or does there not, exist in England a public ready to take intelligent and continuous interest in music-drama *per se* if it had the chance?

It is in order to find out what is the true answer to this question that the present enterprise – the Thomas Beecham Opera Season – has been inaugurated, for unless there is a real demand for opera, any attempt to found a permanent National Opera House in which the best works, new and old, native and foreign, shall be regularly and adequately performed, is at least premature.

The amount of support which the present enterprise is destined to find will go some way towards testing the situation. The repertory speaks for itself, and as regards the casts, the question of expense has not weighed with the management, whose sole aim is to achieve the best possible rendering of each opera on the list.

All the foreign singers whose names appear on the programmes have attained supremacy in their respective countries, and it is believed that many of the native artists engaged are likely to attain similar success if the same chances were afforded them.

In modern opera the Conductor and the Orchestra play as important a part as the singers, and in this as in other departments, including staging, etc., the management has acted on the same principle as in the selection of the casts.

And since neither time nor pains will be spared in the all-important matter of adequate rehearsals, we believe the results of our enterprise – the first of its kind launched in this country – will justify the great amount of interest it is exciting at home and abroad.

In this introduction Beecham was making some very interesting points. He was challenging the supremacy of the singers, notably the prima donnas, whose position, *vis-à-vis* conductors and directors, has steadily declined through this century; and he was anticipating by nearly forty years such institutions as a true National Opera.

That first season covered the months of February and March. Starting on familiar ground, he included two more performances of *The Wreckers*, bringing over Bruno Walter, who had already shown a friendly interest in the piece, to conduct one of them. The German-born conductor and pianist was a protégé of Mahler in Hamburg and Vienna, and became one of this century's best-known musical figures, as director of the Vienna State Opera (before being compelled to leave Austria and Germany by the Nazis) and then principal conductor of the New York Philharmonic Orchestra. In the years to come he was also a regular guest conductor at Covent Garden. *The Wreckers'* indefatigable composer, though, was not entirely happy. For her, the previous year's performances had only been a 'preliminary canter'. Now she grumbled about the singing, and said her opera had 'gone to the wall'. Walter also directed four performances of *Tristan und Isolde*.

Another conductor who shared some of the burden with Beecham during this opening season is largely forgotten today, but was for many years a very well-known and popular figure in British music. This was the composer and conductor Percy Pitt, formerly the Queen's Hall organist, then musical director for the Grand Opera Syndicate, appearing regularly at the opera house, and later musical director of the BBC. He conducted a revival of Sullivan's *Ivanhoe*, lavishly staged and warmly applauded, though by 1910, only twenty years after its première, critics were beginning to call it dated. Pitt was also entrusted with a most unusual double bill, of Humperdinck's charming fairytale opera *Hänsel und Gretel* paired with a stage version of Debussy's early cantata *L'Enfant Prodigue* ('The Prodigal Son'), for which he had won the coveted Grand Prix de Rome. The Scottish composer Hamish MacCunn, whose fine and breezy overture *In the Land of the Mountain and the Flood* still receives an occasional hearing, directed two performances of *Carmen* (in English).

Beecham lovingly directed two performances of Delius's 'music drama' *A Village Romeo and Juliet*, the story of a boy and girl, the children of rival farmers, who seek union in suicide. This opera, as we have noted, had had its première in Germany three years earlier. This was its first British hearing. For one of the scenes, in a fairground, Beecham hired a real merry-go-round, and during one rehearsal took a high-spirited ride on it, to some head-shaking from the more sober members of management and cast. Alas, the work had only a lukewarm reception; and for all his devotion to Delius, Beecham was later to admit that he was a problematical opera composer. So long as the singers were off the stage, he said, the orchestral writing was delicate and enchanting, but the moment they reappeared, the orchestra often struck a more strident note, as though it resented the intrusion. It is certainly true, with regard to *A Village Romeo and Juliet*, that the orchestral interlude 'The Walk to the Paradise Garden' encapsulates in five minutes of poignantly beautiful music the whole sad pastoral mood of the story. Indeed, this interlude is one of Delius's best-loved orchestral miniatures, and the only music from the opera that most people ever hear. Unfortunately, on the occasion of that first London production, this lovely piece was played with the curtain down, and, as Beecham recollected, was almost drowned by chatting among the audience and the thumps and scrapes of scene-shifters on stage. When he later revived the opera he introduced a stage picture and kept the curtain raised, to hold the audience's attention and give the music a chance.

The sensation of the February–March season, the event that really captured the headlines for Beecham, was the first British staging of *Elektra* by Richard Strauss. In 1889, the twenty-five-year-old composer had rocketed to international fame with the dazzling orchestral virtuosity of his symphonic poem *Don Juan*, and soon he was being hailed as heir to the whole German-speaking symphonic and romantic tradition, from Mozart and Beethoven through to Wagner. He was also considered by many to be a shocking composer, literally so with such instrumental effects in his other symphonic poems as the squealing clarinet in *Till Eulenspiegel* while the folk hero dangles from the gallows, tremolo brass to imitate bleating sheep in *Don Quixote*, the use of the wind machine in the same work, and of the thunder machine in *Eine Alpensinfonie* ('An Alpine Symphony'). By 1910, Strauss was well into his forties and no longer a *Wunderkind*; but he had carried his reputation for sensationalism from the concert hall into the opera house. *Elektra*, the fourth of his operas and the first fruit of his long collaboration with the poet, playwright and librettist Hugo von Hofmannsthal, was based on Sophocles' classic Greek drama of Electra's revenge on her depraved mother Clytemnestra for the murder of her father King Agamemnon; and it drew from Strauss a dramatically high-pitched and relentless score. The work had first been given in Dresden the previous year; several other productions quickly followed, and it had created a big stir in the musical world. Now Beecham was bringing it to London.

He had already studied and memorised the score (another example of his prodigious intellectual powers), and in January 1910 hurried off to Vienna to take in some performances there. Returning triumphantly to London with the great composer in tow, he plunged into rehearsals that brought many members of his orchestra, already tackling a large and varied repertory, to the verge of nervous exhaustion. In truth several players did collapse under the strain and had to be replaced. This was the first great age of mass circulation journalism, created by such tycoons as Lord Northcliffe, and the popular press had a field day with this production. The *Sketch*, an illustrated weekly, told its readers, 'The score, both for the singers and the orchestra, is said to be the most difficult ever written'. It also reported that at one rehearsal Strauss was heard to bawl at Beecham and his gallant band, a huge one of about 120 players for the piece, 'Louder! Louder! I still hear some of the voices!' That particular story may well have brought a wicked little smile to Beecham's face, for it was he rather than Strauss who loved to whip up the orchestra at the expense of the singers. Indeed, George Bernard Shaw, then a leading music critic with the pen name of 'Corno di Bassetto', wrote that with Beecham conducting, the opera 'sometimes sounded like a concerto for six drums'. Shaw was not the only one, as we have already noted, who criticised Beecham on this point. As a matter of fact, dancers complained that he often got the orchestra to play too fast. Perhaps in those days he felt his authority in some way challenged, compromised or threatened by those up on stage. The press even got excited about Strauss's inclusion in his score of the heckelphone, a type of bass or baritone oboe (not the same as the cor anglais) with a rather baleful tone, which one reporter claimed had been specially invented for the opera.

The dress rehearsal, meanwhile, was a glittering occasion in its own right, with the French conductor Pierre Monteux (soon to earn his own share of notoriety with the première of Stravinsky's *Le Sacre du Printemps* in 1913) and Granville Bantock among the packed audience, and beefy stewards recruited to keep out gate-crashers (it's not every night of the week that Covent Garden employs bouncers). The opening performance, on 19 February 1910, was attended by King Edward VII and sundry other royal personages from home and abroad. In a reversal of the usual voice-types, the title role was sung by the mezzo-soprano (later soprano) Edyth Walker, one of the first American singers to attain international status; that of Klytemnestra was taken by the Austrian dramatic soprano Anna Bahr-Mildenburg, another protégée of Mahler and already an established star. A doctor stood by in the wings in case either lady collapsed.

The young violin and composition student Eugene Goossens was again on hand to record his impressions from a place in the gallery.

Beecham whipped his hundred players into a lather of such excitement that we were often deafened and lost track of the vocal line quite frequently. I recall someone having provided me with sandwiches to munch during the performance, but such was the crush of people standing that I was unable to retrieve them from the tail pocket of my frock coat for sheer inability to move my arms backwards or forwards.

The press was almost unanimous in its praise, at least of the performance. Everyone agreed that Beecham and his orchestra had covered themselves in glory. There was much praise too for the cast. 'Nothing', wrote the critic of the *Daily Telegraph* about Edyth Walker's Elektra, 'could have surpassed the almost superhuman energy of this richly endowed artist, whether as singer or actress.' Bahr-Mildenburg's acting was also singled out for praise by the critic of *The Times*, who described her performance as 'so vivid a picture of decadence that while she was on stage it was possible to forget all about the music'. That sounds suspiciously like someone who did not really like the music but could not actually bring himself to say so. According to Beecham, an 'eminent British composer' made another oblique attack on the music by declaring that after sitting through one of the performances he went straight home to play the chord of C major twenty times just to satisfy himself that it still existed – apparently overlooking the fact, as Beecham pointed out, that the opera actually finishes with the chord in question, hammered out several times on full orchestra. It was left to Ernest Newman, then music critic of the *Birmingham Daily Post* and future author of such scholarly works as *The Unconscious Beethoven* and *Wagner Nights*, to come right out in the open with his opposition to the opera.

> We don't need to wait for posterity to tell us that much of the music is as abominably ugly as it is noisy. A good deal of the talk about complexity is wide of the mark. The real term for it is incoherence . . . What awestruck worshippers call complexity in *Elektra* would often be more correctly described as impudence at its best and incompetence at its worst.

Shaw, whatever he thought of Beecham's conducting, then sprang to the opera's defence, and these two eminent gentlemen went on sniping at each other in the newspaper columns for weeks to come.

Strauss himself conducted two more performances. He was tall and willowy, with a receding chin, wispy moustache and large balding head, and was slavishly devoted to his wife, the formidable former opera singer Pauline de Ahna, and their son. In appearance and manner, no composer was ever more at odds with the spirit of his music; and in view of some of the wilder reports about him in the British press, the *Daily Mail*'s description of him in the Covent Garden orchestra pit was a timely corrective.

The tall, pale man with the dome-shaped head, the huge, smooth brow, the steel-blue eyes, sat slightly bent forward, with a glow on his delicate features, which are those of a lyric poet rather than of a music-giant. His thin, long hand held the small tapering baton like a pen. His head was immobile, his elbows seemed riveted to his body. The sobriety of his gestures was striking. He seemed a mathematician writing a formula on an imaginary blackboard neatly and with supreme knowledge.

By comparison, Beecham must have been a fireball.

CHAPTER SEVEN

From May to July 1910, Beecham moved to His Majesty's Theatre for what he advertised as a season of 'opéra-comique'. Histori-cally, 'opéra-comique' is a type or style of French opera with spoken dialogue, not necessarily comic at all; but Beecham meant it to suggest a season of relatively light opera, as distinct from operetta. That said, the season at His Majesty's Theatre was signi-ficant in several other ways. Beecham was using it to further the much discussed cause of British or English opera, not so much of the works themselves, but of native talent, and of opera sung in English. Thus his casts of singers blossomed with honest Anglo-Saxon or in some cases Celtic names: his close friend the baritone Frederic Austin, John Coates again, Maude Fay, Walter Hyde, Lewys James, Lena Maitland, Robert Maitland, Agnes Nicholls, Ruth Vincent. There was also Maggie Teyte (born Margaret Tate), a young and beautiful soprano. In fact she was already a rising international star, having studied with the Franco-Polish tenor Jean de Reszke and boldly taken the title role, in Paris, of Debussy's recent opera *Pelléas et Mélisande*. It was because of her French connections that she changed the spelling of her name. In her autobiography, *Star on the Door*, she recalled Beecham's favourite répétiteur (vocal assistant and coach) at this time and for some years to come, another of the splendid eccentrics he attracted through his life. In fact, to judge from the various recollections of him, Tommy Chapman had stepped straight out of the pages of Charles Dickens. He was a big, shambling, scruffy-haired, bearded man, always attired, whatever the weather, in a large, ancient, shabby greatcoat, whose pockets were stuffed with vocal scores, newspapers, banknotes and scraps of food. His equally ancient pocket watch was always crazily wrong. Nobody seemed to know where he lived or what he did with the rest of his life. He arrived mysteriously at rehearsals and just as mysteriously left again. He seemed constantly to be nodding off at the piano. But he knew the repertory backwards and had a mind as sharp as a needle when required. The composer and conductor Julius Harrison, who also worked for Beecham a few years later, called Chapman 'one of the patient oxen of music'.

As well as the singers, and the use of English, for his season of 'opéra-comique' at His Majesty's Beecham cut seat prices and dropped the still almost mandatory wearing of evening dress. Clearly he was out to democratize opera, and in retrospect he can be seen as paving the way, more than anyone else at the time, for such institutions as Sadler's Wells, the English National Opera, Scottish Opera, Welsh Opera, and other strongly British-orientated opera companies.

The three big box-office draws for this season were Offenbach's *Les Contes d'Hoffmann* ('The Tales of Hoffmann'), Johann Strauss's *Die Fledermaus* (even in English-language productions no one ever thinks of changing its title to 'The Bat') and, again, Humperdinck's *Hänsel und Gretel*. Through them Beecham must have hoped to tempt the public to sample some of those French rarities which pleased him so much: Méhul's *Joseph en Egypte*, Auber's *Fra Diavolo*, Massenet's *Werther* and Edmond de Missa's *Muguette* (from all accounts a charming piece of French rusticity, by a composer who had died only recently but has now sunk almost without trace). Moving away from France, Beecham also presented *Feuersnot* ('Fire Famine'), Richard Strauss's second opera, a light-hearted and quite risqué one-acter, far removed from the hothouse world of *Elektra*; *Shamus O'Brien* by Stanford, a successful opera composer in his time; and *A Summer Night* by the *Observer*'s much respected critic, the Australian-born George Howard Clutsam, who later arranged the English version of the sugary stage musical *Lilac Time*, based on Schubert's music, and very loosely on his life.

Finally – all packed into the three-month season – there was what amounted to a Mozart festival. Here was the composer closest of all to Beecham's heart. Through the nineteenth century, in high-minded Victorian Britain at any rate, Mozart had languished in the shadow of Beethoven, Mendelssohn, Wagner and Brahms. He was seen as a kind of periwigged rococo dandy, facile, charming, frivolous, basically insubstantial compared with the romantic giants just mentioned. This kind of image, said Beecham, went against all historical evidence, not only concerning Mozart but eighteenth-century composers in general. They were not, he contended, 'anaemic epicenes, but creatures of overflowing vigour and passion'. Mozart, of course, was for him much more than that; his music was passion and drama combined with perfection of style and utterance.

Beecham, as much as anyone, led the Mozart revival. He included four of the operas in his 'opéra-comique' season: *Le Nozze di Figaro* ('The Marriage of Figaro', billed in Italian), the delightful work billed as *Il Seraglio* (more properly *Die Entführung aus dem Serail*, 'The Abduction from the Harem', since it is an example of German *Singspiel*), the one-act *Der Schauspieldirektor* ('The Impresario') and *Così fan tutte*. The last of these epitomised the still widely current view of Mozart as a frivolous composer. Like *Die Fledermaus*, mentioned above, it is one of that select little group of operas whose title is rarely if ever translated. It means something like 'Women are all the same'. The cynical little storyline, concerning a wager about the inconstancy of women, had been condemned by Beethoven himself as thoroughly unworthy of the composer, an opinion endorsed by, among others, the long-time music critic of the *Athenaeum* magazine, Henry Fothergill Chorley, who deplored the fact that Mozart could waste his time on such a 'tiresome little folly' and declared that 'there is no hope for *Così fan tutte* on the stage as the work stands'. Beecham was thus reviving a neglected masterpiece. It is doubtful if he was much concerned with any of the psychological and sociological undercurrents that have since been read into the work. For him the opera was simply and miraculously 'a long summer's day spent in a cloudless land by a southern sea'.

Unhappily for the season at His Majesty's Theatre, His Majesty died on 6 May 1910. This not only caused a postponement of the opening night, but cast a gloom over London for much of the summer, and upon the whole season of 'opéra-comique'. This vein of ill luck for Beecham continued into the autumn–winter season back at Covent Garden. It was to have opened with the British première, in English, of *Tiefland* ('The Lowlands') by Eugène d'Albert. This cosmopolitan figure was born in Glasgow, lived in France and was German by adoption. He had studied with Liszt, and as well as being an outstanding pianist was highly regarded as a composer. *Tiefland*, a drama of Pyrenean peasant life, was an interesting German example of the Italian school of *verismo* or operatic realism practised so successfully by Puccini. It must have seemed an excellent curtain-raiser to the season. A crisis among the cast, however, forced a postponement, and the season opened instead with *Hamlet* by Ambroise Thomas. Even this had to be delayed for two days, due to sickness among the cast, and when the curtain finally did go up, the opera flopped. The Frenchman Ambroise Thomas was famous for his opera *Mignon*, but when it came to tackling Shakespeare, the London critics decided that he was not in the same league as Verdi. Maybe a certain Francophobia came into it, as the opera has had some formidable champions, including Maria Callas and Joan Sutherland, who both recorded Ophelia's mad scene from it. The *Daily Graphic*'s critic was particularly snooty. 'It is difficult to see what can have induced Mr Beecham, the apostle of progress, to include this feeble and faded work in his repertory.' 'Poor stuff at its best', agreed the *Pall Mall Gazette*, an evening newspaper that circulated within London's plush and exclusive clubland. All this must have been upsetting for the leading soprano, Mignon Nevada, making her Covent Garden début. Daughter of the American singer Emma Nevada, she was born in Paris, and the composer was her godfather (which, presumably, explains her first name). She subsequently sang regularly at Covent Garden, the Paris Opéra and La Scala, Milan, and Beecham said of another of her Shakespeare-inspired roles, that of Desdemona in Verdi's *Otello*, that it was the best he had ever seen. But, to return to that unhappy evening in October 1910, it was probably just as well that he conducted only the national anthem, before handing over the baton to Luigi Camilieri, one of his associates.

An inauspicious start, then, to a truly remarkable season: *Tiefland*, duly presented to a respectful rather than an excited audience, but with critical praise for Beecham; a strong infusion of Wagner – *Tannhäuser* (with the splendidly named tenor Gustav Forchhammer in the title role), *Tristan und Isolde* and *Der fliegende Holländer* ('The Flying Dutchman'); *Carmen* (in English, but a true example of French 'opéra-comique'); *Fidelio* (in German); *Rigoletto* (offering a better chance for Mignon Nevada); *Le Nozze di Figaro* (still in English); *Don Giovanni* (in Italian); *Faust* (also in Italian!); *Il Barbiere di Siviglia* ('The Barber of Seville'); *Hänsel und Gretel*, paired this time with Clutsam's *A Summer Night*; *Les Contes d'Hoffmann*; *Le Chemineau* ('The Tramp') by Xavier Leroux (composed only four years earlier but now a rarity indeed); and one performance of *Pelléas et Mélisande* with Maggie Teyte as Mélisande. These last two were big disappointments for Beecham. 'The production of *Le Chemineau*', wrote one critic, 'must have given Mr Beecham a significant hint of the discouraging attitude towards novelties on the part of the public he is striving so admirably to serve. Xavier Leroux's opera is, of its kind, a masterpiece; the interpretation, under Mr Percy Pitt's skilled direction, could hardly be bettered; but the attendance was quite disappointing.' Nor did Maggie Teyte's growing fame attract a full house for *Pelléas et Mélisande*. Debussy's elusive, fleeting musical imagery, inspired by Maurice Maeterlinck's symbolist play, still puzzled most people in 1910.

There were more performances of *Elektra*. But Richard Strauss, the wizard of the sensational and the shocking, was on hand to supply Beecham with another box-office coup, and to bring the whole amazing year to an end in another blaze of publicity. The new Strauss opera that Beecham set his sights on was *Salome*. This, in fact, dated from 1905, four years earlier than *Elektra*. It was a musical adaptation of Oscar Wilde's verse play which had transformed the Gospel accounts of John the Baptist's imprisonment and death at the hand of King Herod into a sado-erotic drama, in which Salome gratifies her lust for the prophet by having his decapitated head served to her on a platter. Because of its story and its Biblical associations the opera had already run into serious trouble in Germany and in America, and the Lord Chamberlain's office had banned it in Britain, although the purely orchestral 'Dance of the Seven Veils' had been heard three years before at the same Queen's Hall concert as Delius's *Appalachia Variations*, described on page 13. To be fair to them, it was not only these official guardians of public morality who found the story and the mood of the opera objectionable. The French novelist, musicologist and Nobel prizewinner Romain Rolland, a close friend of the composer, wrote to him in 1907:

> Oscar Wilde's *Salome* was not worthy of you . . . There is an undeniable dramatic power in Wilde's poem; but it has a nauseous and sickly atmosphere about it. This isn't a question of middle-class morality, it's a question of health . . . Wilde's Salome, and all those who surround her, except that poor creature Jokanaan [John the Baptist], are unwholesome, unclean, hysterical or alcoholic beings, stinking of sophisticated and perfumed corruption.

In a broader context, Wilde's play and Strauss's setting of it share the same feverish and morbid *fin de siècle* world as the paintings of Edvard Munch, James Ensor, Gustav Klimt and the Secessionists in Vienna, the music of Schoenberg's *Pierrot Lunaire*, much of Mahler, of Debussy's *Le Martyre de Saint-Sébastien* and Ravel's *Gaspard de la Nuit*. This whole period of art, literature and music, together with the pioneer work of Sigmund Freud, also in Vienna, can be seen as lifting the lid off the festering emotions and feelings that lurked behind the moral rectitude of late nineteenth-century society.

Seen in this light, it may be said that Beecham was doing his bit to bring out into the open some of the murkier aspects of the Victorian and Edwardian psyche. He had first to get the ban on the opera lifted. In *A Mingled Chime* he tells how he was lucky enough to meet the prime minister, Mr Asquith, at a country weekend party, and won his way into the latter's good books by playing over and over on the piano the grand march from *Tannhäuser*. As a reward, the PM arranged a meeting between him and representatives of the Lord Chamberlain's department. In 1910 religion, at any rate Christianity, was still deeply ingrained in society; and in England the Anglican Church was still a very real power in the land. Blasphemy, or what might be construed as such, was as serious a matter as it has more recently been among certain fundamentalist Islamic sects. The main and apparently insurmountable objection to the opera, then, was a religious one. Transferring anything from the Bible on to the stage, Beecham was told, was fraught with difficulties. 'But what about *Samson et Dalila*?' Beecham asked, referring to Saint-Saëns's opera, which had been staged at Covent Garden the previous year, though not without problems of its own. Ah! replied the gentlemen in high winged collars and cravats, but that was the Old Testament. The New Testament was trickier still. The ban could only be lifted if the story was removed from its Biblical context by the following changes: the action should be moved from Judaea to Greece; the Jews and Nazarenes were to become Learned Men and Cappadocians; there must be no direct Biblical quotations; John the Baptist must become an anonymous prophet. Moreover, there must be no decapitated head which, in Wilde's play, Salome gloats over and kisses on the lips (though some reports say that a loaf of bread covered by a towel might have been allowed). These changes, of course, destroyed much of the character of the piece; but it was them or nothing, and, as Beecham pointed out, the work was to be sung in German, which most of the audience would not understand in any case.

If it is possible both to beat the drum and still sound dignified, then Covent Garden managed it in their advance press hand-out.

Considerable gratification will be experienced by a vast section of the public, and by all opera lovers, at the announcement now made officially for the first time that the Lord Chamberlain has definitely sanctioned the performance of the much-talked of and world-famous opera *Salome* by Richard Strauss and that it will be sung by the Thomas Beecham Opera Company at Covent Garden shortly . . . Strauss has been described as the stormy petrel of modern music, and *Salome* has aroused more discussion than anything else he has written. Many critics have found its ethic somewhat difficult of digestion, while conservative musicians hold up their heads in horror at its harmonic audacity. The more advanced spirits find a strange, exotic beauty in the weird harmonies and infinitely suggestive orchestration, and contend that a work of art must be judged as such and not as an essay in didactic morality.

When the box office opened, all seats for the first night, on 8 December 1910, were sold within two hours; and the stampede for seats continued for subsequent performances.

Part of the excitement was the leading soprano, the Finnish Aino Ackté, a curvaceous beauty who appeared in the title role in a revealing costume that would have done any Hollywood epic proud. What is more, she performed the 'Dance of the Seven Veils' herself, instead of handing the episode to a professional dancer, which is what usually happened until quite recently. After a long and successful career in Paris, London and New York, Ackté returned to her homeland to become director of the Finnish National Opera. She died in 1944. On the first night, and in the heat of the moment, she and other members of the cast lapsed into the original, forbidden version of the German text. In the dim light of the orchestra pit Beecham broke into a cold sweat, and dreadful thoughts flashed through his mind: of Covent Garden losing its royal charter and of himself banished in disgrace from London's musical and social scene. So he whipped up the orchestra to try and smother the offending words. But hardly anyone seems to have noticed, and at the end of the evening the Lord Chamberlain's party were among the first to congratulate him.

The press were much taken with Aino Ackté. The *Daily Telegraph* declared her 'a superb and often seductive Salome', and that 'she easily surpassed any of her previous performances both vocally and histrionically'. The *Pall Mall Gazette* had some reservations. 'She looked curiously like an Aubrey Beardsley drawing, but she spoilt her effects by monotony; also she did not obtain the real note of sensuality the part seems to require.' Aubrey Beardsley was the brilliant and morbid *fin de siècle* graphic artist, working mainly in black and white, who had illustrated the English edition of Wilde's play. One wonders how many readers of the *Pall Mall Gazette*, sunk deep in their leather-upholstered armchairs, brandy and soda to hand, had ever heard of him. The *Observer*'s critic concentrated on the music.

The work is full of Straussian melody, and the themes, or 'leitmotiven', are clear and pregnant with significance, and I question very much if they received the due attention they require, in the orchestral treatment, brilliantly as the whole thing was carried through by Mr Beecham. This attention to detail and insistence on the essential points of the score cannot be grappled with in a few rehearsals, and it is all to the credit of the English orchestral player that he so finely rose to an emergency that would not have been possible of occurrence at a well-ordered Continental opera house.

(The ability of British orchestras to cope with difficult scores at short notice, due to a lack of proper funding and rehearsal time, is still a fact of life today.) The *Sphere*, a picture magazine that continued into the 1960s, gently mocked the censor's work. One picture showed a cross-section of the stage, with Clarence White-hill (the Prophet) below it, leaning nonchalantly against a pillar, hand on hip, while the Executioner climbs a ladder holding an empty platter. 'The Heroine Apostrophises a Head which is Not There', was the caption to another picture, showing Salome hold-ing aloft the same empty salver, watched by a rather puzzled Roman soldier.

Salome closed the season. Another one-act opera, it is not very long, and on the last night, Beecham preceded it with a rendering of the same composer's symphonic poem *Ein Heldenleben* ('A Hero's Life'), forty minutes of heavy orchestral music; a bonus or, knowing Beecham's roguishness, a penance to be borne by those waiting impatiently for the evening's titillation to begin. The or-chestra, happily, got their own bonus and a day off for their extra effort. Joseph Beecham was left deep in the red. Only four of the operas had been real box office hits: *Elektra* and *Salome* ('short and sensational bloodcurdlers' in Thomas's words), and *Les Contes d'Hoffmann* and *Die Fledermaus* ('tuneful lightweights'). Others had failed dismally. Joseph was philosophical. 'Some people spend their money on the turf. I prefer to devote mine to the popularising of Grand Opera and I do not begrudge the money.' His son was less so. 'There is no audience at all for opera,' he said wildly. 'Get an elephant to stand on one foot on top of the Nelson Column and you will draw a much larger crowd than twenty-five Salomes.'

No doubt physical and nervous exhaustion had much to do with this reaction at the time. The fact seems to have been that even a city the size of London could not digest so much opera, especially when we note that while Beecham was at His Majesty's Theatre, the Grand Opera Syndicate was presenting its own season at

Covent Garden. It must also be said that some of the productions were very hastily and sketchily staged. A performance of *Tristan*, said *The Times*, 'seemed only kept going in pure desperation'. Looking back on the year from the pages of *A Mingled Chime*, Beecham took a much more considered view. In those days, he later admitted, self-indulgence came into it. He would sometimes ignore artistic or commercial considerations and stage an opera simply to satisfy his own curiosity. Putting all that aside, it also became clear to him that a first-rate opera company could not be maintained without some sort of subsidy, private or public. When all was said and done, 1910 was perhaps the most remarkable year of his life.

CHAPTER EIGHT

If 1910 was outstanding, the next year ran it close, with the arrival in London of perhaps the most celebrated and exotic company in the whole history of the performing arts, the Russian Ballet, or, since it had been established in Paris, the *Ballets Russes*. The background story to this 'visitation' was quite complicated. After the company's first big triumph in Paris in 1909, the English art patroness Lady Ripon had invited its charismatic founder and director, Sergei Diaghilev, to start negotiations for a London season. Plans for this, at the Aldwych Theatre during 1910, were upset by the death of Edward VII. The Beechams, father and son, then took up the story. They first planned to bring over the *Ballets Russes* on their own account, a scheme that had strong attractions for Thomas, since the company would come with its own repertory, so relieving him of all the stresses and strains of the previous year. There was, however, Mr Oscar Hammerstein to take into account. The German-American impresario was building an opera house in Kingsway, a new thoroughfare which cut through some old slums between the City and the West End. In the face of this potential competition, Beecham accepted an invitation to join the board of the Grand Opera Syndicate. So it was that the Syndicate approached Diaghilev with proposals for a summer season at Covent Garden, though Beecham, still backed by his father, was the driving force.

Ballet had long been the Cinderella of the performing arts, in Britain at any rate. As an art form in its own right it had begun auspiciously enough, amid the splendours of Louis XIV's court at Versailles, where Louis took his title of 'The Sun King' from one of the many roles he himself danced. It had changed and grown under the stimulus of such celebrated dancers and choreographers as Marie de Camargo, Jean-Georges Noverre, Marie Taglioni and Marius Petipa, French master of the Imperial Russian Ballet. Since Louis XIV's own court composer Jean-Baptiste Lully, Jean-Philippe Rameau, Christoph Willibald Gluck, Léo Delibes, Adolphe Adam and Tchaikovsky had all written fine ballet scores. Even Beethoven (*Die Geschöpfe des Prometheus*, 'The Creatures of Prometheus') and Wagner (the sequence added for the 1861 Paris production of *Tannhäuser*) had contributed music for the ballet. For all this compared with opera or symphonic music it had remained decidedly lightweight. Something disreputable clung to it as well: the girls of the *corps de ballet* at the Paris Opéra, notwithstanding all those beautifully observed studies by Edgar Degas, were regarded in the 1890s as little more than the inmates of a high-class brothel. The artistic integrity of Diaghilev and his Russian Ballet, and the sheer brilliance of his productions, had already changed all that.

Beecham certainly had no doubt that Diaghilev was the greatest of all impresarios, 'the only one among them to realize my full conception of what this most ambiguous of all figures in public life ought to be'. Diaghilev, who had first made a name for himself in St Petersburg as an art critic and sub-director of the Imperial Theatre, had a genius for spotting genius, or the highest order of talent, in others, and mobilising it to his own ends. The list of those composers, writers, artists and designers, choreographers and dancers who worked for him reads like a Who's Who of twentieth-century art and music: Igor Stravinsky, Richard Strauss, Claude Debussy, Maurice Ravel, Manuel de Falla, Erik Satie, Sergei Proko-fiev, Darius Milhaud, Francis Poulenc, Léon Bakst, Alexander Be-nois, Pablo Picasso, Henri Matisse, André Derain, Mikhail Fokine, Léonide Massine, George Balanchine, Vaslav Nijinsky, Anna Pav-lova, Tamara Karsavina, Jean Cocteau. Probably no one else has ever brought together such a galaxy of talent. He was, at the same time, a financial wizard, keeping afloat his enormously expensive company, and maintaining the highest performing standards, in the days of largely private patronage.

It was appropriate that Diaghilev and his *Ballets Russes* had first made their name in Paris, honouring ballet in its historic home and strengthening further the special cultural links between Russia and France going back to the days of Peter the Great. The precision and fire of the dancing, the shimmering stage sets and costumes, the quality of the music, had sent immediate waves of excitement through the artistic world. Paris itself, 'The City of Light', where even the new Metro stations blossomed with the sinuous lines of *art nouveau*, shone brighter yet. Now, with the contracts finally settled and signed – including the very important agreement that Beecham's own orchestra should play throughout the season – it was to be London's turn.

While he was very keen to come to London, Diaghilev also looked forward to the visit with some trepidation. At that time England was truly separate from the rest of Europe, preoccupied with its empire, and with an aristocracy and whole way of life largely untouched by the political and social turmoil that had so much marked the history of Europe since the French Revolution and the Napoleonic Wars. It was an insular country in almost every sense of the word, and pretty much of a mystery to a man like Diaghilev. Moreover, it was Coronation year. What effect would that have on a visiting Russian ballet company?

When the Covent Garden curtain went up on the evening of 21 June 1911 on *Le Pavillon d'Armide*, with music by Alexander Tcherepnin, his worst fears seemed at first to be confirmed. Writing of the occasion some years later, he recalled:

> Our dancers were so nervous that they could hardly dance. The auditorium was even more magnificent than the stage, the walls were hung with over a hundred thousand roses, and the boxes contained almost as many maharajas. Our reception was icy, and neither Karsavina's variations, nor even those of Nijinsky in *Armide*, received the slightest applause. It was only after the dance of the buffoons that the strangest of sounds came to us; the public was gently clapping its kid-gloved hands.

Such discreet applause was quickly swept aside by an unprecedented wave of excitement. The whole of fashionable and artistic London, said Beecham, thought and talked nothing but ballet. He was hardly exaggerating. Here is how it seemed to Leonard Woolf, the liberal writer and publisher, just returned home from what was for him the deadening life of a colonial official in Ceylon (now Sri Lanka).

> Freud and Rutherford and Einstein were at work beginning to revolutionise our knowledge of our own minds and of the universe ... In literature one seemed to feel the ominous lull before the storm which was to produce in a few years *A la Recherche du Temps Perdu*, *Ulysses*, *The Waste Land* ... In painting we were in the middle of the profound revolution of Cézanne, Matisse and Picasso ... And to crown all, night after night we flocked to Covent Garden, entranced by a new art, a revelation to us benighted British, the Russian Ballet in the greatest days of Diaghilev and Nijinsky.

The season (punctuated immediately after the opening night by the coronation itself) ran to the end of July. As well as *Le Pavillon d'Armide*, the company presented *Les Sylphides* and *Le Carnaval*, with orchestral adaptations of the piano music of Chopin and Schumann respectively; the 'Polovtsian Dances' from Borodin's opera *Prince Igor*; *Le Spectre de la Rose*, a version of Weber's *Invitation to the Dance*; *Cléopâtre*, with music by Anton Arensky; and Rimsky-Korsakov's symphonic suite *Shéhérazade*, remembered for its gorgeous sets and costumes by Bakst. Besides Karsavina and Nijinsky the dancers included Adolf Bolm, who possessed much the same electrifying presence as Nijinsky himself. Beecham's orchestra was conducted by Tcherepnin. Confirming everything that Beecham wrote, that summer season was so successful that the company returned for a second season, from October to December of the same year. The repertory now included Adam's *Giselle*, Tchaikovsky's *Swan Lake* and two special excerpts from *The Sleeping Beauty*. The Beecham orchestra was once again in the pit, conducted this time by the imperturbable little Frenchman Pierre Monteux, who has gone down in history as the conductor at the premières of Stravinsky's *Petrushka* and *Le Sacre du Printemps*, Ravel's *Daphnis et Chloé* and Debussy's *Jeux* ('Games'), all Diaghilev commissions.

Away from the heady atmosphere of the Russian Ballet, Beecham did some conducting on his own account. He began the year with a return visit to St Helens, to celebrate his father's second term as mayor. He returned, of course, as a famous man with his own orchestra, bringing with him one of his favourite singers of the time, the soprano Mignon Nevada, to sing four arias in an easy-going programme. Later in the year Joseph was knighted for showering money on his son and thus on the cause of British music. Beecham conducted some more concerts, in London for the Royal Philharmonic Society, and in the provinces, where he made his début with the Liverpool Philharmonic Orchestra and so began a lifelong and affectionate association with them. His programmes were becoming a little less severe in terms of the amount of new music they contained. He was learning to strike a happier balance between the new and the sensational and the more familiar. The reputation of Delius among British concert-goers, he noted, was growing, although it was still a long way behind that of Elgar whom, as he said, the British public had placed on a special pedestal. As a matter of fact, Elgar's Symphony No. 2 in E flat, first given that year by the Queen's Hall Orchestra conducted by the composer, was not so well received. Its dedication to the memory of the old king instead of to the new one, George V, and the valedictory mood of much of it, as though with the passing of the

Edwardian decade something had gone forever, was not what most British people wanted to hear. 'Land of Hope and Glory' was what they liked, even if Elgar himself became sick and tired of it.

There was one more concert during 1911 that Beecham was booked to conduct, but dodged out of at the last moment: an all-Ethel Smyth programme, scheduled, as it happened, for 1 April. Notwithstanding the mutual exasperation that marked their association, Beecham was always a welcome guest at the Smyth family home at Hill Hall in Essex, where he relaxed playing the Bechstein grand or testing his mettle at chess against such opponents as the fashionable portrait painter John Singer Sargent. It was probably through Ethel Smyth's sister and a prominent socialite, Mrs Mary Hunter, that he met Lady (Maud) Cunard. His relationship with her soon confirmed him in many people's minds, after the recent scandal of the Foster divorce, as a bit of a rascal. Lady Cunard was one among quite a number of rich American women who, at around this time, married titled but often impecunious Englishmen, thus giving a shot in the arm to a decaying aristocracy. In fact, her husband, Sir Bache Cunard, was well off; but he loved the life of a country squire at the family home in Leicestershire (good fox-hunting country), while she much preferred the bright lights of society. The name, of course, also conjures up the golden age of the ocean liner. Sir Bache's grandfather had founded the most famous shipping line in the world, and from the time of the *Mauretania* and *Lusitania* of 1907 to the *Queen Mary* of 1936 the name of Cunard was synonymous with everything luxurious and glamorous in sea travel. When she first met Beecham, Lady Cunard had a fourteen-year-old daughter, Nancy (soon to become a famous social and political figure in her own right), was separated from her husband, and lived in London with the Irish novelist George Moore. Her home in Cavendish Square was rented from the prime minister, Asquith, and recently decorated in the exotic style of Diaghilev's most celebrated designer, Léon Bakst. She was fascinated by the arts, though perhaps with no deep understanding of them, and she very quickly fell in love with the handsome, brilliant, dashing Thomas Beecham. Exactly what he felt about her is not so easy to ascertain; but from 1911 and for many years to come she was devoted to him, dragooning royalty and top politicians to his concerts and opera seasons, organising charity balls, receptions and dinner parties, in aid of him in particular and music in general.

Oscar Hammerstein, incidentally, had his own brush with Lady Cunard. This tycoon of the old school, constantly chewing on one of the cigars that had made his fortune and fond of pushing his black silk topper to the back of his head, had built and opened his London Opera House. For all his brashness he genuinely loved opera, and having done much to popularise it in America, had come to London 'to take some of the starch out of it'. All the same, it was probably his mistake to eject Lady Cunard and her party from his theatre for making too much noise; for his enterprise soon failed and he returned dejectedly to New York (perhaps on a Cunard ship). His nephew, Oscar Hammerstein II, later brought real fame to the family, as the lyricist who worked with Jerome Kern on *Showboat* and with Richard Rodgers on such blockbusting musicals as *Oklahoma!*, *South Pacific*, *The King and I* and *The Sound of Music*. Meanwhile, uncle Oscar's opera house was taken over first by C. B. Cochran and then by Sir Oswald Stoll. As the Stoll Theatre it maintained strong musical associations, becoming, briefly, the headquarters of the newly formed Festival Ballet in 1951, then the venue for the first British staging of Gershwin's opera *Porgy and Bess*, before finally closing its doors in 1957.

CHAPTER NINE

The *Ballets Russes* were back in London for the summer of 1912. This time Beecham, who had watched Tcherepnin and Monteux at work and learnt a lot from them, directed his own orchestra in a staging of Balakirev's symphonic poem *Thamar*. Mily Balakirev was the most thoroughly nationalist of all the Russians, *Thamar* ('Tamara') itself, with its exotic flavour and orchestration, having a big influence on Rimsky-Korsakov. Russian music, of course, became one of Beecham's specialities, with a niche in his affections always reserved for Balakirev. This time, too, London was treated to *L'Oiseau de Feu* ('The Firebird'), with the beautiful Karsavina in the title role. With a story taken from Russian legend, this was the first of Diaghilev's commissions from Stravinsky. It was the score that made the composer's name and propelled the *Ballets Russes* into the vanguard of twentieth-century music.

For Beecham himself and his orchestra greater things yet were in store. In the spring of the previous year Beecham's friend André Messager, now director of the Paris Opéra, had secured the orchestra to play for a new production of *Elektra*. This in itself was a great honour – a British orchestra brought to play at the illustrious Paris Opéra (a state of affairs resented in some quarters of the French musical establishment). Now Diaghilev, who personally got on well with Beecham, chose the orchestra, with the experience of three London seasons behind it, to join his company for their visit to Berlin in the winter of 1912. For the great Russian to choose a British orchestra to play for his company in another foreign capital was indeed a unique accolade for Beecham and his musicians.

Berlin was a comparative newcomer among the capitals of Europe. It had been the capital of a united Germany only since 1871. In fact, its real growth and importance went back no further than the time of the Prussian king Frederick the Great (r. 1740–86). But it had come a long way in a relatively short space of time. Such philosophers and scientists as Gottfried Leibniz, Wilhelm von Humboldt, Georg Hegel and Karl Marx had made it a major centre of learning. The flute-playing King Frederick had begun its climb up the musical ladder, bringing to his beautiful palace of Sans Souci at Potsdam the composer Carl Philipp Emmanuel Bach. From that time on, the city was associated with a whole line of great musicians: Felix Mendelssohn (whose grandfather Moses Mendelssohn was another famed Berlin academic), Carl Maria von Weber (the première of his seminal romantic opera *Der Freischütz* took place there), Hans von Bülow, Karl Klindworth, Richard Strauss, Artur Nikisch and Ferruccio Busoni. The founding of the Berlin Philharmonic Orchestra in 1882 added greatly to its musical lustre. It was a handsome city, too, with its Unter den Linden leading to the Brandenburg Gate and the open spaces of the Tiergarten beyond.

For Beecham's players, the visit had its traumas and crises. They made the crossing from Harwich to the Hook of Holland on what was apparently a very stormy November night. The ferry boats of those days were neither as large nor as well stabilised as today's; many of the players were badly seasick and some of their instruments were thrown about and damaged. Having recovered from that ordeal, and installed in Berlin's Kroll Theatre (more famous in years to come as the Kroll Opera under the direction of Otto Klemperer and Alexander von Zemlinsky), the orchestra threatened to go on strike for non-payment of extra rehearsals. Diaghilev hastily scraped the money together, perhaps having second thoughts about employing a bunch of recalcitrant Englishmen. In performance, however, and directed once again by Monteux, they covered themselves with glory. The most important new work for them to play was *Petrushka*, first performed the previous summer at the Théâtre du Châtelet in Paris, the scene of many of Diaghilev's triumphs and scandals. The image of Petrushka ('Little Pete'), as conceived by Alexander Benois and immortalised by Nijinsky, is as famous as that of Odette in *Swan Lake*. The story, of a puppet imbued with human feelings it cannot understand or control – a dark inner world set against the bright outer one of the St Petersburg Shrove Tide Fair – raised ballet to the heights of psychological drama. Stravinsky's score, a big advance on that of the already brilliant *Oiseau de Feu*, established him as a major new force in twentieth-century music. Beecham certainly considered it to be his finest work, notwithstanding *Le Sacre du Printemps* and all that came after.

At the end of the ballet season, Beecham joined his orchestra to conduct two concerts and so concentrate the spotlight on himself and his band of players. Mozart's 'Haffner' Symphony (No. 35), Berlioz's *Carnaval Romain* overture, and an overture by Paisiello were complemented by a number of contemporary, but not too heavy, British pieces, including Vaughan Williams's pastoral evocation *In the Fen Country*, Balfour Gardiner's *Shepherd Fennel's Dance*, Percy Grainger's light-hearted *Mock Morris* (which delighted the usually staid Berliners) and Delius's *Brigg Fair* and *Dance Rhapsody No.* 1 (it should be remembered that Delius was already fairly well known in Germany before Beecham took up his cause). The Berlin press much admired the still youthful Beecham Symphony Orchestra. 'These Englishmen play with a sovereign authority all too rare nowadays anywhere,' Beecham proudly quotes in *A Mingled Chime* – praise indeed from a city of such high musical excellence.

Beecham was also in Berlin to renew his acquaintance with Richard Strauss, and to discuss with him plans for a London production of his latest, and very soon his best-loved, opera, *Der Rosenkavalier* ('The Knight of the Rose'). Beecham had already seen and heard this during its first run in Dresden the previous year, and, thanks once more to his phenomenal memory, already knew much of it by heart. Hofmannsthal's bitter-sweet romance spiced with robust comedy, set in eighteenth-century Vienna, and Strauss's luscious treatment of it were a million miles from the morbid and violent worlds of *Salome* and *Elektra*. The best-known feature of the score is the group of waltzes that accompany much of the action – a dance that came as naturally to the Bavarian Strauss as to his Viennese namesakes. They may be historically wrong for the period of the opera, but add immeasurably to its piquant mood of nostalgia. Indeed, from the time of *Der Rosenkavalier*, a note of nostalgia was to run through nearly all of Strauss's work, turning him from one of music's iconoclasts into one of its longest-living conservatives.

Strauss, a shrewd and opportunist businessman, was delighted with Beecham's proposals. It was at home that Beecham had problems. Despite the earlier success of *Elektra* and *Salome*, he had a tough time winning round his colleagues on the Grand Opera Syndicate, who felt that English audiences might be bored by four hours of Teutonic love and humour. There were also, as Beecham put it, 'my friends of the Censorship at St James's Palace'. The blatantly erotic music at the very start of the opera seems not to have disturbed them. After all, music is music. They were worried about a bed much later on in the action and the lecherous Baron Ochs's references to it. As Beecham observed, such mild hanky-panky could be seen and heard nightly in almost any London music hall or variety theatre, but, in the eyes of the censors, Covent

Garden was clearly supposed to be above such things. Either any reference to the bed must be cut from the libretto, or the bed itself must be concealed. Beecham chose the latter course of action, since, as he said, it was easier to move the furniture around than to tamper with the score.

In spite of such frustrations, Beecham was still able to ring up the curtain on the London première of *Der Rosenkavalier* at Covent Garden on 29 January 1913. The cast on that occasion (it changed later in the run) included Margarethe Siems and Eva von der Osten, the original Marschallin and Octavian; while Beecham specially engaged the Polish soprano Claire Dux, then a member of the Berlin Royal Opera, for the part of Sophie, which became one of her most famous roles. He also brought over the German baritone Hermann Gura, who was also at that time director of the Berlin Comic Opera, and an excellent choice as his producer.

At this point, it is worth quoting from a feature in *The Times*, which appeared the day before the première, and which highlights Beecham's then current status in London's operatic life, as well as the perennial problems of opera in the capital.

> Gallant and debonair, Mr Thomas Beecham is again offering musical London a season of opera. The offering is princely. The modern production of opera exacts stupendous labour, engulfs money and cannot, it seems, be made to repay; a staggering task, which Mr Beecham is not tackling for the first time. The course of opera in London has been strewn with the wrecks of courageous schemes, but Mr Beecham's disappointments have been less merited than anyone's and his courage has surpassed the rest, for a disinterested passion for art is his motive, and he is returning to the charge ... Tomorrow's opera at Covent Garden, 'The Rose Cavalier', is the fourth Richard Strauss opera to reach us, thanks wholly to Mr Beecham, but for whom London would doubtless be still ignorant of them all.

The first night notices were glowing. *The Times* again: 'Mr Beecham came back to the opera last night, bringing wonderful music with him. To an audience of all artistic and fashionable London he gave the rococo Viennese fantasy of 'The Rose Cavalier' of Messrs Hofmannsthal and Richard Strauss and won a new feather for his cap and one of the bravest.' *The Illustrated London News*, opting for its own version of the title, called the opera

> a brilliant work which will reconcile to Strauss many whose sympathies have been alienated by the coarseness of 'Feuersnot',

the unbridled sensuality of 'Salome', the tense, unrelieved gloom of 'Elektra'. 'The Rose-Bearer' is not only brilliant, it is beautiful; not only beautiful but finely considered – the ripe expression of genius.

Together with his father's backing, and the tireless support of Lady Cunard, Beecham now had an invaluable stage manager in Donald Baylis, another in the colourful line (Verdi Fawcett, Tommy Chapman) who were drawn towards him. Baylis had begun as an office boy at the Beecham factory at St Helens, gaining rapid promotion to secretary and then to general manager. He also had a good tenor voice, so Joseph then sent him to Italy, where he had singing lessons and learnt a lot about opera management. Alan Jefferson, in his book *Sir Thomas Beecham: A Centenary Tribute*, suggests that he was Joseph's illegitimate son by one of the servants in the Beecham household, so making him Thomas's half-brother. Be that as it may, he became Beecham's chorus-master and then his right-hand man, dealing with every sort of problem as it arose, sometimes in costume and make-up as he waited in the wings to take to the boards himself, more often, as time went on, ensconced in the theatre bar, sharing to the full his chief's predilection for whisky and soda.

Baylis was worth his weight in gold, as Beecham plunged back into the operatic deep end in that same early season of 1913. As well as *Der Rosenkavalier*, he directed more performances of *Salome* and *Elektra* (according to reports, driving the music harder than ever), and of Wagner's *Tristan und Isolde* and *Die Meistersinger von Nürnberg*. With hardly a pause for breath, he then turned his attention to the next work to come off the Strauss-Hofmannsthal production line. This was *Ariadne auf Naxos*, one of the most unusual of all musico-dramatic works. In its original form, it is not so much a blend as a juxtaposition of straight theatre and opera. It opens with a version (condensed and translated into German by Hofmannsthal) of Molière's play *Le Bourgeois Gentilhomme*, in which he mocked the *nouveaux riches* of his day (the latter part of the seventeenth century). Louis XIV's court composer Lully had originally written incidental music to it, for which Strauss substituted a musical pastiche of his own. Then follows the entertainment which the 'Perfect Gentleman', Monsieur Jourdain, puts on to impress his friends and the lady of his desires, the *Ariadne auf Naxos* of the title. After the musical opulence of *Der Rosenkavalier*, Strauss pared down his orchestra to almost chamber proportions, though the vocal writing is fiendishly difficult in

places. He and Hofmannsthal subsequently revised the work, replacing Molière's play with a new and specifically operatic pro-
logue. But the original version was the one that concerned
Beecham, and the one he always preferred.

The London production had its première at His Majesty's
Theatre on 27 May 1913, drawing into Beecham's orbit two other
famous names. W. Somerset Maugham translated into English
Hofmannsthal's own reworking of Molière's play; while the part of
M. Jourdain was taken by the actor-manager Sir Herbert Beerbohm Tree, at that time in charge of His Majesty's Theatre. Tree,
who founded what later became the Royal Academy of Dramatic
Art, was both a noted Shakespearian and a character actor.
Dressed in comic period costume, from a huge plumed hat to
ribbons on his shoe buckles, and brandishing sword and staff, he
had a tendency to forget his lines and ham it up a bit. The curious
form of the work rather perplexed the public and the press.

> The nymphs and palm trees of Naxos are represented in rococo
> style, but Richard Strauss, whatever he aimed at, has not written
> rococo music. Phrases of other composers from Lully to 'Lohen-
> grin' are carried down undissolved in the torrent, and a whole air
> from Schubert is quoted – indications that parodistic intentions
> were present. But in essence the music is purely and wonderfully
> Strauss – that is, it is music too large for mockery, music too
> purely expressive and passionate to be witty.

Maugham and Tree both came in for some criticism: 'Mr Somerset
Maugham adapted *Le Bourgeois Gentilhomme* out of all recogni-
tion and left it to Sir Herbert Tree to complete the disfigurement.'
Another critic summed up the whole performance thus: 'Take
"Charley's Aunt", tack on the second act of "Tristan and Isolde",
and while the latter is in progress perform the frisky portions of
"Hello Ragtime" ' – very funny copy, all the more so, perhaps, for
a cruel little grain of truth. But it had nothing directly to do with
Beecham, who by then must have been the most experienced and
knowledgeable conductor of Strauss, as well as one of the composer's closest friends.

CHAPTER TEN

In June 1913 *The Times* carried an announcement of Sir Joseph Beecham's forthcoming Season of Russian Opera and Ballet. Joseph was now installed in West Brow, a multi-roomed mansion in Hampstead. This house, judging from descriptions of it, was over-opulent and vulgar, featuring, among other novelties, a very large globular green alabaster 'pill', the source of the family fortunes, placed by the main staircase. We might say this was typically *nouveau riche*. But Joseph clearly loved music and knew a lot about it, especially opera. 'Three Russian operas new to London will be produced,' he himself wrote,

> and their special attraction is that they give us pictures of Russian life with which our public is unacquainted. The whole ceremonial and pageantry of old Russian court life is picturesque and gorgeous and provides splendid material for the stage. The productions approach most nearly, in another form of art, to the historical plays of Shakespeare. Moussorgsky, the composer of two of the works that the Russians will present here, bases his claim to distinction on the fact that he has developed a style entirely his own, and that he is the only great operatic composer who has shown himself to be entirely free from the influence of Wagner.

The striking originality of Modest Musorgsky was not widely appreciated in 1913 – certainly not in London before the season in question – which makes Sir Joseph's comments, assuming they are indeed his own, all the more perceptive.

Such a season was possible thanks once again to Diaghilev, who had already brought to Paris a contingent of the Russian Imperial Opera to join his ballet company. All that was needed – though the operation would still cost a small fortune – was to bring these combined forces, with their ready-made productions, across the Channel. Thomas had first mooted this idea of a combined season of Russian opera and ballet to his colleagues on the board of the

Grand Opera Syndicate. Their worry about the costs and their general lack of enthusiasm brought about his resignation from the Board, and a temporary severance with Covent Garden. Consequently Sir Joseph booked the Theatre Royal, Drury Lane, for a period of just over one month, in the middle of the summer. The Beecham Symphony Orchestra was once again installed in the pit, almost literally a stone's throw from where it had scored some of its earlier triumphs. The conducting was to be entirely in the hands of Monteux and others directly attached to the Diaghilev organisation. Thomas was to be a spectator, although as we shall see even this passive role drew him into the maelstrom of events.

The season opened on 24 June with Musorgsky's *Boris Godunov*, magnificently staged, of course, coming from the Diaghilev stable, and conducted by Emil Cooper, a distinguished Russian despite his name, who had earlier directed the première of Rimsky-Korsakov's *The Golden Cockerel* (often known by its French title, *Le Coq d'Or*) and after the Bolshevik Revolution of 1917 worked mainly in North America. Above all, it had Fyodor Chaliapin, making his British début, in the title role. Tsar Boris, haunted and finally destroyed by guilt, was the part that he virtually created, combining his superb bass voice with a magnetic stage presence. *The Times* next day was ecstatic:

> Stagnation in London musical life is ever dispelled at the name of Beecham. The name has already almost historic association with Richard Strauss and Frederick Delius, not to mention lesser talents. By last night's remarkable opening of Sir Joseph Beecham's Drury Lane season it will be honourably connected with the first introduction of real Russian opera to England.

Boris Godunov itself was 'an opera like no other opera ever written; a vast historical fresco full of vividness and large movement and of epical passions'. As for Chaliapin:

> A man of great stature and handsome mien, M. Chaliapin cannot be imagined to have a rival in this part. His voice is noble, a wonderful organ, but there is not the least tendency to vulgar display. He is first and foremost a great dramatic artist. The scene of Boris's hallucination, though one understood not a word, (the production was sung in Russian) seized one as nothing before seen on the operatic stage. And the death of Boris was an equal achievement, holding everyone spellbound, though the hour was close on midnight, and was applauded as very few operatic performances in London can be remembered to have been.

The *Sketch* carried a full-page illustration of him gorgeously robed as Boris, with a host of spectral figures behind, linking him with Shakespeare's equally guilt-ridden Macbeth.

On successive nights Chaliapin was hardly less impressive as Dosifey in Musorgsky's *Khovanshchina*, another historical drama, completed by Rimsky-Korsakov after Musorgsky's death, and in the title role of Rimsky-Korsakov's own *Ivan the Terrible* (Diaghilev's alternative and certainly more evocative title for *The Maid of Pskov*). The other big picture magazine of the day, the *Sphere*, carried its own artist's impression of the cast of *Khovanshchina* receiving a standing ovation from a packed house. 'The Russians', it said beneath, 'are the rage of the moment in dancing and in acting, and Sir Joseph Beecham has achieved a remarkable triumph with the Russian Opera Company. It is many a year since our national theatre has seen such splendid audiences.' Indeed, the auditorium of the Drury Lane theatre was nightly a-glitter with tiaras, necklaces and pearls, sashes and decorations, the snapping open and shut of elegant fans. And to the delight of those with a sharp eye and a knowledge of the contemporary art and literary scene, Ethel Smyth was joined by another lady of masculine aspect, the American avant-garde writer and friend in Paris of Picasso, Matisse and Braque, Gertrude Stein.

The dramatic importance of the chorus in these Russian operas, and the splendid singing and acting of this particular ensemble, were not overlooked by the critics. They were certainly a force to be reckoned with in more ways than one, as Thomas Beecham discovered on the night of a royal gala performance of *Boris Godunov*. Arriving late, but in time for the Coronation scene, he instantly knew something was wrong. Only a fraction of the chorus was on stage. He hurried backstage with Donald Baylis, where he learnt, through an interpreter, that a dispute had broken out between the chorus and Chaliapin over the matter of the night's box-office takings. The chorus, apparently, understood it to be their benefit night. Chaliapin, it seems, thought otherwise. At that moment the great man himself came off stage in a towering rage, started arguing fiercely with a member of the chorus and knocked the man down, whereupon his colleagues set upon Chaliapin, in Beecham's words, 'like a pack of wolves'. The police were called. Baylis, who unwisely intervened, received a bump on the head 'as big as a fair-sized plum'. It must have made an amazing spectacle: Chaliapin in the gold and jewel-encrusted robes and crown of the Tsar (together weighing close on thirty kilos), being set upon by a crowd of 'serfs', like a sudden eruption of real-life Russian history in the heart of London's West End, with King George V and Queen Mary just out of sight on the other side of the footlights. Equally remarkable, according to Beecham, was how quickly the volatile Russians calmed down again, allowing the performance to continue almost as though nothing had happened. Indeed, the audience seems to have known nothing of the fracas. 'By way of prelude,' *The Times* reported sweetly next morning, 'the Russian mob [the chorus] turned to the audience and sang 'God Save the King' in recognisable English. At the end the chorus came forward again and sang the noble Russian anthem, M. Chaliapin in their midst.' M. Chaliapin, their reporter might have been alarmed to know, had by then two loaded revolvers concealed about his person. The episode tells us much about Chaliapin himself. He was born into near poverty in provincial Russia, and for him as for many another famous star who has pulled himself up by his boot-straps, money was something of an obsession. He had also been brutally used as a boy, learning very quickly the hard lesson that attack is the best form of defence. Since he had the build and something of the demeanour of a heavyweight boxer, it was a lesson well learnt.

Because of their novelty, and the towering presence of Chaliapin, the visiting Russian singers rather stole the headlines from the dancers. Yet the *Ballets Russes* brought back with them a programme that was in many ways their most remarkable ever. *Prélude à l'Après-midi d'un Faune* was a realisation of Debussy's early orchestral masterpiece, inspired by Stéphane Mallarmé's poetic evocation of mythical Greece. The sets and costumes, sensual enough in themselves, were by Bakst, while Nijinsky's choreography, expressing both sexual awakening and something of the dancer's own sexual ambivalence, had already caused quite a scandal. London received it politely. *Jeux* was new to the Diaghilev repertory. Nijinsky and Bakst had collaborated again, while this time the score had been specially commissioned from Debussy. The nebulous scenario, of sexual dalliance on a tennis court, never really caught on, and for a long time Debussy's score, his last major orchestral work, was cast aside with it, often cited by critics as evidence of his declining powers. Today the music of *Jeux* stands securely on its own, as a seminal work of twentieth-century music. There was also *La Tragédie de Salomé*, with music by the French composer Florent Schmitt, conceived originally as a mimed drama, then choreographed for Diaghilev by Boris Romanov, who later formed a ballet company of his own. Schmitt is an attractive composer, unhappily marginalised by the work of his contemporaries, primarily Debussy and Ravel, with whom his own music has points in common. It was Karsavina in the title role that was the main talking point at the time of the ballet's London staging. She certainly invited comparison with Aino Ackté's earlier operatic portrayal of the same character, with some daring designs stencilled onto her legs which once again invoked the name of Aubrey Beardsley.

The other new production of Sir Joseph's season was *Le Sacre du Printemps* ('The Rite of Spring'), a celebration of pagan Russia. This had just hit the artistic world like a sledge-hammer. The sets and costumes by Nicholas Roerich, who was ideal for the job in view of his scholarly interest in prehistoric Russia, and the choreography by Nijinsky, were startling enough in themselves. But it was the music that all the fuss was about. Nothing, not even certain passages in *Petrushka*, nor even such a score as *Elektra*, had prepared anybody for it. Stravinsky himself remembered from his childhood 'the violent Russian spring that seemed to begin in an hour and was like the whole world cracking'. He had now compressed that experience into his epoch-making score, so causing his name, for the next fifty years at least, to send a thrill of horror through the breast of every maiden aunt in the land. The circumstances of the world première, at the Théâtre des Champs-Elysées, Paris, on 28 May 1913, the catcalls, the fighting, the arrival of the police, while Nijinsky frantically went on calling out the steps from the wings and Monteux and his orchestra battled on in the pit, are all well enough known. What is not so well known is that, under Thomas Beecham's aegis, some of the preliminary rehearsals had taken place in the Aldwych Theatre in London. Now 'The Crowning of Spring', to quote from the programme, was back. The audience was to be prepared by a pre-performance stage talk from the British music critic Edwin Evans, a future president of the International Society for Contemporary Music. On the evening of the first of four scheduled performances, 11 July, he got the slow handclap from a restless and impatient audience.

So, to those cold and desolate opening strains on the highest register of the bassoon, the curtain went up on Roerich's strange, doll-like figures of pagan Russia, a million miles from the wings and white dresses of *Les Sylphides*. The subsequent effect of the music is summed up by one keen London balletomane, Cyril Beaumont, author of *The Diaghilev Ballet in London*: 'The maelstrom of rhythm, immensely vital and as dominating, as remorseless, and as irritating to the nervous system as the continuous thudding of a savage's tom-tom.' The young Lytton Strachey, soon to write *Eminent Victorians* and to emerge as one of England's prominent men of letters, described the evening as 'one of the most painful experiences of my life'. Someone was heard to remark that he wanted to howl like a dog, but didn't bother because he couldn't have been heard. Eighty years on, the music can still come as just as much of a shock at first hearing. The evening did not end in another riot. London society liked to think itself above such mayhem. But it was just as stunned, as the majority of press notices made clear. *The New Statesman*, a new voice of the intellectual Left, launched only two months earlier, was one of the few publications to take a more considered and perceptive view, with the opinion that whether one liked the music or not, the ballet as a whole achieved a new kind of artistic synthesis.

Beecham's orchestra, it is worth adding, had only eight rehearsals with Monteux, compared with over twice that number for the Paris première. It might be argued that the French players were the very first, in every sense, to face the music. But the score, with its unprecedented time-signatures, must have been just as shocking to the men of the Beecham Symphony Orchestra. Said Eugene Goossens, then a youthful orchestral violinist, 'Feats of sight-reading performed in a minimum of rehearsal time during that season have never been equalled anywhere, before or since.' Monteux was certainly impressed. This reputation among British orchestras for sight-reading new and difficult scores is, of course, just as strong today. Monteux, incidentally, was not so happy with the music itself. The man so closely associated with *Le Sacre* for the rest of his very long life later declared that he had only agreed to direct the work in the first place after much pleading from Diaghilev, and never liked it. Beecham clearly did not like it either. After his enthusiasm for *Petrushka*, he could only bring himself to refer diplomatically to *Le Sacre du Printemps* as 'this striking and interesting work'.

In the autumn he was able to escape from London and the Diaghilev hothouse and into a situation which showed him in his finest light. Ernst Denhof was a German-Swiss impresario now operating an opera company which toured mainly in the North of England. It was a formidable operation: a company of nearly two hundred, an orchestra of around eighty players (including, as circumstances permitted, members of the big London orchestras), and an ambitious repertory that encompassed *Elektra* and *Der Rosenkavalier* as well as *Der fliegende Holländer*, *Tannhäuser*, *Tristan und Isolde* and *Die Meistersinger von Nürnberg*. Beecham admired Denhof's enterprise, and for the latter's projected tour of autumn 1913 agreed to conduct, among other things, a production of the

Ring, no less. But disaster soon struck. Box-office takings fell woefully short of the very high production costs, and the season foundered in Manchester. A call for help went out to Beecham, still in London, and he and Baylis duly hurried north to the rescue. They went straight from the station to Manchester's Theatre Royal, where Beecham called everybody on stage and told them that the show *would* go on. Then he and Baylis started phoning the other scheduled theatres, reaffirming bookings, poring over seating plans and prices, consulting auditors and accountants, and drumming up financial support from local philanthropists. They also hit on a novel publicity campaign, appealing through the press to the sporting instincts of each town and city to support the tour, as though they were calling for support of the local football or cricket team.

The Lady Cunards of this world would surely have been totally lost in such a scenario. Beecham, the Liverpudlian, was back in his element. He could relish such incidents as the night when members of the orchestra (locals, one assumes, not Londoners) refused to play on stage during the last act of *Meistersinger*. They were, they told him, musicians and respectable men, not 'bloomin' actors'. This was the voice of Methodism, rising from the hills and dales, the smoke-begrimed mills of cotton, wool and steel, where the Stage was looked upon askance, if not with an even more baleful and withering eye.

CHAPTER ELEVEN

The next year Sir Joseph Beecham begged to announce, in a large printed copperplate hand, a Grand Season of Russian Opera, German Opera and Russian Ballet. The cover of his new prospectus looked like a very stiff and formal invitation to a society wedding. Another great season was in store. The wheeling and dealing that lay behind it is of some interest, because it involved the French impresario Gabriel Astruc. From 1907, Astruc had largely promoted the Diaghilev company in Paris. Thus the world has him to thank, almost as much as Diaghilev himself, for *L'Oiseau de Feu*, *Petrushka* and *Le Sacre du Printemps*. Now Astruc had gone bankrupt, due partly to the costly failure of *Le Sacre du Printemps* in his newly-built and beautifully appointed Théâtre des Champs-Elysées, and the enormous production costs of *Boris Godunov* and *Khovanshchina*. The Beechams had stepped quickly into the breach, acquiring from Diaghilev the productions of both these operas. They also loaned to Diaghilev the sum of money the latter had already agreed to pay to Richard Strauss and Hofmannsthal for their new ballet *Josephs-Legende*, though, as we shall see, this was not such a shrewd piece of business.

The season, from 20 May to 25 July, again at the Theatre Royal, Drury Lane, was going to be as brilliant as any that the Beechams had so far brought to London. Up the road at Covent Garden they had Nellie Melba, Emmy Destinn, Enrico Caruso, John McCormack, Antonio Scotti and Giovanni Martinelli; but even this galaxy of stars could not compete with 'The Lane', as fashionable London now dubbed it. In the prospectus, Chaliapin Nights were picked out in coloured ink. The great man himself was the bane of hostesses from Hampstead to Cheyne Walk, suddenly left with an empty place at their dinner tables because some guest had been hijacked by the last-minute offer of a ticket or a place in a box for a 'Chaliapin Night'. Not so welcome were all the social hangers-on, arriving late, leaving early, whispering, chattering, giggling. The correspondence columns of *The Times* broke out in a rash of letters of complaint. Still, it did mean that every night was a sell-out.

The season opened with Thomas Beecham back in the pit, directing his own valiant orchestra in the German part of the programme. His further performances of *Der Rosenkavalier* have a special niche in operatic history because they included the twenty-six-year-old Lotte Lehmann, then on the threshold of fame, though her appearances on that occasion went virtually unnoticed. *Die Zauberflöte* was another landmark in Thomas's rehabilitation of Mozart. While *Così fan tutte* had for so long been dismissed as trivial and in poor taste, *Die Zauberflöte* ('The Magic Flute') was written off by most people, including Sir Joseph, as a sort of tedious aberration. It is written in the much less familiar idiom of Viennese *Singspiel*, with spoken dialogue instead of sung recitation (which, it must be admitted, can become rather tedious if it is not well acted), and the work is an odd blend of pantomime, fairy tale and masonic ritual. Moreover, some of the good and bad characters switch round halfway through. It certainly can be a minefield for any theatrical producer. Thomas, however, had conducted some performances on his recent tour with the 'Denhof-Beecham Grand Opera Company', which had no doubt sharpened his own judgment of the work. For Drury Lane, he simplified the settings, speeded up the numerous scene changes and cut some of the dialogue, allowing the music, alternately Mozart at his most innocent and most elevated, to shine through. His service to Mozart extended to his casting. For the extremely taxing role of the Queen of the Night he brought over from Germany the soprano Frieda Hempel, already famous in her own country and now acclaimed in London. His casting of Claire Dux (his Sophie in *Der Rosenkavalier*) as Pamina was an even greater revelation. Melba, Destinn and Caruso all came down the road to hear her, and Melba, not one to hand out compliments lightly, hailed her with the words 'You are my successor', though in terms of international fame Claire Dux never reached that level. An extra performance of the opera, by public demand, must have been very gratifying to Beecham himself.

Then came the Russian repertory: together with revivals of *Boris Godunov*, *Khovanshchina* and *Ivan the Terrible*, the big new operatic attraction was Diaghilev's production of Borodin's *Prince Igor*, one more work completed by Rimsky-Korsakov with help from Glazunov after its composer's death. It was also another marvellous vehicle for Chaliapin, who this time took the two strongly contrasted roles of the profligate Russian Prince Galitzsky and the wild but noble Polovtsian chieftain Khan Konchak, while the ballet company was on hand to repeat the 'Polovtsian Dances' in Act II, which had so thrilled London in previous seasons. As recalled by Beecham, the run-up to the first night was show business at its craziest. Drury Lane, he said, was more like a railway station than a theatre, with dressmakers, wigmakers and scene-shifters all milling about and getting in each other's way. Much of the scenery, it was soon discovered, had only been sketched out, and there and then had to be laid out on every available square inch of floor space for painting. The orchestral parts, with cuts, were full of errors, which took days to correct. Chaliapin had another fight, this time with the baritone Paul Andreev in the title role, the chorus, as Beecham put it, 'taking sides with as much ardour as if they had been Capulets and Montagues'. The hysteria reached a climax over one weekend. A general rehearsal was conducted while the elaborate stage sets, many of them still wet with fresh paint, were positioned with much commotion. This went on into the small hours of Monday morning, until the conductor, Leon Steinberg, finally collapsed and had to be carried off to his dressing-room. After a break of a few hours, the full dress rehearsal began, and went on for another seven hours. At one point Chaliapin, now close to tears, begged for a postponement. Indeed, as Beecham wrote, 'It now seemed impossible that the work could be ready on time.' Yet for once, at any rate, that old chestnut, 'It'll be all right on the night', worked like a charm. After all the chaos and the hysterics, the first performance was, again in Beecham's words, 'as flawless as it was exhilarating'. If such a thing were possible, it was greeted with even more rapture than *Boris Godunov*. Soon after, Joseph was awarded a baronetcy to go with his knighthood, while the Tsar bestowed upon him the Order of St Stanislas.

The other new Russian operas turned from history to fantasy. Rimsky-Korsakov's *May Night*, based on a fairy tale by Nikolai Gogol, is rarely staged today, for all its charm. *The Golden Cockerel*, on the other hand, has become Rimsky's most famous and successful opera. It was his last major work, inspired by another fairy tale, this time by Pushkin. It had at first been banned in Russia itself, because the authorities suspected it of mocking Tsar Nicholas and his government after the fiasco of the Russo-Japanese War of 1905, when an antiquated Russian fleet sailed halfway round the world and was then blasted out of the water. Classified in the programmes as an 'opera-ballet', *The Golden Cockerel* was tailor-made for Diaghilev, and the start of its international success lies with him. Fokine, who directed and choreographed the production, decided, regardless of cost, to have both a singer and a dancer for each of the principal roles, the former being placed on either side of the stage, a bit after the manner of a Greek chorus, while the dancers performed in the middle. This upset the composer's son Alexander, who protested in a letter to *The Times* that it was going against his father's intentions; another instance, perhaps, of the often rather misguided ways in which so many descendants or otherwise self-appointed guardians of famous artists try to protect their work and reputation. Above all, there were the sets and costumes of the avant-garde Russian painter Natalia Gontcharova, one more in the company of composers, artists and choreographers who fully justified Diaghilev's faith in them. Gontcharova's sets and costumes were another feast of colour, epitomising, with those for *Petrushka* and *Daphnis et Chloé*, the Diaghilev era. The *Sphere*, which carried an artist's impression of one of the scenes, spoke of 'the thrill of aesthetic pleasure' they generated. Other critics were full of praise for the production ('amazing gusto and originality'), and for the work itself, with some allusion to its political troubles at home. 'So rough and hearty is the satire of human authority in King Dodon (danced by Adolf Bolm), that it is small wonder Rimsky-Korsakov's work has been prohibited in his fatherland.'

Stravinsky's *Le Rossignol* ('The Nightingale') occupied much the same sort of middle ground between opera and ballet. Based on another fairy tale, an oriental one by Hans Christian Andersen, it must have come as a disappointment to those musical shock troops now hardened to *Le Sacre du Printemps*, and as a relief to everyone else. It has not enjoyed anything like the fame of the early ballets, but it is an interesting work, begun before *L'Oiseau de Feu* and completed after *Le Sacre du Printemps*, so marking in an unassertive but fascinating way the evolution of Stravinsky's style. It also exists in a concert version, as *Le Chant du Rossignol*.

The prospectus also gave notice of an opera called *Dylan*, whose title sat rather awkwardly in the company of *Boris Godunov*, *Prince Igor*, *The Golden Cockerel* and all the other splendours from Mother Russia. It was the second part of an operatic trilogy based on Celtic mythology, *The Cauldron of Anwen*, by Joseph Holbrooke. Oscar Hammerstein, while still in charge of his London Opera House, and true to his promise to promote native British talent, had already staged the first part, *The Children of Don* (conducted, surprisingly, by Nikisch). Little good had it done him. Now Thomas Beecham, in much the same altruistic spirit, introduced and conducted this recently completed second part, with no more success. The production created quite a few headaches: it included a filmed flock of birds, whose image was supposed to be projected onto a screen while a choir gave voice to their song. At several points in the action the stage also had to be plunged suddenly into darkness. 'Blackout, 'Arry!' one electrician kept shouting to another during rehearsals. When, on one occasion, this did not happen, Beecham made a sarcastic remark about 'our friend 'Arry' that instantly became a backstage joke. It was in ways like this that he kept the common touch.

There was not much else he could do for the opera. Perhaps because Holbrooke took himself so seriously, he was always slipping on his own banana skins. With *Apollo and the Seaman* of five years earlier (another piece requiring pitch darkness), it was an over-enthusiastic clash of cymbals that had brought unwonted levity to the occasion. Now, with *Dylan*, the unhappy hero, clearly in poor voice on the first night, entered with the line, 'I sing, I have sung, I can sing better.' The *Tatler*, so polite as a rule, was for once quite withering, putting its finger on what its critic still saw as the general state of English music, notwithstanding Elgar, Delius and Vaughan Williams. *Dylan*, he said, was 'a sad example of what England can do. It is typically modern English because it is so typically Victorian German. We can't yet hear our own thoughts for the echo of the boom of Wagner.'

The season's ballets were commemorated in a beautiful souvenir programme, with a cover picture in full colour of Michel and Vera Fokine dancing in *Shéhérazade*. Nijinsky was conspicuously absent, following his marriage to the dancer Romola de Pulszky and his traumatic dismissal from the company by his former lover Diaghilev. Monteux, however, was on hand to carry the bulk of the season on his stoic shoulders, except for the day he rushed home to Paris to be with his wife and their newborn daughter; thereupon Beecham stepped in to conduct his own orchestra in a performance of *Petrushka*, still, let it be remembered, one of the trickiest of modern scores for any conductor to handle, especially at such short notice.

The new productions offered nothing as sensational as *Le Sacre du Printemps*. Some, indeed, were rather tame. *Papillons* ('Butter-flies'), taking its title direct from the piano pieces by Robert Schumann, orchestrated by Tcherepnin, was danced in Dickensian period costumes – a hark back to the more anodyne world of *Les Sylphides*. *Midas*, which had had its première in Paris only on 2 June, was danced by Karsavina and the strongly masculine Adolf Bolm, with music by Maximilian Steinberg. He provides an interesting link between pre- and post-revolutionary Russian music, as

Rimsky-Korsakov's son-in-law and the teacher at the St Petersburg Conservatory of the young Dmitri Shostakovich. His own score, alas, did not make much of an impression. Billed with *Le Rossignol*, the music for *Midas* to the ears of one critic 'sounded conventional after Stravinsky'.

One of the two big new productions was *Daphnis et Chloé*, first performed two years earlier at the Théâtre du Châtelet in Paris, with choreography by Fokine, who partnered Karsavina in the title roles, and with another of Bakst's most famous scenic designs, of an antique and mythical Grecian landscape. The music was by Maurice Ravel; it was the composer's most ambitious and most ravishing orchestral score, and it created problems purely on that account. 'The beauty of the scenes,' wrote the critic of *The Times*, 'the poses of the groups of Grecian figures, the dances alike of the individuals, the masses of youths and maidens, and of the pirates, seem to take their places in the scheme primarily as illustrations of the symphonic poem played by the orchestra.' That was the trouble. The music is, really, a superb evocation of atmosphere, and in the theatre it must have risen up from the pit like some thick and heady incense, overwhelming any action on the stage. The full score includes a large wordless chorus. For the London performances Diaghilev wanted to dispense with this, provoking Ravel to write indignantly to *The Times*. Diaghilev's stated reason was a saving of money, but perhaps he was also trying to lift some of the weight from the musical sound. There were to be revivals in the years to come. But the ballet was never a complete success, and today the title *Daphnis et Chloé* calls to most people's minds one of the great works of the orchestral repertory, with scant regard for its origins. Indeed, the most famous part of the score, depicting sunrise and the dawn chorus, with its slowly rising theme on the strings and rippling woodwind, is a part of the fabric of twentieth-century music, shamelessly plundered by every other Hollywood studio musician called upon to accompany a thousand more dawns, a sailing ship cresting the waves, or any number of other romantic images. What is a little curious is Beecham's lack of interest in Ravel, a composer embodying just those Gallic qualities that he admired so much in others: style, elegance, exquisite refinement.

The other big new production, recently given its première in Paris, was soon to become an historical curiosity. This was *Josephs-Legende* ('The Legend of Joseph') by Richard Strauss, a Biblical piece to a scenario by Hofmannsthal and Count Harry von Kessler, a longtime friend of both Strauss and Hofmannsthal. It was bolstered by another impressive show of Diaghilev talent: sets by José-Maria Sert (husband of the Russian-born Paris socialite and Diaghilev confidante Misia Sert), voluptuous costumes by Bakst (prominently illustrated in the souvenir programme), choreography by Fokine, and, dancing the title role, the seventeen-year-old Leonide Massine, the rising star of the Russian Ballet. Karsavina took the seductive role of Potiphar's wife. Dr Strauss was to conduct. The first night was a glittering event, *The Times* and other journals taking the trouble to list all the celebrities present, headed by the prime minister, Asquith, and his wife. Disappointment soon set in. 'It is amazing that the composer of such works as 'Salome' and 'Rosenkavalier' should have given us this music, which shows so little invention, so little that is even exotically beautiful' (the *Daily Chronicle*); 'A triumph of workmanship, but not of inspiration' (the *Morning Post*). Beecham himself seems suddenly to have taken against the composer. Writing to Delius in June 1914, he speaks of 'German blather and vulgarity' in contrast to the unaffectedness and refinement of Russian opera. 'Strauss is practically finished in London, though his Ballet will provide the usual sensation of the moment – welcomed as a masterpiece and relegated next year to the dust bin.'

Beecham may have been right as far as *Josephs-Legende* was concerned. The first night, however, proved to be a poignant occasion. Strauss took his curtain calls. He was joined on stage by Sir Joseph, a multi-millionaire maybe, but a rather small and humble figure caught in the spotlight's glare, clutching a gilded wreath presented to him by a grateful public. He promised another season next year. Within three months the Beechams, on one side, and Richard Strauss, on the other, were to be divided by one of the greatest catastrophes in history, when a good deal more than *Josephs-Legende* would be lost beyond recall.

CHAPTER TWELVE

In another letter to Delius, written in October 1914, Beecham returned to his attack on German music, now in the context of war. 'I think that on the whole it will be a splendid thing for us, for this means the actual end of the long German influence and domination here in musical matters, which is bound sooner or later to produce a healthy reaction in our own people.' Taking what was presumably another swipe at Richard Strauss, he continued, 'It is not as if Germany had still something vital and first-rate to send us; on the contrary, in music, and most especially in thought, she is a bankrupt nation.'

The First World War, the Great War for those who were a part of it, began for Britain on 4 August 1914 in a mood of jingoistic gusto coupled with a happy belief that it would be over by Christmas. There were rumours and there was paranoia. As Britain's small regular force (referred to by the Kaiser as a 'contemptible little army', which gave rise to their proud nickname 'The Old Contemptibles') embarked for France, friendly Russian troops were reported arriving in Scotland with the snow still on their boots (never mind the time of year). Shops with German-sounding names received bricks through their windows; even dachshund dogs were kicked in the street. It was whispered that Lord Haldane, a member of the Liberal government, who had been educated in Germany, was the Kaiser's illegitimate son, and he was forced to resign from office. Music was by no means immune from this hysteria. The English-born Gustav Holst – just starting work on his *Planets* Suite, with its ominous opening movement of 'Mars, the Bringer of War' – felt threatened on account of his part-Swedish, part-German ancestry, and hastily dropped the hereditary 'von' from his name. The more venerable names of Bach, Haydn, Mozart, Beethoven, Schubert, Weber, Mendelssohn, Schumann and Brahms disappeared overnight from concert programmes. Henry Wood dropped his Wagner Nights from the Proms. Henry Coward, another well-known conductor of the time, then suggested that only German music written after 1870 (the time of Bismarck's creation of the German Empire) need be shunned. This would have meant that *Lohengrin* might be heard but not *Parsifal*, Brahms's first piano concerto but not the second. The war produced some strange adversaries, too. There is Arnold Schoenberg staring morosely at the camera from beneath his spiked (*Pickelhaube*) helmet, and another photograph of Vaughan Williams looking not much happier in puttees and service cap. Of more immediate musical concern was the fact that hostilities instantly deprived British orchestras and British concert life of hundreds of excellent German, Austrian and Hungarian musicians, who were forcibly repatriated or interned.

One of Beecham's first wartime acts was to send a gift of money to Stravinsky, stranded in Switzerland on his way back to France from Russia when war was declared. The composer was to spend the war years in very straitened circumstances. Beecham, meanwhile, mobilised all his money and his energies on behalf of music at home. With the exit, first of so many good German-speaking musicians, and very soon afterwards of more native ones into the armed forces, every British orchestra and musical institution faced a crisis. Beecham came to their rescue wherever he could.

His relations with the Hallé Orchestra in Manchester had been somewhat ambivalent ever since he had made his precocious, and in some quarters unwelcome, début with them on the day of his father's inauguration as mayor of St Helens in 1899. He had conducted them again since then, to much critical praise. He may then have been piqued by the fact that upon Hans Richter's retirement as chief conductor they had not even considered him, but had gone straight to another German, Michael Balling, as Richter's successor. With the war, Balling departed and they were in trouble. Beecham wrote of Balling as a solid and painstaking hack, and poked fun at the Hallé Orchestra, whose future, he said, seemed dark and dismal without the guiding hand of their true-blue Teuton. Be that as it may, he at once offered his services as unpaid conductor (and subsequently as musical director), and these were gratefully accepted by Gustav Behrens and his colleagues of the Hallé Concerts Society Committee.

Elgar conducted the opening concert of the Hallé's 1914–15 season. Landon Ronald (knighted in 1922), the Belgian Henri Verbrugghen (who as a distinguished violinist gave the British première of the Sibelius Concerto), and the Russian Vasily Safonov (who had taught Alexander Scriabin and Nicolai Medtner) were other guest conductors. But Beecham shouldered most of the season's work. His programmes certainly reflected his own tastes, with a good helping of French, Russian and English music, much of it new to Mancunian ears. He included a performance of Granville Bantock's *Omar Khayyam*, a large-scale setting of Edward Fitzgerald's translation of the 'Rubaiyat', which he himself took over at short notice when the composer fell ill. Delius, of course, was well represented, with a performance, among other works, of his Piano Concerto, played by Robert Forbes, who had studied at the Royal Manchester College of Music and went on to become their principal. The *Manchester Guardian*'s critic, Samuel Langford, liked the concerto, but it is not often heard today, despite Beecham's advocacy of it.

A performance in the same programme of *Sea Drift* prompts an amusing digression. Delius and his wife Jelka were in England as Beecham's guests, following the early German advance to the river Marne, which brought the invaders alarmingly close to Paris and to the composer's home at Grez-sur-Loing. Delius had accompanied Beecham to Manchester where, prior to the concert in question, the latter had addressed the Royal Manchester College of Music (now the Royal Northern College of Music) on what he regarded as the poor state of academic musical training in Britain as a whole. Dante's famous legend over the Gates of Hell (*Lasciate ogni speranza voi ch'entrata*, 'Abandon All Hope You Who Enter'), he said, should be inscribed over the entrance to every musical college and academy in the land. He then challenged the college to provide a singer good enough to take the baritone part in *Sea Drift*. The composer would be the judge. The composer duly obliged by choosing, with very little fuss, a young baritone named Hamilton Harris, who sang the part to the general satisfaction of all concerned, except perhaps of Beecham, who had had the wind fairly taken out of his sails. Never again, he vowed, would he entrust the casting vote of decision to the unaccountable impulse of a composer! While Delius was in England, living at Beecham's country home at Grove Mill House, near Watford, he was often visited by the young Philip Heseltine, better known as Peter Warlock, composer of the perennially popular *Capriol Suite* for strings and the deeply melancholic song cycle *The Curlew*. Heseltine, who committed suicide in 1930, was another of the composer's champions.

Beecham took over the 1915–16 season of Hallé concerts. These included several concerto performances. Adolph Brodsky played the Tchaikovsky Violin Concerto; he had given the first performance of this in 1881, after the work's dedicatee, Leopold Auer, had pronounced it unplayable. After a period as leader of the New York Symphony Orchestra, Brodsky took over leadership of the Hallé Orchestra and was Principal of the Royal Manchester College of Music. The Beethoven Violin Concerto was played by Arthur Catterall, one of Brodsky's pupils, who in turn became the Hallé's leader and later leader of the BBC Symphony Orchestra. Fanny Davies, who had studied with Clara Schumann and performed with Joachim, Casals and Alfredo Piatti, played Mozart's C minor Piano Concerto (K491). She had also been the first to play Debussy's piano preludes in England, when they had just pushed the frontiers of aural perception and technique to new limits. The piano part in d'Indy's *Symphonie sur un Chant montagnard français* was taken by Robert Forbes, who had earlier played the Delius Concerto. The Australian William Murdoch, who played Franck's *Variations Symphoniques*, formed a partnership with Albert Sammons (one of Beecham's protégés).

Back in London, Beecham came to the rescue of the Royal Philharmonic Society. This already venerable institution, founded just over a hundred years earlier in 1813, had strong associations with Beethoven. It had commissioned from him his Ninth Symphony (though this was first performed in Vienna) and sent him a further generous sum of money during his last illness. In 1870 it commemorated the centenary of his birth by striking a gold medal that soon became (and remains) one of music's most coveted awards. In 1914, the players in its orchestra faced the dismal prospect of half-pay for their concerts, even if these continued. Beecham stepped into the breach by conducting, again without a fee, five out of the seven concerts of their 1914–15 winter season at the Queen's Hall, and underwriting the orchestra's full wages out of his own pocket. The programmes, compared with those of the Hallé Orchestra (which had included a Wagner Night), were much more anti-German. Even the revered Beethoven was excluded, while Mozart hung on by a single symphony. The most substantial work was Berlioz's setting of the *Te Deum*, for which Beecham brought the Hallé choir down from Manchester to sing with the boys of the London College of Choristers. The organist at this, as at other Philharmonic Society concerts, was Henry Goss Custard, who supervised the installation of the organ in Liverpool's new Anglican cathedral, the largest cathedral organ in England. During subsequent Royal Philharmonic Society seasons through the war, Beecham shared the platform with several notable figures, including the pianists Artur Rubinstein and the eccentric Vladimir de Pachmann, and the great Belgian violinist Eugène Ysaÿe.

He also helped to keep the London Symphony Orchestra on its feet in the early war years. As temporary chief conductor, he opened their 1915–16 season with a typical Beecham programme of Berlioz, Mozart, Delius, Elgar and Rimsky-Korsakov. There was, however, some Beethoven and Brahms in subsequent programmes alongside such native talents as Ethel Smyth and Bantock, reflecting a diminishing of the initial anti-German fever that had gripped the London musical scene. The Brahms Double Concerto was played, under Beecham, with Beatrice and May Harrison as soloists. Delius had heard them perform the same work in Manchester, and their playing almost certainly inspired his own Double Concerto. (Beatrice Harrison also recorded the Elgar Cello Concerto with the composer, and made a famous recording for the BBC playing her cello to the sound of a nightingale.) Beecham shared the rostrum during these concerts with, again, Henri Verbrugghen and Vasily Safonov, and with Emil Mlynarski from Poland, who had studied with Leopold Auer, and who became director of the Warsaw Conservatory and later taught at the Curtis Institute in Philadelphia.

Beecham's association at this time with Landon Ronald was not so successful. Ronald already had a distinguished career behind him, as Nellie Melba's accompanist on one of her American tours, and as conductor of, among other orchestras, the London Symphony and the Berlin Philharmonic. At the outbreak of war he was Principal of the Guildhall School of Music (continuing in that post right up to his death in 1938) and conductor of the New Symphony Orchestra which, of course, Beecham had founded in 1906 and with which he had parted company two years later. For 1915, Beecham and Ronald arranged and invested in a series of summer 'Promenade Concerts' in the Royal Albert Hall. Several factors conspired against their success. The cavernous size of the Albert Hall was still pretty intimidating in those days. This factor was not helped by the programmes; these were full of new British music, which may have struck a laudably patriotic note, but were not good box office. And the series coincided with some of the first Zeppelin raids on London which, contrary to Beecham's belief that they would drive people into concerts and other entertainments, kept more of them away.

Delius and Jelka returned home to Grez in November 1915, by which time the war was well over a year old. An attempt to break the deadlock with the Allied landings at Gallipoli in the Dardanelles was a disaster, and the Western Front had settled into the grim stalemate of trench warfare. Beecham, never one to remain within the ivory tower of music, was much concerned with the worsening state of the war and with its conduct. One thing that especially concerned him, as a Lancastrian, was the continued export of cotton, an ingredient of some explosives, to Germany. He helped to organise a protest meeting in the Queen's Hall against this scandalous trade, which soon afterwards was stopped by the government. His campaign against other examples of war profit-eering and graft involved him for a time with an outspoken polit-ical journal, *New Witness*, and brought him into contact with G. K. Chesterton (whose brother Cecil was the journal's editor), Hilaire Belloc, Bernard Shaw and other literary giants.

For almost anybody else, all this activity would have been more than enough. For Beecham, the greater part of his energy was still reserved for the world of opera. Covent Garden was closed to opera for the duration of hostilities, the Diaghilev Opera and Ballet company was struggling to keep going on the continent, and opera in Britain was everywhere in the doldrums. During 1915, Beecham accordingly formed a new opera company, recruiting singers not already in the forces from among those who had sung under his baton in earlier London seasons or with the old Denhof company, and orchestral players from his own former Beecham Symphony Orchestra, which had been disbanded at the outbreak of the war. The indispensable Donald Baylis was also on hand, as were Tommy Chapman (still going strong), and the conductors Percy Pitt from Covent Garden, Hamish MacCunn, Julius Harrison, who had worked with Nikisch and Felix Weingartner and at Covent Garden, and Landon Ronald. When, incidentally, some of these gentlemen became eligible for call-up, it was probably Beecham who quietly arranged for them to join the Royal Flying Corps and be posted to RFC headquarters in Regent's Park, from whence they could still work, part-time at least, for the new Beecham Opera Company.

For his first season, Beecham joined forces with Robert Court-neidge (father of the musical star Cicely Courtneidge), who was then manager of the Shaftesbury Theatre (bombed out in the Sec-ond World War). This theatre already had quite a musical history, presenting the first London production of Mascagni's *Cavalleria Rusticana*, then the stage musicals *The Belle of New York* and *The Arcadians*. Earlier in the year, Courtneidge had presented his own season of opera favourites. Now, on 2 October 1915, the curtain of the Shaftesbury went up on Gounod's *Roméo et Juliette*, mark-ing the commencement of 'Thomas Beecham's and Robert Court-neidge's Season of Opera in English'. *Faust*, *La Bohème*, *Tosca*, *Madama Butterfly*, *Carmen*, the already popular pairing of *Caval-*

leria Rusticana and *Pagliacci* ('Cav and Pag') and *Les Contes d'Hoffmann* were all scheduled for that first season. There were also two novelties on the way: *The Critic* by Stanford and *The Boatswain's Mate* by Ethel Smyth.

It was in connection with these last two pieces that Beecham brought into the circle of his aides and assistants the young man who had been so excited about the Beecham Symphony Orchestra and had stood in the packed gallery at Covent Garden for a performance of *Elektra*. This was Eugene Goossens, junior, now twenty-two, a violinist with the Queen's Hall Orchestra (exempted from military service on medical grounds) and a budding composer. He belonged to a whole dynasty of highly gifted and famous Anglo-Belgian musicians, including his conductor father, Eugène, his oboist brother Leon and two harp-playing sisters, Marie and Sidonie. Beecham saw and heard him conduct one of his own pieces, *Symphonic Prelude*, at a War Emergency Concert, and asked the young man to call round next morning at his Cavendish Square home. Goossens describes in his autobiography how he duly arrived at Cavendish Square, to be greeted by Beecham in pink pyjamas and mauve silk dressing-gown. The latter told him of the two new works mentioned above, said he was tired and needed a holiday, and asked Goossens if he would like to take over their direction. Goossens answered 'certainly', while, as he put it, veering towards the nearest piece of furniture for support. Beecham's sharp and instant recognition of high talent (something he shared with Diaghilev) had again paid off handsomely. Goossens remained with him for the next five years as his principal assistant conductor, before moving on to a distinguished conducting career of his own.

The 'holiday' Beecham mentioned in passing was, in fact, a semi-official visit to Rome. Italy had entered the war on the Allied side, but there was reckoned to be strong sympathy in some quarters for the Central Powers, going back to the country's historical connections with the Austro-Hungarian Empire. The debonair British conductor was to be a kind of cultural ambassador for the Allies, with luck swinging any doubtful sympathies their way. He did not start off too well, by including in his first programme at Rome's Augusteo concert hall Delius's *Paris: the Song of a Great City*. This proved far too advanced a piece for most of the audience who started talking and then whistling, at which point Beecham stalked off the platform. Then, no doubt recalling why he was there, he hastily returned to conduct another of his own favourite pieces, and a much more acceptable one to the Romans, a tuneful little overture by Paisiello. From a musical point of view, he found the Eternal City at that time fairly moribund and conservative. There were, however, one or two interesting diversions. One was his meeting with the baritone Antonio Cotogni, born as long ago as 1831, a friend of Verdi and teacher of, among others, Jean de Reszke and, more recently, Beniamino Gigli. Cotogni reminded Beecham of the curiously insular attitude of opera singers of his generation, Italian ones at any rate, who might render their own part to perfection, but had little knowledge of or interest in the opera when they were not on stage. As blinkered as this approach obviously was, Beecham wondered whether it was still better than that of some singers of his acquaintance who might know an opera inside out but left much to be desired when it came to their own part in it. Another diversion was a number of visits to the Teatro Dei Piccoli to witness some marionette performances of otherwise long neglected or forgotten operas, including Paisiello's *Il Barbiere di Siviglia*, a very popular piece until eclipsed by Rossini's treatment of the same story. All in all, Beecham probably did more for the Allied cause with his champagne dinners and suppers, 'where the provision for the carnal man exceeded in length and importance that for the spiritual'.

He returned to England early in 1916 and to a knighthood. His response, as expressed in *A Mingled Chime*, was engagingly modest and witty. Among other things, he said, a title meant that you were expected to tip more handsomely. You just murmured 'noblesse oblige' and tried to look as if you had been doing it all your life!

CHAPTER THIRTEEN

Nineteen-sixteen was the year of Verdun and of the Somme offensive, when all hopes of a swift and conclusive end to the war were finally dashed. Tucked away in the records of *Hansard* for the grey November of that year there is an entry headed 'Sir Thomas Beecham'. A question was asked in the House of Commons, of the Secretary of State for the Home Department, 'whether, in view of the fact that Sir Thomas Beecham is of military age, he can say what tribunal exempted him from military service'. Another government spokesman, the Financial Secretary to the War Office, replied that 'enquiries are being made'. There the matter seems to have rested. Perhaps the mission to Rome had something to do with it. What can be said without much fear of contradiction is that the thirty-seven-year-old conductor was already giving his all for his country. In August 1916 he wrote to Delius of a 'very strenuous and harassing year', and that he was beginning to feel a little tired. 'I have given forty consecutive weeks of opera and have directly or indirectly been responsible for over eighty concerts . . . This, in the midst of business annoyances, has been rather a strain.'

At the beginning of the year he came back from Italy to extend his opera season at the Shaftesbury Theatre from six weeks to ten. As often happens in wartime, people were turning to music and the arts for solace. Thousands of young men in khaki, plus thousands more from the hugely expanded wartime ministries and from the munitions factories dotted about the capital, were flocking to the Shaftesbury to listen to Gounod, Puccini and Offenbach. They were offered some contemporary British fare as well. The two new pieces in the repertory that Beecham had left in rehearsal were first given during January 1916. Stanford's *The Critic*, based on a play by Richard Brinsley Sheridan, went down very well with *The Times*, which praised also the conducting of Eugene Goossens ('quite admirable') and the singing of the tenor Frank Mullings ('just that blend of seriousness and absurdity which is the essence of the piece'). A few nights later came the première of *The Boats-*

wain's Mate, based this time on a fairly light-hearted story by
W. W. Jacobs (best remembered today for his classic horror story *The
Monkey's Paw*), which Goossens had also taken through rehearsal.
'At the last moment,' he wrote afterwards of its redoubtable composer, Ethel Smyth, 'she took over the baton, thinking herself the
heaven-sent conductor she was not. This necessitated additional
last-minute rehearsals, which she directed with a maximum of fuss,
pomposity and ineptitude.' *The Times* was not very impressed with
the piece. 'All the goodwill of a very enthusiastic audience could
not help the sense of anticlimax as the music laboured towards its
end . . . It wants just the thing which makes Jacobs the best of light
reading, the capacity to make a joke and leave other people to see
it.' Writing with a touch more humour than his young assistant
conductor, Beecham said that he had often thought of suggesting to
Ethel Smyth how she might revise the piece, lightening some of its
heavier passages. He had, however, always drawn back, for fear of
releasing a flood of correspondence in its defence 'that would have
done credit to the dialectical brain of St Thomas Aquinas'.

Meanwhile, he was busy, in the face of all the restrictions and
other frustrations of war, building up his company and his repertory, and in the process taking another step towards the creation of
a truly national opera company. With hardly a pause for breath, he
moved first of all from the Shaftesbury to the Aldwych Theatre,
now owned, in name at any rate, by his father as part of a huge
financial deal that, as we shall see, was to have disastrous repercussions for Thomas when the war was over. There he mounted
another brief, two-week season, conducted entirely by himself. At
the same time, he was finalising plans for a much more ambitious
season in Manchester, creating what he saw as the first of a number
of links between London and the main provincial centres. For this
he was going to include a revival of *Boris Godunov*, using the
costumes and sets he and his father had acquired from Diaghilev
before the war. It was to be sung, rather incongruously, in French,
because the Belgian bass-baritone Auguste Bouillez, in the title role,
did not have time to relearn his part in English. Indeed, with time
swiftly running out for everybody, Beecham came up with another
example of his very special blend of showmanship and enterprise
by commandeering a railway coach, furnished with a piano, in
which sections of the chorus – such a vital part of the opera – could
rehearse en route. So their train steamed north from London,
trailing a drama of sixteenth-century Muscovy across the green
rolling shires, and astonishing passengers and staff at Rugby, Staf-
ford and Crewe, perhaps in some cases the same ones who had

earlier jumped half out of their skins to the detonations of the once-famous 'Fireworks Orchestra'. As further evidence of the haste with which everything had to be done, Goossens recalls that the productions he was in charge of were presented without separate orchestral rehearsal. 'A grilling test of apprenticeship', as he put it.

'Sir Thomas Beecham's Great Manchester Season of Grand Opera' opened at the city's New Queen's Theatre on 10 May 1916, this time with an augmented Hallé Orchestra in the pit, including Archie Camden on first bassoon, the doyen of British bassoonists for many years to come and another famous British orchestral musician closely associated with Beecham. The latter, with his intimate experience of Diaghilev's Russian Opera seasons, con-ducted a first night *Boris Godunov* to great acclaim, while the magnificent sets and costumes, reminders of a more peaceful and a more opulent age, were something new to British theatre outside the metropolis. During that season, Beecham also conducted two other great and contrasted masterpieces of the repertory. Verdi's *Otello*, sung in Italian, starred Frank Mullings in the title role and Mignon Nevada as his Desdemona. Mullings, very much a Beech-am protégé, was perhaps the finest British 'heroic' tenor of his generation. Beecham later wrote warmly of him, while recalling that when Mullings attacked certain high notes he, Beecham, some-times feared for his health and safety! Mignon Nevada, of course, he already knew well, likening the colour of her voice 'as ivory is to white'. Wagner's *Tristan und Isolde* exemplified the contrariness that was a part of Beecham's personality and his brilliance. Having excoriated so much German music in speech and writing, he thenceforth conducted *Tristan* with such understanding and com-mitment that it became one of the best-loved operas of the war years, so proving, given the circumstances of the time, that great art certainly can transcend all barriers. He subsequently added *Tann-häuser* and *Die Walküre* ('The Valkyrie', the second part of the *Ring*) to his wartime repertory, answering press charges of un-patriotic policy by pointing out that Wagner was the favourite composer among the thousands of young soldiers in his audience.

A less elevated note was struck one evening by another member of the company, the tenor Frederick Blamey, in a performance of Saint-Saëns's *Samson et Dalila*. With, it seems, a good deal of liquid refreshment inside him, he came on stage, with a certain aptness perhaps, as the blind Samson, led by a small boy. He sang all right, then collapsed between the temple pillars instead of bringing them down. Beecham's stage manager, George King, yet one more in the ranks of his sturdy lieutenants, saved the situation with a swift dowsing of the lights and fall of the curtain. The Manchester season also introduced into the programmes one interesting curiosity: a production of *Phoebus and Pan*, a satirical secular cantata by J. S. Bach, the nearest he came to writing an opera, which, thanks to Beecham, was staged as one.

The company was back in London at the Aldwych Theatre for a six-week summer season starting in the middle of June. Lord Kitchener had just been drowned on his way to Russia, and press notices for the season appeared cheek by jowl with pictures of that well-known face ('Your Country Needs You') and appeals for his memorial fund. The repertory, growing all the time, made for some odd but interesting programmes, Bach's *Phoebus and Pan* sharing the bill one night with Puccini's *Manon Lescaut* and with *The Boatswain's Mate* on another. The big new highlight was the production of Mozart's *Die Entführung aus dem Serail*, or *Il Seraglio*, as it was billed for that season. This was Mozart's first major work in the Viennese *Singspiel* style, originally in German and with spoken dialogue. At the time of its composition the western borders of the Ottoman Empire were still quite close to Vienna, giving rise to a fashion in things Turkish, reflected by Mozart's high-spirited use of janissary-type percussion and his delightful handling of the menacing but comic Osmin, keeper of the harem (written for a bass, which makes it twice as funny when we remember that such functionaries were supposed to be eunuchs). For Beecham the work introduces the audience to a new operatic world. Gone, he said, were the pallid heroes and heroines of antiquity and all the other artificial paraphernalia so dear to the eighteenth-century librettists. In their place were recognisable people, expressing their joys and sorrows in music as fresh and spontaneous today as it must have sounded to the first Viennese audience all those years ago.

The circumstances of the first night, on 24 July 1916, are remarkable in themselves. The event was turned into a benefit night for the six orphaned children of the Spanish composer Enrique Granados, someone else who had recently been drowned, with his wife, when the ship bringing them back to Europe from America was torpedoed and sunk in the Channel by a German submarine. The auditorium of the Aldwych was draped with Spanish shawls, and society ladies, including Lady Cunard, wore Spanish costumes and sold souvenir programmes. *The Times* spoke of 'the awkwardness of combining an expression of public sympathy with the appearance of a festival'. But, the reviewer went on, 'Mozart put all right, for his delicious comedy carried us away at once into the realm of pure imagination, the realm of artists in which the conventions of behaviour do not count.' As well as plaudits for Beecham and his orchestra, there was more praise for Mignon Nevada, now in the very different role of Constanze, and for Robert Radford's Osmin ('one scarcely expected such drollery from a singer whose chief parts this season have been King Mark and Sarastro'). There was mention too of the 'luxurious scheme of colour' provided by Adrian Allinson, one of Beecham's stage designers who had supplied earlier and more controversial sets for *Tristan und Isolde* (notably an enormous Hokusai-type wave as backcloth to Tristan's ship in Act I).

With the Aldwych playing to packed houses, Beecham became involved in Birmingham's plans to form a municipal orchestra. As he observed, 'It was surprising that what had proved impossible in peace time should be regarded as feasible in the middle of a world war.' Nevertheless, he threw his weight wholeheartedly behind the scheme. 'In Birmingham', he suavely told the city fathers,

> you do not know very much what an orchestra means and what it would cost. An orchestra is something of a bogey to you. It is the simplest thing in the world to have an orchestra and to run it. It entails no great responsibility and little liability; and after you have listened to it a great deal you will find it a very nice thing to have. By the time the orchestra is able to play well you'll be quite proud of it.

The Lord Mayor and future prime minister, Neville Chamberlain, was not personally convinced, for the present at any rate, whereupon Beecham himself rallied local support by offering to help form and to engage a new orchestra for a guaranteed number of concerts each year.

While all this was afoot, Goossens was unexpectedly summoned one morning in October 1916 to West Brow, Sir Joseph Beecham's Hampstead home. Thomas was waiting for him. Sir Joseph had died in the night. Handing over to his young principal assistant a pile of scores and directing him to proceed forthwith to Liverpool to conduct that evening's concert, then straight on to Manchester, then on to Bradford (an insight into his own punishing work schedule), Beecham turned to the arrangements for the funeral. Years later, in *A Mingled Chime*, he set down the omissions, misunderstandings, regrets, and the few fond memories, that marked his relationship with his father. He had, said Thomas, been a very shy man at heart and one who found it almost impossible to unburden his deeper thoughts and feelings to anyone. He had married against his family's wishes, and his wife had for many years been an invalid. Nor did he seem to get on very well with his children. Thomas sadly recalled their own quarrel and reflected on the pain this must have caused his father at a time when he most needed friendship and support. Music was his one sure joy and consolation in life. *Lohengrin*, apparently, was his favourite opera, and he must have seen and heard it a hundred times in different opera houses around the world.

There was another sad aspect to the business of Sir Joseph's death. Just a few hours before he died in his sleep, Utica and the two boys, Adrian and Thomas, had visited him at West Brow, where he played the organ for Adrian and promised to take Utica to the opera. For years now, they had stood on the side-lines of his son's illustrious life.

CHAPTER FOURTEEN

The tragic death of Granados symbolised the growing bitterness and desperation of the war. In 1917 the Germans introduced unrestricted submarine warfare against Allied shipping in answer to the tightening British naval blockade. Civilian populations on both sides began to feel the pinch. The new British offensive on the Western Front, the Third Battle of Ypres, or Passchendaele, proved even more costly and hideous than the Somme. The United States entered the war on the Allied side, but the Bolshevik Revolution took Russia out of it, so releasing huge numbers of German men and guns for use against the Western Allies. In Britain, David Lloyd George (the 'Welsh Wizard') had replaced Asquith as prime minister, but the war seemed set to go on forever.

Beecham's own almost superhuman energies showed no sign of flagging. He was very busy in the orchestral and concert field. In London, perhaps a shade mischievously, he threatened (in the politest way) to withdraw his support from the Royal Philharmonic Society, whereupon that august body handed over to him and Baylis almost complete control. Through his influence and efforts Birmingham gained its orchestra, though unhappily this was soon disbanded again when the government requisitioned the famous Town Hall (where Mendelssohn had conducted the first performance of his oratorio *Elijah*) as food offices. In Manchester Beecham inaugurated a series of 'promenade concerts' given by the Hallé Orchestra, which were very successful, due partly to the wartime boom in cotton and coal production, which was putting money in local people's pockets.

His main thrust, though, continued to be down the path of opera. The Beecham Opera Company returned to Manchester (with the Hallé Orchestra again in the pit), and also visited Birmingham, Glasgow and Edinburgh. Back in London, Beecham moved from the Aldwych to the much more suitable Drury Lane Theatre, scene of all those pre-war triumphs organised in partnership with his father and now also technically a part of the disastrous property deal already alluded to. 'Sir Thomas Beecham's Season of Grand Opera in English' opened there on 30 May 1917 with Verdi's *Otello*, which he conducted. Frank Mullings, Mignon Nevada, and Beecham's old friend and erstwhile mentor Frederic Austin as Iago all came in for critical praise. The biggest accolade was reserved for Beecham himself. 'Beecham is undoubtedly our most valuable and instructive British musical institution; and by the sheer strength of his capacity he has brought his company up to a pitch of excellence that makes it a truly national asset.' Over twenty works of an amazing diversity were packed into the season. *Boris Godunov* was joined (in English translation) by those other pre-war triumphs of the Russian Opera, *Khovanshchina*, *Ivan the Terrible* and *The Golden Cockerel*. Beecham was also preparing Glinka's *A Life for the Tsar (Ivan Susanin)* to add to this strong Russian complement. At a Royal Philharmonic Society concert in December 1916 he conducted members of his opera company in excerpts from it. But the abdication of Tsar Nicholas II early in 1917 and the fall of the Romanovs then made it seem painfully inappropriate to the times, and it was dropped. To turn from things Russian, Charpentier's *Louise*, Puccini's *La Fanciulla del West* (his least-known major opera), *Aida* and a sparkling new production of Bizet's *La jolie Fille de Perth* ('The Fair Maid of Perth') now entered the repertory.

Among fellow conductors for that season Beecham brought in Eugène Goossens senior, to work alongside his son, and the Australian Aylmer Buesst, who later worked for the BBC and wrote a very interesting book about Wagner's *Ring*. Among other singers apart from those already mentioned, the New Zealand soprano Rosina Buckman shone as Isolde to Mullings's Tristan, also as Aida and Mimì. She made a pioneer recording of *Madama Butterfly*, in English, with Goossens conducting. There were some interesting diversions as well: a screening right in the middle of the season of D. W. Griffith's silent film epic *The Birth of a Nation*; and a gala performance in aid of the French Red Cross Society, at which Beecham accompanied the extraordinary contralto Clara Butt in all of Arthur C. Benson's verses of 'Land of Hope and Glory'. He once said of her that on a clear day she could quite easily be heard in France, which suggests something of the power of her voice but not her way of descending through throbbing tenor almost to baritone when God and Empire were being invoked. Meanwhile, the centrepiece of the season, and another major landmark in Beecham's career, was a new production of *Le Nozze di Figaro*.

Beecham's observations about *Die Entführung aus dem Serail* could be applied even more cogently to *Le Nozze di Figaro* ('The

Marriage of Figaro'), the first and in some ways the most remarkable fruit of Mozart's collaboration with the Italian librettist Lorenzo da Ponte. The latter fashioned the French playwright Pierre Beaumarchais's highly subversive play into Italian *opera buffa* (comic opera), but the work is far more than that: a marvellously observed social and domestic drama, still with a radical cutting edge, realised through a score of near-miraculous beauty, subtlety and dramatic mastery. Nothing like it had been seen or heard before. Composed three years before the Fall of the Bastille in 1789, *Le Nozze di Figaro* was a revolution in itself.

Beecham, in fact, decided to restore to his production something of the mood and style of Beaumarchais's original play, with all its political connotations, as he explained in his Drury Lane programme notes:

> The present production of 'The Marriage of Figaro' lifts the play from its setting in medieval [*sic*] Spain to the France of Beaumarchais' own time. For the Spanish setting was but a ruse by which Beaumarchais strove to conceal his revolutionary purpose from the powers of reaction. By using again the scene and characters of 'The Barber of Seville' he hoped to palm it off as a similar piece of pure fantasy, and he trusted that if the Count Almaviva were clothed in *l'ancien costume espagnol* his identity with the graceful and corrupt soul of the aristocracy would be concealed from all but the intellectuals to whom it was desired to speak. By abandoning this when setting and restoring the play to eighteenth-century France we release Beaumarchais' work of art from a restriction imposed by a century not ready for it.

To this end he commissioned a new translation of Da Ponte's libretto, at the same time replacing the traditional Italian recitative with spoken dialogue. And he brought in Nigel Playfair to produce it. Playfair, one of the big names in British theatre, had already worked with Herbert Beerbohm Tree (as had Beecham in connection with Strauss's *Ariadne auf Naxos*). Most important of all, from Beecham's point of view, he was the acknowledged expert on eighteenth-century theatre, later producing a famous revival of *The Beggar's Opera*. He coached the cast very thoroughly in period acting, and in their diction. For stage and costume designs he turned again to Hugo Rumbold, who had worked on *The Critic* and *The Boatswain's Mate*. Rumbold was another in the great stable of Beecham 'characters'. The son of a British ambassador, he painted all his own scenery, always dressed as though ready for lunch at the Ritz, combining a stutter with a droll sense of humour – the very antithesis, one imagines, of someone like Tommy Chapman.

The first performance of the new production, conducted, it goes without saying, by Beecham, was on 11 July 1917. *The Times* review next day, though relegated to the foot of a column by all the wartime lists of killed and injured, promotions, postings and decorations, was little short of ecstatic:

> It is difficult to know where to begin, or having begun, to stop, over the delights of Figaro last night. The whole thing well repaid the very great pains that had been spent on it. The audience were so charmed with the setting that they could hardly listen to the music, and so wrapped up in the music that they forgot to talk when it stopped.

The reviewer also spoke of the 'eighteenth-century frankness' of the translation. 'The whole thing represents quite the highest point the Beecham company has reached.' There was high praise too for the cast: for Frederic Austin as the Count, Miriam Licette as the Countess, Desiree Ellinger as Susanna, Bessie Tyas as Cherubino, and the Irish baritone Frederick Ranalow as Figaro himself. Singing with Beecham, Ranalow was also a notable Hans Sachs in *Die Meistersinger von Nürnberg* and Papageno in *Die Zauberflöte*, and a few years later teamed up again with Austin, singing Captain Macheath in the Playfair revival of *The Beggar's Opera*.

A later performance of *Figaro* was badly disturbed by an air raid, with anti-aircraft shrapnel rattling noisily down on the roof of the theatre, and Lady Cunard, who hardly missed a night of the season, valiantly urging the audience to stick it out with the singers and orchestra. Compared with the devastation of the Blitz some twenty-five years later, the Zeppelin airship and Gotha bomber raids over London were small-scale affairs. But at the time they were a terrifying new extension to warfare, and as well as causing damage they killed or wounded nearly three thousand civilians. They symbolised, too, the apparent hopelessness of the struggle. With the arrival of 1918, the anticipated German offensive in the West, following the collapse of the Russian front and Lenin's negotiated peace, was duly launched. All the Allied gains of the previous three years, made at appalling cost, were lost in a matter of days, and once again the enemy was dangerously close to Paris. The shells from 'Big Bertha', the giant German gun mounted on railway tracks and nicknamed after a member of the Krupp family, descended on the boulevards.

Beecham's own campaign suffered a reverse when the composer, scholar and board member of the Royal Philharmonic Society Thomas Dunhill led a kind of rebellion against Beecham's autocratic control, resulting in the latter's resignation as a director and that of Baylis as secretary. Otherwise, he carried on with as much vigour and enterprise as ever. He launched new opera tours covering Manchester, Sheffield, Leeds, Bradford, Birmingham, Glasgow and Edinburgh. In London his spring season at Drury Lane lasted through March, April and May. As a kind of appendage to this, he had a hand in a Grand Charity Matinee for the war wounded, sharing the stage (excerpts from *Aida* and the ballet music from *Faust*) with a juggler, a ventriloquist, the celebrated music-hall comic George Robey ('the prime minister of mirth') and a certain Mr George Mozart, 'in song and patter'. The programme cover depicted a wounded soldier in a wheelchair kissing the hand of an angelic, white-robed nurse. Sentimentality apart, it throws into stark relief some of the advertisements still regularly appearing in other Drury Lane programmes, for ostrich-feather stoles and wraps, the latest chauffeur-driven limousines, the finest wines, afternoon teas or late-night suppers at the Waldorf Hotel, in that, the fourth and most desperate year of the war.

The summer season, at the same theatre, from early June to the end of July, concluded with another Beecham novelty. This was a production, in association with the Incorporated Stage Society, of Byron's verse-drama *Manfred*, with Schumann's incidental music. The composer made several unsuccessful attempts to break into the theatre; in this case the overture survives as perhaps his finest single piece of orchestral music. 'This fine but gloomy drama', Beecham called it, and enlivened the production with ballet sequences danced to orchestrated versions (very hastily provided by Eugene Goossens and Julius Harrison) of some of Schumann's piano pieces. A young Edith Evans appeared in the cast list.

As one of England's major poets and one of Germany's major composers were thus brought together on the stage at Drury Lane, the First World War went through its final convulsions. With the aid of fresh American divisions, the new Allied supreme commander, Maréchal Ferdinand Foch, first halted the Germans, then went over to a last and this time victorious offensive of his own. By the time of the armistice, on the eleventh hour of the eleventh day of the eleventh month of 1918, the forces of the Central Powers had been pushed back almost to their starting point, the German navy had mutinied, and the German people were on the verge of starvation and revolution. The Kaiser abdicated and fled the country.

Through the most dreadful war in history Beecham had sustained, musically and financially, the Royal Philharmonic Society, the London Symphony and Hallé orchestras. He had not only kept opera alive, he had enormously enriched it, and carried it to every corner of the land – even in the closing weeks of the war setting down brave and exciting proposals for a new Manchester opera house. He had, perhaps, done more than any other single person, among all the belligerent nations, to keep alight the beacon of music, beauty and decency.

CHAPTER FIFTEEN

While President Woodrow Wilson and Prime Ministers Georges Clemenceau and David Lloyd George debated the terms of the peace amid the splendours of Versailles, the rest of the postwar world took shape. It was going to be a vastly changed one, of motor cars and buses – air travel too for those who could afford it – of electric lighting and heating, of radio and the cinema (the picture palace). The war had also given political and industrial clout to the Suffragettes' cause. In Britain, women's vital war work earned them the vote, first at the age of thirty, then at the same age as men. Fewer and fewer of them knew the drudgery of domestic service, the old 'upstairs, downstairs' lifestyle of the rich. There was, to begin with, an understandable desire to forget, as far as it was possible, the 'war to end all wars'. This was the Jazz Age, of cocktails and parties, short skirts, straw boaters, high heels and co-respondent shoes, of the Black Bottom, the Charleston and the other dances that were the rage of fashionable London, Paris, New York and the French Riviera, the new playground of the rich. Jazz was not confined to dance halls and parties. Its rhythms and harmonies infected the music of Stravinsky and Ravel, of Darius Milhaud, Francis Poulenc and the new clutch of French composers known collectively as 'Les Six'; of Kurt Weill and Ernst Krenek in the Berlin of the Weimar Republic; and of George Gershwin in Prohibition America, with that first electrifying wail of the clarinet in *Rhapsody in Blue*. In London there was the scandal of *Façade*, with Edith Sitwell reciting Dadaist poems into a megaphone behind a painted curtain, to racy and witty music by the young William Walton. Noël Coward, not much older than Walton, lampooned her as the cranky poetess Hernia Whittlebot.

Beecham, at forty, regarded the postwar scene with a somewhat jaundiced eye. There were, he said, five or six million ex-servicemen looking for jobs, the National Debt had risen from seven hundred and fifty to six thousand million pounds, and the annual budget from two hundred million to a thousand million, yet everybody was just out to have a good time with no thought for the morrow. Something, however, of the old pre-war spirit seemed at first to have survived. In 1919 the Diaghilev Ballet, having struggled through the war, returned to London, this time to the Alhambra Theatre, for the world première of one of its most celebrated productions: Manuel de Falla's ballet *El sombrero de tres picos* ('The Three-Cornered Hat'), based on the same scenario as Hugo Wolf's opera *Der Corregidor*, which Diaghilev had suggested to Falla back in the dark and uncertain days of 1916. Choreographed by Massine, with decor by Pablo Picasso, and conducted by the French-Swiss Ernest Ansermet (founder of the Orchestre de la Suisse Romande), this brilliant splash of Spanish warmth and colour must have seemed, momentarily, like a return to the glorious old days at Drury Lane.

Beecham himself appeared to enter the peace in good shape. Under the conditions inherited from his father, to which we shall soon return, he moved back to Covent Garden (used as a storehouse throughout the war), in harness with the Grand Opera Syndicate. Through 1919 and into 1920 he staged summer and winter seasons at Covent Garden itself, with forays to Manchester and other provincial centres. For these seasons he was able to call upon a remarkably rich and diverse company of singers: those of enduring fame (Nellie Melba, Emmy Destinn, or Ema Destinnova as she now called herself in recognition of Czech independence, Giovanni Martinelli); those who were big names in their day (the French bass Edouard Cotreuil, the Algerian baritone Dinh Gilly, the tenors Fernand Ansseau from Belgium, Alessandro Dolci from Italy and Ulisse or Ulysses Lappas from Greece, the Italian soprano Gilda Dalla Rizza); and an exceptionally strong contingent of British and Commonwealth artists, many of whom had now been singing with him for years (Norman Allin, Frederic Austin, Rosina Buckman, Louise Edvina, Desirée Ellinger, Joseph Hislop, Walter Hyde, Miriam Licette, Frank Mullings, Mignon Nevada, Agnes Nicholls, Robert Radford, Frederick Ranalow, Margaret Sheridan, Edna Thornton). Beecham shared the conducting with Aylmer Buesst, Albert Coates, Eugene Goossens, Julius Harrison, Percy Pitt and the Italians Gaetano Bavagnoli and Leopoldo Mugnone. The last of these had conducted the premières of *Cavalleria Rusticana* and *Tosca*, and seems to have been of the same temperamental mould as Toscanini. (Beecham tells the story that Mugnone was always threatening to walk out of productions. One day he called his bluff by handing him a one-way ticket back to Milan. 'I will never leave you!' cried the Italian maestro.)

He opened his first 1919 season on 12 May with *La Bohème*, probably the opera most closely associated with him. His Mimì was Nellie Melba, by now aged fifty-eight, in the part most closely associated with *her*. *The Times* reported next day:

> The Royal Opera opened its doors last night for the first time after four years of silence and admitted a wonderful and wondering audience. The audience was wonderful not only by the fact that the Royal box was occupied by the King and Queen, Queen Alexandra, and many other members of the Royal Family, and that the stalls and boxes contained more than the usual number of distinguished patrons; it was wonderful in its heterogeneity and its homogeneity, the one shown in the contrasted decorousness of the boxes and the hilarity of the gallery, the other in the feeling of eager good will with which all assembled. It was a wondering audience because everything promised to be so very familiar, so that one asked, Will it be just the same, and can we really settle down to the old mixture of social and musical pleasure as though nothing had happened?

Melba did not think so. 'I had the feeling that I was singing to an audience of ghosts ... It was that night at Covent Garden that made me realise the full extent to which London had changed.' Perhaps her first encounter with Beecham impressed upon her how much times had changed. Apparently she had burst into his office one day demanding to know why her old dressing-room had been repainted green. He retaliated by pretending not to know who she was, asking sharply who the deuce gave her permission to come barging in like that, and adding for good measure that as far as he knew the room in question did not belong to her or anybody else. The great Australian diva (taking her stage name from her native city of Melbourne), the embodiment of the old-style autocratic prima donna, had clearly met her match.

Beecham had reservations about her as an artist. The voice itself, he said, was beautiful and bright and perfectly even throughout its range. Her sense of accent and rhythm could hardly be faulted. Moreover, she was a shining example to everyone in her attitude to her work, always punctual at rehearsals, dedicated and disciplined. But, in his opinion, there was some essential quality lacking in her as an artist, which he could only describe as a genuine spiritual refinement. Perhaps, he added, with a sly dig at his compatriots, this explained why she was not so popular on the Continent as she was in England, where the subtler and more elusive aspects of singing and acting were not so highly valued.

That review of the opening night, it is worth adding, also spoke highly of a new and exciting English tenor, Thomas Burke, who, in a sense, was inheriting the mantle of Caruso, by singing Rodolfo to Melba's Mimì. Puccini himself said of Burke, 'I have never heard my music sung so beautifully.'

There were some interesting or notable novelties that same season. Ravel's one-act *L'Heure Espagnole* ('The Spanish Hour'), first given in Paris in 1911, is, on the face of it, a light-hearted sexual farce. But at a deeper level, with its exquisite orchestration, it forms an important part of the composer's lifelong fascination with Spain. Beecham's production had another striking decor by Hugo Rumbold. The work was warmly welcomed by the critics. 'It might have waited indefinitely for a production in this country had it not been for the recent coalition of operatic interests between Sir Thomas Beecham and the Grand Opera Syndicate. The whole was a brilliant performance of a wonderful little masterpiece of comedy.' Mascagni's *Iris* was one of that composer's many attempts to repeat the phenomenal early success of *Cavalleria Rusticana*. Here the *verismo* element of life in the raw is transferred from Sicily to Japan, as the eponymous heroine throws herself into a stinking sewer with the sacred Mount Fujiyama in the background. Its reception was only lukewarm, though the opera has been revived several times. *Naïl* was an exotic melodrama by Isidore de Lara. This London-born composer is now a forgotten figure, with not even a mention in many musical dictionaries. Yet in the last years of the nineteenth century and the early years of this one he had operas staged at Monte Carlo, Paris and the Metropolitan Opera, New York, as well as at Covent Garden. Beecham considered him an adroit and knowledgeable opera composer with an attractive lyrical vein, but one who was unable to sustain dramatic momentum or breathe real life into his characters. Despite excellent scenery and costumes by the composer's friend, the painter Charles Ricketts, and Beecham's own care for the production, the opera made little impact, and people spoke of it as 'a nail in Beecham's coffin'. The season also contained some interesting operatic and theatrical footnotes. The cast in the revival of *Prince Igor* included Darrell Fancourt, before he joined the D'Oyly Carte Company to become the archetypal Ko-Ko and other comic leads in the operettas of Gilbert and Sullivan. *La Traviata* featured, as *première danseuse*, the young Ninette de Valois, who went on to found the Sadler's Wells (later Royal) Ballet.

Throughout July, while the Carl Rosa Company was playing at the Lyceum, Beecham offered rival entertainment at Drury Lane with a brand-new production of *La Fille de Madame Angot*, one of several highly successful operettas by the nineteenth-century French composer Alexandre Lecocq. It featured the mezzo-soprano Gladys Ancrum, another well-known British singer of the period. His enterprise was not rewarded. Goossens, who conducted, notes in his memoirs that 'Hugo Rumbold carried out scenery and costumes and the production was on a lavish scale, with a slick, up-to-date translation, but the public tired of it after three or four weeks, so the run was brought to a close.'

For the winter season of 1919–1920 Beecham was back at Covent Garden and in Manchester with, among much else, a revival of *A Village Romeo and Juliet*, Verdi's great comic swansong *Falstaff*, and English-language versions of *Die Meistersinger von Nürnberg* and, more exceptional still, of *Parsifal*, with Frank Mullings in the title role and Gladys Ancrum now in the very different part of the spiritually tormented Kundry. This latter production experienced several mishaps. During one performance the swan killed by Parsifal landed on the head of an extra and stunned him, while on another evening Klingsor's spear, held by its invisible wire, got stuck in mid-flight – as though the wrath of Cosima Wagner, who some years earlier had appealed to the Kaiser himself to protect the work from performance anywhere but at Bayreuth, let alone, one assumes, in translation, were at work.

The summer season appeared to show Beecham, as impresario and conductor, still in top gear. He brought back *Pelléas et Mélisande*, so giving Debussy's solitary operatic masterpiece more and still much needed exposure. *The Times* critic certainly appreciated this revival. 'Its unique quality is that it, almost alone among modern operas, really fulfils the canon of the union of the arts, preached in their several generations by such masters as Monteverdi, Gluck and Wagner.'

Even more notable as an historical event was the British première of Puccini's *Il Trittico*, his triptych of one-act operas of contrasting mood and style: *Il Tabarro* ('The Cloak'), a grim little drama of infidelity, jealousy and murder on a river barge, very much in the prevailing *verismo* style; *Suor Angelica* ('Sister Angelica'), a quiet tragedy with an all-female cast, set in a convent; and *Gianni Schicchi*, a tale of chicanery over a will, and Puccini's only essay in comedy. This time, however, the critic of *The Times* had his reservations. 'When the violent ending comes,' he wrote of *Il Tabarro*, 'one wonders whether all the careful working up was really worth while.' Of *Suor Angelica*, he said that 'tunes which faintly recall the second act of *Madama Butterfly*, and harmonies of the sugared ecclesiastical type, soon cloy, and the conventional ending seems to throw a doubt on the sincerity of the whole thing.' *Gianni Schicchi* fared much better. 'A succession of well-made musical points, and in opera of this kind one asks for nothing more. The pity is that it occupies only the last third of a long evening.' Puccini must have been very disappointed, especially over the reception of *Suor Angelica*, which, apparently, was his own favourite. According to Beecham, he didn't help by insisting that the set for this opera should be modelled exactly on a real Tuscan convent, with the result that much of the action could not be seen by the audience. Beecham took it off after one or two performances, leaving *Il Tabarro* and *Gianni Schicchi* (both with Tom Burke in the tenor lead) together, or pairing them with other pieces. This led an irate Puccini to speak of Beecham as 'The Purge' (perhaps with those pills also in mind). At all events, *Gianni Schicchi*, with its much-loved aria 'O mio babbino caro' ('Oh, my beloved Daddy') – in the context of the work a clever and witty piece of self-parody – soon took off with a life of its own, leaving its two companion works rather sadly in the shade.

Beecham had problems of a different kind with his staging of Gluck's *Orfeo*, starring Clara Butt. She was made a Dame of the British Empire in the same year, but her performance in the title role of Gluck's opera came in for some quite tough comment. One critic said, 'She played fast and loose with the time and spoiled the phrasing.' 'Perhaps', the *Tatler* commented more sympathetically, 'the ordeal of appearing on stage – which is so different from the concert platform – affected her.' Beecham's revival of Bizet's *Les Pêcheurs de Perles* ('The Pearl Fishers', sung in Italian) must, by comparison, have been pure joy. His leading lady, in the role of the Brahmin priestess Leila, was the Spanish coloratura soprano Graziella Pareto, singing in her only season at Covent Garden. Beecham recalled her voice as one of exquisite purity and of haunting pathos, at the same time classing her with Claire Dux as one of those artists of exceptional talents who, for whatever reason, never make it to the very top of their profession. She died in 1973, aged eighty-four.

An appendage to this season, though an important one, was the presence of the Diaghilev Ballet (as distinct from its separate return to London of the previous year). One of its offerings was *Pulcinella*, choreographed by Massine and with sets and costumes by Picasso. Stravinsky's score was a clever reworking, for chamber orchestra and vocalists, of music mainly by the eighteenth-century composer Giovanni Pergolesi. This was the new neo-classical Stravinsky, very much in tune with post-war musical tastes. It had a companion piece, *Le Astuzie Femminili* ('Feminine Wiles'), this time based on music by Domenico Cimarosa and arranged by Ottorino Respighi, who had earlier provided Diaghilev with arrangements of Rossini for the ballet *La Boutique Fantasque* ('The Fantastic Toyshop'). Diaghilev's conductor once again was Ansermet. These pieces, however, failed to set the season alight, as in the old days. Beecham attributed this to a fickle public and press who expected an exact repeat of all the triumphs and sensations of former years and turned against them when these were not forthcoming. It was against this rather anxious and unhappy background that Diaghilev, fearful for his own finances, suddenly cancelled the rest of his performances and issued a writ against the Beecham Opera Company.

Both of them, in fact, were in financial trouble. In Beecham's case he had, through the war years, exhausted his own funds with his unstinting support for every orchestra and musical institution in a crisis, while earning hardly a penny from conducting. The return of peace had not restored his fortunes. The pre-war days of widespread private patronage were gone. Few people now bought a box or a grand tier seat for a whole season. At the same time, that mass wartime craving for the arts had quickly fallen away in the face of rival entertainments. To add to his troubles, Donald Baylis, his right-hand man for so long and a tower of strength in any crisis, had just died. The Beecham Opera Company bravely went on tour in the run-up to Christmas 1920. It gave a final performance, of *Carmen*, in Glasgow early in December, then went into voluntary liquidation.

All this, however, was only a small part of his troubles. The huge black cloud that loomed was the matter of the Covent Garden Estate, to which we have alluded already. The genesis of this went back ten or eleven years, to the Chancellor of the Exchequer Lloyd George's budget of 1909, which introduced new taxes on wealth and property and prompted the eleventh Duke of Bedford to sell off the large area of land and property he owned around Covent Garden. In 1914, after protracted negotiations, Sir Joseph Beecham became the purchaser of this prime chunk of the West End, encompassing the famous fruit and vegetable market, the Royal Opera House, the Aldwych, Drury Lane and Strand theatres, the National Sporting Club, the Waldorf Hotel and numerous restaurants and pubs. The whole deal, involving hundreds of millions of pounds at today's values, made good financial sense in peacetime. But the war wrecked the whole complicated arrangement of loans and repayments. The worry undoubtedly hastened Sir Joseph's death. Now the burden of it, linked as it was to the terms of Sir Joseph's will, fell largely upon Sir Thomas's shoulders, while his younger brother Henry presided over the family business from St Helens. The whole matter went to the court of Chancery, while Sir Thomas himself, from an office in the Strand, wrestled with the problem of paying off the huge debt on the estate and disposing of as much of it as he could. A particular sadness was the sale of West Brow (not, of course, part of the estate itself), Sir Joseph's large if not very architecturally distinguished mansion in Arkwright Road, Hampstead. This property, rather ironically in view of Sir Thomas's scornful opinion of trades unions, was bought soon after by the Associated Society of Locomotive Engineers and Firemen (ASLEF) as their headquarters, which it remains to this day, planted high above the once smoky tunnels of the main line in and out of St Pancras station.

For three whole years the problems of the Covent Garden Estate kept Beecham away from music. In many ways he considered this a blessing in disguise. For him the settled routine of office work was like a balm after the punishing hours and the endless crises and traumas of the theatre, both conducting and managing productions. He had time to reflect, and also time to do some travelling on his own account. He visited Germany to survey the postwar musical scene, where he also saw early evidence of the horrendous inflation that was to undermine the authority of the Weimar Republic and pave the way for Hitler. He proceeded to France, where he made the fairly short journey south from Paris to visit Frederick and Jelka Delius at their home by the placid waters of the river Loing. The disease that was to kill the composer, after lying dormant for so long, was now affecting his sight and the use of his limbs. Beecham remembered the vital and athletic figure of years gone by. 'He was not yet sixty and had no business to be looking like that.'

CHAPTER SIXTEEN

In 1923 Beecham began to see light at the end of his long financial tunnel. Large parts of the Covent Garden Estate had been sold off. The rest was soon to be combined with the family business to form a new company, Beecham Estates and Pills Limited. He began to ease himself back into music and public life. During that year he entered into a happy association with the Phoenix Society, an enterprising group founded in 1919 for the revival of Elizabethan and Restoration drama. His very broad and deep knowledge of English literature and theatre was put to good account, working with the society on a recreation of the pastoral play *The Faithful Shepherdess* by the seventeenth-century dramatist John Fletcher, best remembered for his long collaboration with his fellow playwright Francis Beaumont. Beecham set to music the play's various songs and choruses, and added, as incidental music, arrangements for small orchestra of selected pieces by Handel, Mozart and other eighteenth-century composers. The staging of this revival, well received by the critics, had an amusing sequel. Beecham one day received a communication from the Inland Revenue, asking for the playwright's address. Wishing, he said sweetly, to be as helpful as possible, he directed them to the south aisle of Southwark Cathedral, where the aforementioned playwright had resided for quite some time and was probably not planning an early move. (The tax men, he remembered, had made similar inquiries about the authors of *The Beggar's Opera* at the time of its revival, three years earlier, by his friends Frederic Austin and Nigel Playfair, at the Lyric Theatre, Hammersmith.)

He took up the baton again in March 1923, to conduct the Hallé Orchestra in the Free Trade Hall, Manchester. The pieces by Weber, Delius, Berlioz and Mozart constituted a quintessential Beecham programme. The novelty was Hamilton Harty's First Piano Concerto, with the composer as soloist. The Irish composer-conductor, whose popular 'Handel-Harty' arrangements of the *Water Music* and *Music for the Royal Fireworks* tended to overshadow his own very attractive works, had recently been appointed the Hallé's principal conductor. The next month Beecham made a more emphatic return to public life in London at the Royal Albert Hall, with nearly two hundred musicians on stage from the combined London Symphony and Albert Hall orchestras. He was joined, once again, by the formidable Clara Butt, this time in her element. She appears, however, to have been rather put out when her customary encores were interrupted by calls for Beecham. He then gave the audience 'The Ride of the Valkyries' and Strauss's *Ein Heldenleben*, which must have reached the ears of Prince Albert himself, seated pensively beneath his extravagant gothic canopy across the road in Kensington Gardens.

It was the prelude to a decade of busy concert work. Beecham made some excursions abroad, notably in January 1927 to Prague to conduct the Czech Philharmonic Orchestra, founded as an act of political faith back in 1901, well ahead of their country's actual independence. 'The Walk to the Paradise Garden' was one of the pieces they played with him. For most of the time he remained at home, striking up a particularly close association with the London Symphony Orchestra. He was in equally distinguished company. Many of the most famous international conductors of the interwar period appeared with the orchestra at this time: Wilhelm Furtwängler, Felix Weingartner, Bruno Walter, Serge Koussevitzky. From abroad there were also Hermann Abendroth, later principal conductor of the Leipzig Gewandhaus Orchestra and a frequent guest conductor at Bayreuth; Georg Schneevoight, Finnish conductor and cellist, who founded orchestras in Helsinki and Riga and worked also in Germany and America; and Leo Blech, a colleague of Erich Kleiber at the Berlin State Opera. Among his fellow countrymen, Beecham shared the London Symphony Orchestra rostrum with Elgar, Sir Hugh Allen, Professor of Music at Oxford University and Director of the Royal College of Music (from his pictures in concert programmes of the time looking uncannily like Stalin's foreign minister, Molotov), and a fresh-faced young John Barbirolli, who had played the cello with the Beecham Opera Company during the war. Beecham's own programmes featured more eminent contemporaries: Pablo Casals, playing the Haydn Cello Concerto; Arthur Catterall, by now leader of the Hallé Orchestra, playing the Beethoven and Brahms concertos; the Austro-American violinist Erica Morini, who had made her début in Vienna aged twelve, playing one of Karl Goldmark's concertos; Joseph Szigeti, who had made his début with Beecham in 1907, playing one of Mozart's. Lionel Tertis, who had played in the Beecham Symphony Orchestra in

1909, took the solo part in the *Rhapsody* for Viola and Orchestra by the London Symphony Orchestra's own leader, W. H. Reed. Other soloists who appeared with him have since all but vanished from view and memory: the violinist Quiroga, taking the solo part in Lalo's *Symphonie Espagnol*; the pianists Martha Baird and Mischa Levitski.

These years with the London Symphony Orchestra were notable also for their vocal and choral music. The Scottish baritone Roy Henderson, at the start of a long and distinguished career, took the solo part in a performance of *Sea Drift*. There was an all-Wagner evening at the Albert Hall, with the Australian soprano Florence Austral, a fine Brünnhilde in her time, from Melba's home city of Melbourne. Another delightful young soprano, Dora Labbette, a favourite with Beecham for years to come and indeed another of his loves, joined John Coates, Margaret Balfour and Harold Williams in Beecham's own revised edition of *Messiah* (his 'farewell' concert in January 1926 before an abortive sally to America). Beecham's association with *Messiah* is interesting. With its strong Germanic origins, it stood for that aspect of English musical life that he so often attacked as philistine. But it was sung and loved by English people of every class and creed, and Beecham, coming from the heart of old Industrial England, never lost the common touch. His 1926 performance, in fact, though musically inflated by today's standards, brushed away many of the cobwebs of institutional piety that had clung to the work for so long, and marked the beginning of a Handel revival by Beecham.

The great and sturdy Hanoverian was given another good dusting down by him on 22 March 1928. This time the work was *Solomon*. The text, long since bowdlerised to spare Victorian blushes over King Solomon's sex life, was restored and spruced up, along with the score. Among the soloists, Dora Labbette was this time joined by the soprano Lilian Stiles-Allen (who years later coached the stage and film musical star Julie Andrews), Clara Serena and the tenor Walter Widdop. This was a Royal Philharmonic concert. The Society and Beecham had parted company, not on the best of terms, in 1918. Now they were making it the occasion to honour him with their Gold Medal. So, to the joyous strains of 'The Arrival of the Queen of Sheba' – a great Beecham concert favourite in the years to come – he joined the illustrious company of other gold medallists, beginning with Sir William Sterndale Bennett in 1871 and including, up to Beecham's own award and well beyond it, Charles Gounod, Joseph Joachim, Hans von Bülow, Johannes Brahms, Adelina Patti, Ignaz Paderewski,

Eugène Ysaÿe, Pablo Casals, Sir Henry Wood, Alfred Cortot, Frederick Delius, Sir Edward Elgar, Ralph Vaughan Williams, Gustav Holst, Sergei Rachmaninov, Jean Sibelius, Richard Strauss, Felix Weingartner, Arturo Toscanini, Dame Myra Hess, Sergei Prokofiev, Sir Adrian Boult, Zoltán Kodály, Igor Stravinsky and Dmitri Shostakovich.

In November of that same year, Beecham conducted the first performance of the Swedish composer Kurt Atterberg's Sixth Symphony. Atterberg was a big name in contemporary Scandinavian music, but it was the circumstances surrounding his new symphony that gave the event its special interest. The Columbia Graphophone (*sic*) Company had organised a competition for a new work, to mark the centenary of Schubert's death. An international panel of judges included Franco Alfano (who had recently completed Puccini's last opera *Turandot*), Denmark's greatest composer Carl Nielsen, Alexander Glazunov (who used the event as a chance to quit the Soviet Union), the German-American conductor Walter Damrosch, and the English scholar and critic Sir Donald Tovey. That other great English music critic Ernest Newman caused quite a stir at the time by suggesting that Atterberg had won the competition, and the handsome prize money that went with it, by making his symphony a kind of pot-pourri, with something in it for each of the judges – a touch of Rimsky-Korsakov for Glazunov, a touch of Elgar for Tovey, and so on. 'Very adroit' was *The Times*'s own more discreet opinion of this curiosity. Their critic was much less happy with Beecham's handling, in the same programme, of Mozart's Requiem Mass, notwithstanding his fine group of soloists (Isobel Baillie, or Bella Baillie as she was billed, the mezzo-soprano Astra Desmond, Francis Russell and Robert Easton). Not every Beecham concert, even featuring his beloved Mozart, was a red-letter day. At the Leeds Triennial Festival of 1928, he conducted the concert suite from Stravinsky's most recent ballet, *Apollon Musagète*, clearly out of sympathy with the music; the performance very nearly came to grief.

Deprived of Beecham's energy and initiative, opera in Britain, meanwhile, was rather in the doldrums. Two quotes serve to illustrate how important Beecham had been to British opera through the war years and immediately afterwards, and how much he was missed. In 1919, the conductor and composer Albert Coates (born in Russia but of English parents) had declared in the *Daily Telegraph* that there could be 'no appreciation too high' for the work Beecham had done in the cause of English opera. When Beecham's own company went into liquidation soon afterwards the English bass Robert Radford, in a letter to the same newspaper, called it 'the most calamitous happening that has occurred in British music for many years'. His words would certainly seem to have been borne out by the fact that from 1920 up to the summer of 1922 Covent Garden had staged only twelve weeks of opera, given by the visiting Carl Rosa Company (the longest-surviving touring company in British operatic history), filling up the rest of the time as best it could with seasons of pantomime and films, even with boxing matches. The formation of the British National Opera Company in 1922 brought some new light to this gloomy scene. Beecham, then immersed in his private affairs, was not directly involved, but he was, to a large extent, its inspiration, since the new company inherited many of his old singers and orchestral players, together with a quantity of scenery and costumes. The British National Opera Company included among its directors Percy Pitt, and among the singers Robert Radford, Norman Allin, Walter Hyde and Agnes Nicholls, all old Beecham comrades. Other leading singers in the company were the baritone Percy Heming, the tenors Frank Mullings and Heddle Nash, and Eva Turner, soon to become one of the finest dramatic sopranos of her time. John Barbirolli, Adrian Boult and Malcolm Sargent, all rising stars of the new generation of British conductors, also worked for it. 'It will be of deep interest', commented the *Daily Mail*, 'to see how far they manage to repair the sad gap that was made in England and English musical affairs by the cessation of the Beecham enterprise in 1920.' The same article also spoke of 'this daring project of running opera by a committee rather than by the one despotic head always heretofore considered necessary in the opera house.'

For the rest of the decade, the British National Opera Company, with Beecham's spirit still very much at its heart, toured the provinces, attracting such big names as Melba (*La Bohème*) and Maggie Teyte (*Madama Butterfly* and *Hänsel und Gretel*), staging the premières of Vaughan Williams's now neglected historical drama *Hugh the Drover* and Holst's witty one-act operatic parody *The Perfect Fool*, and presenting, at Covent Garden, an English-language *Ring* cycle. The company survived until 1929. Beecham himself conducted them in an English-language performance of *Die Meistersinger* at His Majesty's Theatre on 18 July 1924. The cast included Miriam Licette, who had also sung with the old Beecham company, and Walter Widdop. For them, and for many others in the company, having Beecham back in the pit hurling insults and witticisms during the morning rehearsal must have been like a giddy breath of ozone. The blazing heat of that particular July day, and the whole gloriously festive and optimistic mood of Wagner's opera, added to the excitement.

To the great disappointment, no doubt, of many members of the company, it was a one-off appearance for Beecham. As far as the stage was concerned, ballet next claimed his attention. In 1926 he renewed – under happier circumstances this time – his association with Diaghilev. The great Russian impresario, now nearing the end of his life, had recently been drawn across the Channel from the bright, chic Parisian world of Poulenc, Milhaud and 'Les Six' to the cooler, more whimsical climes of Chelsea and Bloomsbury. He had commissioned the ballet *The Triumphs of Neptune*, 'an English pantomime in ten scenes', to a scenario by Sacheverel Sitwell, with choreography by Georges Balanchine and music by Lord Berners. The latter was one of the most colourful figures in contemporary British cultural life. Educated at Eton, Sir Gerald Hugh Tyrwhitt-Wilson, as he was before succeeding to the title of fourteenth Baron Berners, had a beautiful eighteenth-century country house near Faringdon (now in Oxfordshire), a town house in London and another in Rome, where he had served in the diplomatic corps. He once dyed the feathers on some fantail pigeons, and built what was reputedly the last folly in England, to the designs of a descendant of the Duke of Wellington. To this extent he might be thought a fine example of an English aristocrat and eccentric, hardly to be taken seriously. But as Diana Mosley says in her book *Loved Ones*, 'he was talented, civilized, hospitable and extremely funny. He liked the company of people who appreciated beauty, intelligence, elegance and jokes; he created an atmosphere in which these qualities combined to make perfection.' He wrote poetry and novels, painted pictures and composed music. He was a dilettante but, as far as his music was concerned, he earned the respect and friendship of Stravinsky, Constant Lambert and Walton, who dedicated to him his oratorio *Belshazzar's Feast*. *The Triumphs of Neptune* had its première in London in 1926, and soon afterwards Beecham was invited to conduct a gala performance of it in honour of a visit by the future King Farouk of Egypt. The event had a direct bearing on Beecham's own career, because it resulted in a commission from Diaghilev to provide the music for another ballet.

The scenario for this, originally titled *Les Deux Mendiants*, was similar in character to that of *The Faithful Shepherdess*: a charming 'pastoral' in which a humble shepherd and a serving maid are transformed into deities from classical antiquity. For his score Beecham selected and arranged pieces by Handel. The result was the one-act ballet *The Gods Go A-Begging*. This opened at His

Majesty's Theatre on 16 July 1928, with choreography again by Balanchine, using some of Bakst's sets from the first production of *Daphnis et Chloé*, costumes by the Spanish painter Juan Gris, taken from an earlier production, and with two of Diaghilev's newer star dancers, Alexandra Danilova and Leon Woizikovsky, in the leading roles. 'Sir Thomas Beecham's interest in Handel has borne new and refreshing fruit', *The Times* reported next day:

> Sir Thomas Beecham, who conducted the first performance last night, has selected a number of short movements from the less familiar works of Handel, orchestrated them with full wind, which occasionally sacrificed something in clarity for the sake of increased sonority, touched up the piquant spots with instruments so diverse as a harpsichord and a tubular bell, and made of it all a thoroughly serviceable suite for dancing. So the rescue of Handel by process of editorial selection from oblivion brought on by over-production proceeds profitably.

And, just as Beecham had recently joined the august company of Royal Philharmonic Society gold medallists, so he was now numbered with Stravinsky, Debussy, Ravel, Falla, Prokofiev, Bakst, Benois, Picasso, Matisse, Nijinsky, Pavlova, Chaliapin and all the other composers, artists, dancers and singers who had worked for Diaghilev.

The Gods Go A-Begging enjoyed several later revivals as a ballet, notably in 1936 with new choreography by Ninette de Valois. The orchestral suite, along with Hamilton Harty's own Handelian arrangements, was also popular for many years to come. Beecham, meanwhile, had other and much grander schemes afoot. The life of a top conductor, and of a clever and talented arranger, was not nearly enough for him. In 1928, concertgoers found leaflets tucked into their programmes. 'Join the Opera League Today', they were urged in strong black lettering. 'If already a member, please pass this on.' The leaflets came from an office in New Bond Street, London, headquarters of The Imperial League of Opera, founder, Sir Thomas Beecham, Bart. Among the League's trustees was Sir Eric Hambro, Chairman of Hambro's Bank. Sir Landon Ronald and Frederic Austin were also on hand.

'It is the eventual aim of this organisation', Beecham went on to explain,

> to build and endow an opera house in London and to assist in the building and endowing of opera houses in some of the leading provincial cities. But for such a large enterprise public opinion is

not fully ripe. As yet it remains unconverted to a belief in the need for opera houses, nor is it wholly convinced that the artistic resources of this country are equal to the task of creating institutions which shall compare favourably with those that flourish in Continental capitals.

It is waste of time to criticise the general public for this attitude of mind. Owing to limited opportunity the bulk of the public has never heard Opera.

But although of moderate dimensions, there does exist a select public which patronises Opera in London and in the provinces, and there is no actual insufficiency of first rate artists of British origin on the modern operatic stage.

Many of these artists, however, are rarely heard in England. They sing regularly in the United States, France, Italy, Germany, Austria and indeed almost everywhere except on a stage in London, the heart of the British Empire.

The plain reason why they are not here is that there is no home to house them. Such a home has long been overdue and it is the immediate purpose of the Imperial League of Opera to bring it into existence.

There was an accompanying enrolment form. The basic subscription was £1 for two years, in advance.

In speeches up and down the country, Beecham used a more populist approach. As reported in the *Yorkshire Post*, he told an audience in Leeds, to cheers and laughter, that he would give them the finest opera in the world for what amounted to, per head, tuppence a week – 'the price of half a glass of ale, a bun or a slab of Yorkshire pudding!' Lady Cunard, as ever, was by his side, moved to add some words of her own on the beauty and worth of opera. 'It is not only great music,' she wrote, 'but music set to epic poetry . . . The melting voice breathes a finer knowledge, like the soul of things.' More to the point, perhaps, she contributed £5000 to the League, still a very tidy sum in those days, a good deal more, certainly, than tuppence a week.

CHAPTER SEVENTEEN

The euphoria of the early 1920s did not last long. Already, in 1921, Benito Mussolini had marched on Rome with his Blackshirts and imposed fascism on Italy. Rampant inflation in Germany, caused partly by the huge burden of war reparations, destroyed millions of people's lives and their faith in the Weimar Republic. Adolf Hitler was writing *Mein Kampf*. The wretched condition of British coal miners in 'The Land Fit for Heroes' brought about the General Strike of 1926. Beecham had hardly been in a euphoric mood in any case. *The Faithful Shepherdess* and *The Gods Go A-Begging* were happy enough projects, and there was the special honour of the Royal Philharmonic Society gold medal. But it was not, overall, a very happy decade for Beecham. He settled the affairs of the Covent Garden Estate, but continued to accumulate debts. He suffered periodically from ill health and a lameness that made it painful and difficult for him to conduct. He was often rude to people, scathing about the state of the world. The Bolsheviks were 'Asiatic mongrels'. Britain's own Labour Party, now replacing the Liberals as the main party of the Left, 'preached a gospel of thieving and stealing'. The root of his troubles, probably, was that he had no opera company, no orchestra of his own. He must have felt rudderless.

The sad fate of the Imperial League of Opera crowned, if that is the word, this period of restlessness, frustration and general malaise. Beecham got as far as planning the League's first season for 1930, which included such exciting projects as a staging of Berlioz's *La Damnation de Faust* and a production of Smetana's comic masterpiece *The Bartered Bride*, with designs by the Welsh artist Augustus John, noted especially for his striking portraits of such figures as the Portuguese cellist Guilhermina Suggia. The repercussions from the 1929 Wall Street stock market crash soon dealt a blow to all his hopes and plans in this direction. Subscribers and funds to the League fell away. There was, however, more to it than that. Beecham had been discussing an amalgamation with the

Grand Opera Syndicate. But when he learnt that Covent Garden was to receive what amounted to a subsidy from the incumbent Labour government, he broke off his talks with the Syndicate. How, he asked angrily, could he justify all the money people had paid voluntarily into the League, if opera was now to be funded out of taxes? It was an ironic situation. He had spoken, often enough, of the benefits, the need even, of municipal or state subsidies for music, as enjoyed in other European countries. Now, it seemed, his fondest hopes were being sabotaged by the first pioneer moves in that direction by a British government. Perhaps the fact that it was a Labour administration had something to do with his anger. We have just read what he thought of the Labour Party. At all events, it left the League more or less stranded. To add to this unhappy picture, the same government's entertainments tax proved the last straw for the already shaky finances of the British National Opera Company (which, we may remember, had largely been founded on Beecham's former company), though this was resuscitated for a while longer as the Covent Garden English Company, with John Barbirolli as its musical director.

In 1929, however, one event temporarily absorbed all of Beecham's energies and devotion. In that year Delius was made a Companion of Honour. In his biography of the composer, Beecham tacitly acknowledges that despite all his own efforts so far, it had taken this belated act of official recognition to bring him to the notice of most British people.

> The immediate result was a ripple of curiosity in circles wider than those of the musical profession itself . . . There grew rapidly a desire to know more about the mysterious Englishman who had lived his life far from home, and who, according to the experts, had written a mass of strange and beautiful music, which for some reason or other had failed to achieve the popularity of those respectable expressions of national taste, 'Land of Hope and Glory' and *Merrie England.*

Beecham decided on a festival. He invited Philip Heseltine (Peter Warlock) to help him plan and publicise it. We have already noted Heseltine as another Delius devotee and close family friend. By 1929, as Beecham put it, his 'first fine careless rapture' for Delius's music had somewhat waned. 'But for all that,' Beecham went on, 'he knew far more about the composer and his music than anyone else in England and possessed a skilled and facile pen, together with a capacity for fiery energy, when his interest was aroused.' A year before his suicide, Heseltine willingly joined Beecham in the task in hand. Through that summer the two of them consulted with Delius in Grez-sur-Loing on the planning of the programmes. They also discussed the question of whether the now blind and largely paralysed composer, also often racked with pain, could attend the festival in person. In the event he did, journeying with Jelka by car to Boulogne, taking a night crossing and resting the next day in Folkestone before proceeding to the Langham Hotel in Portland Place for the duration of the festival.

This took place in London during October and the beginning of November. Beecham's claim in his advance publicity that 'such an event is without parallel in the history of music in England' was hardly exaggerated. No other British composer had ever been honoured in such a comprehensive way. The BBC Orchestra (not yet the BBC Symphony Orchestra, as we shall see shortly), the Columbia Graphophone Company and the Royal Philharmonic Society were joined by a host of top British instrumentalists (Albert Sammons, Arthur Catterall, Beatrice Harrison, the pianist Evelyn Howard-Jones, the Virtuoso String Quartet), choirs and vocalists (Pauline Maunder, Miriam Licette, Astra Desmond, Dora Labbette, Olga Haley, Heddle Nash, John Goss, John Armstrong, Dennis Noble, Roy Henderson, the London Select Choir). There were six concerts, four orchestral and choral ones in the Queen's Hall, two more of songs, instrumental and chamber music in the smaller Aeolian Hall in Bond Street. The programmes ranged from songs written as early as 1888, including several notable settings of Verlaine, to the first performance of the recently completed orchestral piece *A Late Lark*; and from such central works as *Brigg Fair* (which opened the festival), *A Song Before Sunrise* and *Summer Night on the River*, to such comparative rarities as the first performance of *Cynara*, a setting of a poem by Ernest Dowson for baritone and orchestra, and 'Mazurka and Waltz for a little girl' from the Five Piano Pieces of 1923. At the final concert, on 1 November 1929, Beecham conducted *A Mass of Life*.

'It was a memorable occasion,' *The Times* reported next day, of that last concert.

From a musical point of view the performance was nearly perfect. At the end there was prolonged applause for Mr Delius and for Sir Thomas Beecham. In a short speech of thanks for the enthusiasm which had been shown towards the festival, Sir Thomas Beecham reaffirmed his belief that Mr Delius had written a greater quantity of beautiful music than any other living composer, and said he wished to correct any notion that this festival had exhausted the store of works from Mr Delius's great workshop; on the contrary, he could supply more than enough for another festival next week. Since this was in the nature of a leave-taking – Mr Delius would soon be returning to his home in France – he called for cheers for him.

In reply to this ovation, Mr Delius, from his chair in the circle, briefly expressed his thanks to the audience, to the collaborators in the organisation and execution of the festival, and, most of all, to Sir Thomas Beecham for his inspired leadership. The festival had, he said, been 'the time of his life'.

Filling almost the whole of an adjacent column was another feature, a 'Retrospect' of Delius's music, much of which is as apposite today as it was in 1929:

> The strength and weakness of Delius is his solitariness. He belongs to no school, follows no tradition, and is like no other composer in the form, content, or style of his music. He constantly presents to those who would study him a paradox. It might reasonably be expected, for example, that a composer whose music is so all-over alike in style, idiom and subject matter would weary his audiences by monotony. But this festival has revealed a very great variety within this undeniable sameness, and an undoubted capacity to sustain whole programmes single-handed.
>
> Another true enough generalization would be that Delius's music is contemplative rather than emotional – the emotion either is recollected in exceptional tranquillity or it has never been experienced direct at all. Delius is no romantic worshipping his own emotions; he is almost always quite detached.
>
> Unhurried contemplation permits an acute sensibility to record its own aching sense of the beautiful. The spirit of today asks rather for the naked truth than what is pleasing to its sense of beauty. In that respect Delius certainly belongs to the last century rather than to this, but in all else he belongs to no nation or period or school, for there are in him too many contradictions. This constitutes the strength of his appeal. He is as little likely to influence those who come after him as he has been influenced by those who have gone before. He is himself alone, and his uniqueness will ensure him a lasting shrine in one of the quiet and shady groves of the temple of music.

Such a lengthy, deeply considered tribute in what was then still widely regarded as the most authoritative newspaper in the world

1 & 2. *Cartoon of a dandified young Thomas Beecham and* (below) *a portrait photograph of him in about 1908.* (Hulton Deutsch Collection Ltd)

1

2

3

4

5

3. *The Finnish soprano Aino Ackté, sensational star of the 1910 production of* Salome. (Royal Opera House Archives)

4. *Sergei Diaghilev. The Beechams brought his ballet and opera company to London.* (Royal Opera House Archives)

6. *Beecham in 1927, with the familiar goatee beard already in evidence.* (Hulton Deutsch Collection Ltd)

5 & 7. *Two more pictures from the late 1920s: (opposite, below) with the Russian-American conductor Serge Koussevitzky; and (below) handling mail for his Imperial League of Opera.* (Hulton Deutsch Collection Ltd)

6

7

8

Lisa Perli

8. *The English soprano Dora Labbette, alias Lisa Perli, one of Beecham's loves. It seems fairly common knowledge that she bore him a son.* (Royal Opera House Archives)

9. *Delius and his wife Jelka at home in Grez-sur-Loing in 1928, the year before Beecham's festival of his music.* (Hulton Deutsch Collection Ltd)

9

10

10. *With Wilhelm Furtwängler (third from left, top table) in 1937 at the Savoy Hotel dinner in honour of the Berlin Philharmonic's London visit.* (Royal Opera House Archives)

11. *The Norwegian soprano Kirsten Flagstad, one of the great stars Beecham brought to Covent Garden, as Brünnhilde.* (Royal Opera House Archives)

11

12. *Rehearsing with the London Philharmonic in the Royal Albert Hall, November 1944.* (Hulton Deutsch Collection Ltd)

13. *Beecham with Richard Strauss in London, 1947. Their association went back nearly forty years.* (Hulton Deutsch Collection Ltd)

12

13

14

14. *Relaxing at home.*
Playing the piano and chess
were two of his favourite
pastimes. (Hulton Deutsch
Collection Ltd)

15. *Beecham in 1949,*
listening to the playback of a
radio talk about Delius.
(Erich Auerbach/Hulton
Deutsch Collection Ltd)

15

16. *Left to right: Oliver Messel, Beecham, Karl Ebert and the actor Miles Malleson at the time of the 1950 Glyndebourne production of* Ariadne auf Naxos. (Hulton Deutsch Collection Ltd)

17. *With the Russian-American violinist Isaac Stern in 1952 in the Royal Festival Hall, the building he had called 'a chicken coop'.* (Hulton Deutsch Collection Ltd)

16

17

must have given Beecham particular satisfaction. From our standpoint, right at the end of the century, it may also strike a more poignant note. For all the claims that Beecham made for the music, for all the time and love he lavished upon it, Delius has indeed remained a 'solitary' composer, certainly not one of the commanding musical figures of the age. In the years to come, Beecham may privately have accepted this. For the moment, the festival had been a personal triumph, every bit as much for him as for Delius. In his biography he recorded a touching postscript to the whole event. On the homeward-bound crossing from Folkestone to Boulogne the composer, who in the past had so often railed against the land of his birth, asked for his wheelchair to be turned towards the receding cliffs of Dover, though, of course, he could no longer see them.

CHAPTER EIGHTEEN

Three years after the Delius Festival, the BBC moved into its brand new home at Broadcasting House, Langham Place. The big white stone building, shaped rather like the prow of a ship, was very much a product of its time, with its touches of art deco and sculptures by Eric Gill, the graphic artist whose display lettering was the model for the typography used by the London Underground. Radio broadcasting began in Britain in 1920, with the Marconi Company, modestly based at Chelmsford in Essex. Two years later the British Broadcasting Company was formed, transmitting from studios at Savoy Hill (with their call sign 2LO) off the Strand in London. In 1927 the company became a public corporation, financed by a radio ('wireless') fee, and with a guaranteed monopoly of broadcasting within the British Isles. Its Director General was Lord (John) Reith, the son of a Scottish Free Church minister, gaunt and craggy-faced and fired by a sense of mission and moral rectitude. The lives of whole generations of Britons were coloured by Lord Reith's BBC, whose announcers spoke with impeccable accents (and read the news in evening dress, though no one could see them), and where each day began and ended with 'Lift Up Your Hearts' and 'The Epilogue'. Millions switched to Radio Luxembourg as soon as they got the chance. But however morally superior and stuffy the BBC may have been in many ways, it was a magnificent friend and patron of music. Percy Pitt, already a much-loved figure in British musical circles, was its first Controller of Music. It gave work to many musicians, took over the running of the annual Promenade Concerts (thereby probably saving them) and began its long tradition of commissioning new music.

Beecham had watched all this with something less than enthusiasm. Early experiments in the broadcasting of music, especially of opera, had provoked some of his most apoplectic outbursts. 'The most abominable row that ever stunned and cursed the human ear ... It sounds like horrible chattering, gibbering, chortling, shrieking devils and goblins . . . It's insanity.' When technical standards improved, he saw broadcasting as a sign of moral decay in the British people. 'We are the laziest nation in the world already,' he said. 'Now we are becoming comatose. People are having their music brought to them. I feel sure that in another fifty years Englishmen will never even get out of bed in the morning, if this present tendency goes on.' Nevertheless, by the end of the 1920s, the BBC was a power in the land, and could not simply be mocked or pilloried. Beecham, for his part, was fifty, distinguished by his greying hair and the now familiar goatee beard, and widely recognised as Britain's musical elder statesman (a state of affairs much resented by Sir Henry Wood, who was ten years his senior). Almost inevitably, therefore, Beecham was drawn into discussions with the Corporation about the creation of a new orchestra.

One idea was for an orchestra, owned jointly by the Corporation and by Beecham at the head of a financial consortium, which he would help to form and, of course, conduct. Another was to reconstitute the London Symphony Orchestra, because of Beecham's already close associations with it. Beecham also proposed a new concert hall, with a capacity of nearly four thousand, at a site in Russell Square. On the face of it this was an attractive idea, especially when it came to the Proms. For it made the BBC independent of the Queen's Hall (though this was so conveniently sited just across the road from Broadcasting House), and of the music publishing firm of Chappell and Co., who presently owned the lease on it. Throughout 1929 and into 1930 discussions went on, committees were set up, memoranda circulated through the corridors of the BBC. They and Beecham got as far as planning a pilot series of concerts. But nothing was settled. One stumbling block between Beecham and the Corporation seems to have been the balance between live concerts and broadcast music. In the end the Corporation went ahead on its own. In 1930 it created its own BBC Symphony Orchestra, with a permanent strength of over a hundred players, and with Adrian Boult, this time ten years Beecham's junior but with a career of solid worth already behind him, as their chief conductor. (One of Beecham's funniest and cruellest jibes was reserved for the upright, sober and conscientious Boult, whom he described as 'reeking of Horlicks'.)

It was probably all for the best. The flamboyant, independent Beecham and the bureaucratic, paternalistic BBC never hit it off. Down to the smallest matters they were poles apart. ('Mean bastards', Beecham said years later, when he brought his own bottled refreshment to studio rehearsals, in defiance of their ban on alcohol.) In that winter of 1929–30, at any rate, he left them to their own devices, while he came to the rescue of an undergraduate opera group from Oxford, whose ambitious season at the Scala Theatre, London, presenting such rarities as the Restoration composer Matthew Locke's *Cupid and Death*, was floundering badly. For four days, and halfway into the nights, Beecham rehearsed them in Weber's *Der Freischütz* ('The Freeshooter'), that landmark of German romantic opera, with its thrilling note of diabolism, which he then conducted for five performances (without a fee) to packed houses. He also directed a production at the Royal College of Music of a new comic opera, *The Devil Take Her*, about a poet who restores his wife's voice and then regrets it. The composer was one of the College professors, the Australian-born Arthur Benjamin. This and his other operas have rather fallen by the wayside, but his name is kept alive by his delightful *Jamaican Rumba*, one of the many attractive pieces of light orchestral music in a field led by Eric Coates who, we may recall, had played viola in the Beecham Symphony Orchestra before the First World War. Beecham and the German-born businessman and impresario Robert Mayer then took over the arrangements for a visit to London of Wilhelm Furt-wängler and the Berlin Philharmonic Orchestra, when the concert promoter and agent Lionel Powell suddenly died. Powell, a big name in the London musical and theatrical scene, had also been handling Beecham's own affairs.

The biggest event of this fairly brief but hectic period was Beech-am's direction of a season of Russian opera and ballet. Diaghilev had died in 1929, and his Russian Opera and Ballet Company was now managed by Colonel W. de Basil. The latter's real name was Vassili Grigorievich Voskresensky, and he was rumoured to have been a Cossack general. 'A charming, world-weary, cynical Russian', was how the *Observer* described him in an interview. Beech-am's season with the company was presented during May and June of 1931 at the Lyceum Theatre. The company was composed largely of former Diaghilev singers and dancers, headed by the still charismatic Chaliapin, now fifty-eight, and making what proved to be his last London appearances. His fellow Russian, the soprano Oda Slobodskaya, on the other hand, though forty-three herself and already a well-established international name, was making her London début. The repertory included *Boris Godunov*, *Prince Igor*, Rimsky-Korsakov's lesser-known *Sadko* and *The Tsar's Bride*, Glinka's *Ruslan and Ludmilla*, and Alexander Dargo-myzhsky's *Rusalka*, based on Pushkin's version of the old Slavonic fairy tale, about the water-nymph who wishes to marry a prince.

Time has been rather unkind to the pioneer Russian composer Dargomyzhsky. He has been overshadowed by his slightly older contemporary Glinka. His *Rusalka* has been neglected in favour of Dvořák's own operatic treatment of much the same story. His only real claim to fame today is his later, unfinished opera *The Stone Guest*, based on Pushkin and telling the same story as *Don Giovanni*, though few people can have heard a single note of the music. At a gala performance, Chaliapin sang extracts from another role he had made famous, not a Russian one this time, but that of the dying knight in Massenet's *Don Quichotte*. While Beecham conducted most of the operas, Eugene Goossens handled the ballet: performances of Falla's *El Amor Brujo* ('Love, the Magician'), his most intensely Spanish stage work, Stravinsky's *Pulcinella*, and Prokofiev's early and now largely forgotten ballet *Chout* ('The Jester', or 'The Buffoon'). The orchestra was billed as 'The Russian Opera Orchestra'. There were not many Slavic faces to be seen in it. Beecham had recruited some of the best British orchestral musicians then around – Eugene Goossens's brother and sister, the oboist Leon and harpist Marie, the violinist George Stratton, James Bradshaw on timpani – and it signalled some very exciting times just around the corner.

The fairly short but glamorous season attracted as much publicity as a gala night at Covent Garden, and London society duly turned out for it. The covers to the programmes matched the occasion with their coloured patterns and insignia of old Imperial Russia. Inside they carried an advertisement for Balkan Sobranie cigarettes, the classiest brand on the market. 'Yes,' it declared, 'Chaliapin smokes.' Quite a few famous singers did in those days, including Caruso, often pictured in fur-lined coat and spats, with a fat cigar in his hand, looking like Al Capone.

CHAPTER NINETEEN

The early 1930s were a time of swift change in British orchestral life. Old practices such as independent bowing among the strings gave way to the standardised bowing we have long taken for granted. Standards of playing themselves improved, notably among the woodwind, which Sir Henry Wood prettily called 'the flower garden of the orchestra'. Altogether, there was a much brisker, clearer, more businesslike sound and feel in the air. This was the background to the formation of the crack new BBC Symphony Orchestra, and, coming close on its heels, the orchestra which many people regard as Beecham's greatest single achievement.

At the beginning of that decade his future seemed to lie with the London Symphony Orchestra. After a flirtation with Willem Mengelberg, principal conductor of the Amsterdam Concertgebouw Orchestra since 1895, the London Symphony turned again to Beecham. Throughout 1931 and into 1932 – during some of the worst months of the Depression – they gave a concert season at the Queen's Hall, which included the fifteen-year-old American-born Yehudi Menuhin playing the Beethoven Violin Concerto. They followed this with a tour of the provinces, returning to London for another prestigious concert, this time with Fritz Kreisler (who had given the first performance of the Elgar Violin Concerto in 1910) playing Bach's D minor Concerto. Everything pointed to Beecham as the new man at the helm of the London Symphony Orchestra. A problem was that they were self-governing, and every member was a shareholder. Such a democratic arrangement was not something Beecham was used to. He could not easily hire and fire players as he chose, even in the very best musical interests of the orchestra.

At this juncture Malcolm Sargent made a providential entry into the Beecham story. The dapper, thirty-six-year-old organist, composer of the attractive orchestral piece *Impressions of a Windy Day* and an exciting choral conductor, had recently been asked by the millionaire industrialist and art patron Samuel Courtauld to form an orchestra to play at a new series of concerts. Not usually one to shrink away from the limelight, Sargent was also prudent enough to believe that he probably still lacked the experience to recruit and train an entirely new orchestra. So he approached Beecham. With the BBC Symphony Orchestra now widely accepted as the best in the country, Beecham was presented with one of the strongest and most exciting challenges of his life. He took it up with the same gusto, flair and nose or ear for talent that had served him over twenty years earlier when he formed the Beecham Symphony Orchestra, plus all the extra knowledge, experience and authority that the intervening years had brought with them. He was backed by a board that included Samuel Courtauld himself, Robert Mayer (the founder of the long-running series of children's concerts, who lived to the age of 106) and Baron Frederic d'Erlanger (shrewd, long-time member of the Grand Opera Syndicate). With this money and support behind him, Beecham set about his task in buccaneering spirit. He took key players away from existing orchestras, including the BBC Symphony and London Symphony orchestras. In the latter case he even tried to buy their famous name from them. He was not popular in some quarters. Less controversially, he snapped up much of the best new talent just coming out of the music academies and colleges. His chosen leader was Paul Beard, from the City of Birmingham Orchestra, formed in 1920 in the wake of Beecham's own wartime efforts on behalf of that city's musical life. Among other top orchestral musicians who joined him were: George Stratton, leading the second violins; the Argentine-born Anthony Pini, principal cello; Leon and Marie Goossens, principal oboe and harp, respectively; Reginald Kell, clarinet; Gerald Jackson, flute; Gwydion Brooke, bassoon; James Bradshaw, timpani. So was born the London Philharmonic Orchestra.

It was always Beecham's contention that Britain possessed many of the best orchestral players in the world, but that British orchestras lacked the resources and support enjoyed in one form or another by the top orchestras on the Continent or in America. Sixty years later, nothing much seems to have changed in this respect. But, at the start at any rate, Beecham lavished on his newest orchestra all the money, time and care in the world. It may be true that he sometimes took a cavalier attitude towards rehearsals. It all depended on the music and the occasion. For the London Philharmonic's opening concert he was the most meticulous and assiduous of conductors. He prepared and marked the orchestral parts down to the finest detail. He worked through these with his principals and section leaders, often at the piano, like an opera conductor taking his leading singers through their roles. He held six or seven rehearsals for individual sections. 'He rehearsed the violas for three hours', recalls Leo Birnbaum, who had gone straight into the orchestra from his studies at the Guildhall School of Music. 'I was, of course, very excited to play under England's greatest conductor. He was absolutely charming the whole time.' Finally came rehearsals for the whole orchestra, held in the basement of the massive Liverpool and Victoria building in Bloomsbury Square. Beecham himself, once so notoriously unpunctual, set a shining example, arriving for each one on the dot, stepping briskly up onto the podium and stripping down to shirt and braces.

The London Philharmonic Orchestra and Sir Thomas Beecham made their début at the Queen's Hall on 7 October 1932. 'Come along, Mr Beard, let's show 'em what we can do!' Beecham is reported as saying to his leader just before they joined the rest of the orchestra on the platform. Berlioz's *Carnaval Romain* overture was the opening piece (as it had been for the début of the Beecham Symphony Orchestra in February 1909). Then came Delius's *Brigg Fair* and Mozart's Symphony No. 38 ('Prague'). 'When Tommy came on again after the interval,' Mr Birnbaum remembers, 'we couldn't start for several minutes because of the applause.' It was even more prolonged and deafening after the performance of *Ein Heldenleben*. 'At the end of the concert', he adds, 'my chest must have expanded several inches with pride!' Public and critical opinion was well summed up by the doyen of British music critics, Ernest Newman – he who had lambasted *Elektra* back in 1910 – writing in the pages of the next edition of the *Sunday Times*:

> Sir Thomas Beecham's new orchestra began its operations in Queen's Hall on Friday evening. He began with a performance of Berlioz's *Carnaval Romain* Overture that had an air about it of 'You Londoners want to know what an orchestra ought to be like? Well, just listen to this.' The demonstration was certainly complete enough; nothing so electrifying has been heard in a London concert room for years. The tone was magnificent, the precision perfect, the reading a miracle of fire and beauty, and the enthusiasm of the audience could not have been greater.

Beecham and his London Philharmonic Orchestra ('London Pillharmonic' as the wags were quick to name it) were instantly projected into the very centre of British musical life. Menuhin, now a year older, played a Bach and a Mozart violin concerto with Beecham, and then the Elgar Concerto with the seventy-five-year-old composer (with whom he had already struck up a remarkable partnership). The orchestra was in demand everywhere. They were booked for the Leeds and Norwich Triennial Festivals. They were constantly in demand in the recording studios (their own and Beecham's recording career is covered in the appendix to this book). One of the first, closest and happiest of their associations was with the Royal Philharmonic Society. Their opening concert had also opened the Society's one hundred and twenty-first season. Up to that moment, the Royal Philharmonic Society had traditionally provided its own orchestra for these seasons. This, as Robert Elkin points out in his book *Royal Philharmonic*, was not a permanent ensemble but one brought together, season by season, from among the best available players in other orchestras – rather like selecting the best individual players at club level to form a national team. With the advent of the London Philharmonic Orchestra, the Royal Philharmonic Society decided they could not do better themselves. Thenceforth, for a long time to come, the London Philharmonic Orchestra was their chosen instrument.

For the rest of that 1932–33 season, Beecham and his orchestra appeared with a clutch of notable soloists. In the second concert of the season, Myra Hess, who had made her concert début with Beecham in 1907, played Mozart's Concerto in C minor (K491). The concert ended with the Symphony No. 99 in E flat of Haydn, the other classical master whom Beecham delighted in playing. (At that time, incidentally, the last twelve and most famous of Haydn's symphonies, written for London, were often numbered as such, 1 to 12, of the 'Salomon set'; they are still often referred to as the London Symphonies). At another concert the Russian-born Vladimir Horowitz, the virtuoso pianist *par excellence*, thundered through Tchaikovsky's First Piano Concerto in B flat minor. (Later, after settling in America, he married Toscanini's daughter.) In February 1933, there was the Brahms Centenary Concert (celebrating his birth), at which the Double Concerto was played by two more notable soloists. The Hungarian-born violinist Jelly d'Arányi, who became a British subject, had several works dedicated to her, including Bartók's two violin sonatas and Ravel's well-known *Tzigane*. The Spanish cellist Gaspar Cassadó studied with his compatriot Casals, giving his first recital aged nine, but never enjoyed the latter's great fame. Albert Sammons and Lionel Tertis, who had first played together with the Beecham Symphony Orchestra in 1909, joined him again in Mozart's Sinfonia Concertante for Violin and Viola (K364). In the last concert of that particular season Beecham shared the rostrum with Ildebrando Pizzetti, who conducted the first performance in England of his *Rondo Venezia*. This Italian teacher and composer was quite a big name. One of his later works was the opera *L'Assassinio nella Cattedrale*, based on T. S. Eliot's *Murder in the Cathedral*. As a postscript to that year's concert work, Beecham conducted *The Prison*, a type of choral symphony or large-scale cantata, one of the latest compositions of Dame Ethel Smyth, still in fine and combative fettle at seventy-five and celebrating the fact with a mini-festival of her music.

During subsequent Royal Philharmonic Society seasons, Beecham and the London Philharmonic teamed up with more international celebrities, some now legendary: the violinists Jascha Heifetz and Adolf Busch; the cellist Gregor Piatigorsky; the pianists Moritz Rosenthal, Artur Schnabel, and the tall and lugubrious Sergei Rachmaninov, giving the first London performance of his recently composed *Rhapsody on a Theme of Paganini*. At these seasons Beecham was also called upon to do the honours in presenting the Society's Gold Medal, which, of course, he had received in 1928. In April 1934 the recipient was the Welshman Sir Edward German, the immensely popular composer of the light operas *Merrie England* and *Tom Jones*, Edwardian images of a never-never land of maypoles and Good Queen Bess. Rather shamefully, we might think, none of his tuneful music was included in that evening's programme.

In November of the following year, the Finnish Minister in London received the Gold Medal from Beecham on behalf of Sibelius. Jean Sibelius, of course, is another composer closely linked with Beecham. In fact, Beecham was a fairly late convert to his cause. Granville Bantock and Sir Henry Wood had been promoting him – to the point where, in Britain at any rate, Sibelius was widely regarded as the greatest composer of the age – long before Beecham showed much interest in his music. Indeed, Beecham's new enthusiasm for the Finnish master surprised many people at the time. Walter Legge, who also played quite an important part in Beecham's career, wrote as follows of a concert the latter gave in 1937 of three of the symphonies:

> Such uncivilised and uncomfortable music as this is at the very antithesis of Sir Thomas Beecham's personality and outlook. Sibelius's basic English, so to speak, is poles apart from his exquisite choice of the finely moulded phrase of apt polysyllables. He cast his innate grace and polish aside as if it were a mere top dressing of soil and came to grips with Sibelian granite in a way which must have surprised and shocked his most devout admirers.

Be that as it may, from the 1930s until the end of his life, Beecham is now remembered as one of the staunchest supporters and finest interpreters of 'Old Sib', as he liked to call him. He had conducted the Sixth Symphony at that 1935 Royal Philharmonic Society concert. As an interesting footnote, he included in the same concert a cello concerto credited to Arnold Schoenberg (soloist Emmanuel Feuermann), a composer emphatically not associated with Beecham. To put the record straight, this was Schoenberg's arrangement of a keyboard concerto by the eighteenth-century Austrian Georg Monn – much more, we may assume, to Beecham's taste.

CHAPTER TWENTY

For almost anybody else, the formation and management of a great new orchestra would have been more than enough to cope with. Not so with Beecham. Opera was beckoning again. The Royal Opera House was now controlled by the Covent Garden Opera Syndicate Company, with the Hungarian financier F. A. Szarvasy as chairman and Lt-Col. Eustace Blois as managing director, an interesting man who had turned from the army to composition and opera administration. Opera was suffering from the current economic slump as badly as everything else, and during May and the first few days of June 1932 the Syndicate tried to revive their flagging fortunes with a four-week 'Wagner Festival Season'. They had an experienced cast of British and foreign singers, a large contingent of the London Symphony Orchestra in the pit, and, sharing the conducting with Robert Heger (a regular visitor from Germany), Charles Webber and John Barbirolli, they also had Beecham, back at the Royal Opera House after twelve long years. The festival went well, with the result that Beecham entered into negotiations with the Syndicate, the BBC and other interested parties. He emerged as Covent Garden's new Artistic Director. It was a decisive move. The rest of the decade at Covent Garden belonged to Beecham and to the London Philharmonic Orchestra, which he brought with him. Not only the name of the orchestra, but a full list of players thenceforth appeared in many opera and ballet programmes.

Together, on 1 May, they opened the 1933 season with *Der Rosenkavalier*. The German-American soprano Lotte Lehmann, perhaps the favourite singer of her generation, was the Marschallin, her best-loved part, and Alexander Kipnis, another in the stable of great Russian basses, was Baron Ochs. Heddle Nash, rising steadily in the operatic ranks, was the Singer in Act I. 'Brilliant in the fullest sense of that overworked word,' was the *Daily Telegraph*'s verdict on that opening night. 'The most devoted Edwardian at the Royal Opera last night, as his eyes ran round that lovely auditorium – the most beautiful theatre interior in the world – must have admitted that in smartness 1933 fully held its own with 1903 or 1913.' There was a drawing of the audience in the *Sketch*, and smart they certainly were, in the fashion of the day, the women with their permanent waves, the men with short back and sides and the occasional clipped moustache, like the cast of *Private Lives*. A cameraman from the *Sketch* also snapped Ivor Novello, with his mother, among the first-night celebrities.

The rest of the season – especially the German part of it – glittered with big names. Beecham conducted the German soprano Frida Leider and the Danish tenor Lauritz Melchior in *Tristan und Isolde*. Leider and Melchior formed the perfect Wagnerian partnership, Melchior every inch the classic *Heldentenor*, big, barrel-chested, rigged out in gleaming helmet and chain mail. For all the fame and prestige of these two great singers, it was Beecham and his orchestra whom *The Times* singled out for praise. 'If the singers did much, Sir Thomas Beecham did even more, for the poetry of his reading and the lyrical playing which he draws from the orchestra carry the whole drama forward in a ceaseless flow.' Robert Heger came back to conduct a *Ring* cycle, with Leider and Melchior as Brünnhilde and Siegfried, backed up by the Hungarian-born Friedrich Schorr as Wotan and Lehmann as Sieglinde. A strong English-speaking contingent included Walter Widdop, Norman Allin, Florence Austral (who took over in later performances as Brünnhilde) and a newcomer, Mary Jarred, who earned critical praise in the smaller parts of Erda and Fricka. Again, though, it was Beecham's orchestra that seems to have stolen the show. 'It touches on the marvellous', said the *Daily Telegraph*, 'that a newly formed orchestra should, after only a week's rehearsing, have played as the London Philharmonic did last night.' This part of the season involved two other interesting singers. During the *Tristan* run, Leider was suddenly taken ill. Frantic phone calls brought the soprano Henny Trundt flying in from Cologne to sing with Melchior that same evening. Henny Trundt is hardly a household name today, but she was warmly applauded, and deservedly so, by the Covent Garden audience that night. Her airplane dash, a portent of the jetsetting age, also caught the fancy of the London press. A revival of *Parsifal* brought in Gertrude Rünger as Kundry. Like Henny Trundt, and very many others, Gertrude Rünger is not widely remembered today, yet she had an impressive career, with both the Vienna and Berlin State operas, at Salzburg, at the Metropolitan Opera, New York, and for a time after the Second World War with the East Berlin State Opera.

The Italian and French sections of the season appeared to lack the same Teutonic solidity. The Italian part opened with *Aida*. Eva Turner was reportedly very good in the title role; but the Italian tenor Francisco Battaglia as Radames – in one of those acutely embarrassing situations where the audience probably suffers even more than the performers – almost cracked up during his rendition of 'Celeste Aida'. In subsequent performances (conducted by Barbirolli), Eva Turner was joined by two other British singers, Muriel Brunskill, who later slipped into a different gear to sing regularly in Gilbert and Sullivan operetta, and the baritone Dennis Noble, a well-known figure in English oratorio and opera until after the Second World War. Melchior sang the title role in *Otello*, but in German, and got booed for it. Beecham's revival of *Don Carlos* – its first airing at Covent Garden for nearly seventy years – was, from all accounts, vocally below par. He also staged, for the first time in England, Berlioz's 'dramatic cantata' *La Damnation de Faust*, something he had wanted to do with his Imperial League of Opera. Alas, the singers again seem to have let him down, and his orchestra, once again, was 'the true hero of the evening'.

There were two gala performances in June by the Camargo Ballet Society, of great importance in the history of British dance since it led first to the formation of the Vic-Wells Ballet under the aegis of the remarkable Lilian Baylis, then the Sadler's Wells Ballet, and finally to the creation of the Royal Ballet at Covent Garden. On this occasion Beecham shared the conducting with Constant Lambert, a new and rising name in British music as both conductor and composer, while the dancers included such big stars as Anton Dolin, Ninette de Valois, Karsavina and Alicia Markova.

The real talking point at the end of the season was the future of the Royal Opera House itself (something not finally settled until 1980, when the government granted it the freehold of the Covent Garden site). The existing lease, held by the Covent Garden Opera Syndicate, had expired. Beecham, addressing the last night audience, wondered whether they had all just shared an historic and melancholy event – the last performance at the present theatre. There was, indeed, a real possibility that the building might be pulled down. Ernest Newman, writing in the *Sunday Times*, made this prospect of demolition the excuse for an attack on the Covent Garden audience. 'To some of us it seems too good to be true; and if it should turn out, after all, that next year, and year by year after that, the place is to be given over again to Italian and German tenors, we shall merely pass the hand of fortitude over the brow of resignation, and once more, in due time, prepare for the worst.' He went on,

> The devotees of the German season are not so bad. It is true that they are ludicrously limited in their receptivity [but] they are, in the main, musical people, and they have standards of sorts . . . It is when the Italian season begins that the whole aspect of Covent Garden changes. It is painfully manifest that they [the audience] have no standards whatsoever . . . All they want is an occasional ringing high note; they are not even critical of the quality of the high note, so long as the rude power is there.

The orchestra, Newman concluded, were the real star performers, whose musicality and skill were wasted – another feather in the cap of Beecham and the London Philharmonic, though, given the tone and burden of Newman's words, one they might have found a trifle embarrassing.

If the worst had really happened, Newman would surely have been as saddened as everybody else. For all the faults and failings of sections of the audience, the Royal Opera House was an integral part of London. Indeed, what great city could call itself truly civilised without such an institution? In the event, before the year was out, the *Observer* was able to announce: 'Covent Garden Opera House has been reprieved . . . In spite of all the elaborate planning schemes for the neighbourhood, and in spite of all the powerful local marketing interests, the Opera House is to remain.' A new administrative syndicate, the Royal Opera House Company Limited, with Geoffrey Toye as managing director and Beecham remaining as artistic director, had secured a new lease. At the same time, building improvements and renovations were to be put in hand to meet London County Council safety regulations and to provide more office space and dressing-rooms. New stage lighting was also to be installed, notably a 'cyclorama', a great battery of electric lamps controlled from a console that produced multi-coloured back projections and made the rear of the stage look more like a film studio. The *Daily Telegraph* sent somebody along to see how things were going. 'The ambition seized me', wrote their man-on-the-spot,

> to be the first member of the public to use the new stairway to the gallery that opens on Bow Street. I fell over a pile of washing basins. I inspected the commodious new quarters for which they were destined. Duly impressed, I at last reached the amphitheatre. It was wrapped in ghostly gloom. Escaping from its dark

silence, I found myself on a platform high in the wings. Here electricians were engaged upon the mysteries of their calling. After falling over some cordage I returned to the sunlight of Bow Street. There I admired the newly cream-painted façade. The two ladies in their lofty niches symbolised more satisfactorily than ever the eternal soprano and the eternal contralto. There was about them and the shining Corinthian pillars of the portico a Roman air of permanence.

In this upbeat mood, the 1934 season got under way on 30 April with Beecham conducting a new production of *Fidelio*. Next morning, the *Daily Mirror* splashed the occasion across its front page. 'Sir T. Beecham in Opera Scene. "Stop Talking" shout to the audience.' There was a photograph of him inset into a full-page one of the first-night audience standing for the National Anthem. He had created a sensation by shouting out a reprimand to noisy latecomers while he was conducting the overture. The *Daily Mirror*'s version of events was really quite mild. Others said Beecham's words were, 'Shut up, you barbarians.' The performance was being broadcast, and some listeners apparently misheard 'barbarians' – if that was the word – for something much worse. *The Times* tried to pour a little oil on the troubled waters Beecham had stirred up. 'The first thing the new management must do is to educate its audience and perhaps it would have been better to wait a little before casting Beethoven before them.' Perhaps Newman's attack on the philistine ways of Covent Garden audiences had raised Beecham's own ire. At any rate he seemed quite unrepentant, and made it a rule that latecomers would not be admitted until the first intermission. Such was his authority that patrons, however high and mighty, uttered hardly a whisper in protest. The cast included Lotte Lehmann as Leonore, the German tenor Franz Völker, a familiar voice at Bayreuth and Salzburg during the 1930s, as Florestan (later replaced by Melchior), and Kipnis as Rocco the jailer. The *Daily Telegraph* singled out Lehmann for special praise. 'She beautifully succeeded where so many have fallen into disaster. Truly, that voice, with its sweet yet gallant ring, its dauntlessness and tenderness, is Leonore's voice.' The same newspaper also said that Beecham's conducting gave the work 'all the eager vitality that it needed to make it a thing of simple – if rather naive – grandeur.' There was praise too for the stage sets, traditional but striking, by Rex Whistler, the English painter, graphic artist and stage designer (no relation to the American James McNeill Whistler).

Beecham, for the first time at Covent Garden, also conducted two complete *Ring* cycles. It was a new production, with sets and costumes by the well-known scenic artist Gabriel Volkoff (though they look traditional enough by today's abstract and symbolist standards). *The Times* wrote that Volkoff's Valhalla 'gleamed rosy as a peak of the Dolomites against an azure sky'. Leider and Melchior were back as Brünnhilde and Siegfried, Lehmann and Völker as Sieglinde and Siegmund. The performances also brought together some of the top Wagnerian baritones and basses of the day: Kipnis again, Rudolf Bockelmann, Hans Nissen and Emmanuel List. Gertrude Rünger returned to sing Fricka and Waltraute. 'The "Ring" performances at Covent Garden', the *Daily Mail*'s music critic wrote, 'are getting more and more thrilling. *Die Walküre* was a triumphal progress from act to act . . . Frau Leider and Herr Bockelmann (Wotan) rose to wonderful heights in the concluding scene.' Writing in the *Sunday Times*, Newman again turned the spotlight on conductor and orchestra. 'In *Siegfried*, the orchestra, under Sir Thomas Beecham, was again supreme; never before, in any performance of the "Ring", have I heard an orchestra sing and soar like this.'

Beecham handed over the baton to the visiting Austrian conductor Clemens Krauss (making his own début at the Royal Opera House) for two new operas. *Schwanda the Bagpiper*, by the Czech composer Jaromir Weinberger, was a setting of an old Slavic folk tale about the eponymous hero's adventures with Queen Ice Heart and the Devil (reminiscent in places of the plot of Stravinsky's *L'Histoire du Soldat*). Krauss's Romanian wife Viorica Ursuleac sang the role of Schwanda's wife Dorota. After the epic proportions of the *Ring*, this charming enough work seemed very lightweight. Another eminent critic, Richard Capell of the *Daily Telegraph*, summed up the general reaction to it. 'Weinberger's "Schwanda" was voted good fun at its first performance last night at Covent Garden. It was a curious evening, with a flavour about it of a first night at the Coliseum rather than at Covent Garden.' (The Coliseum theatre in St Martin's Lane, in due course home of the English National Opera, was at that time noted for such hit musical shows as *White Horse Inn* and *The Vagabond King*.) The opera came and went without making any deep impression, though two excerpts from it, the 'Polka' and 'Fugue', have helped to keep the composer's name alive. Richard Strauss's *Arabella*, his last collaboration with Hugo von Hofmannsthal before the librettist's death in 1929, had had its première (conducted by Krauss) in Dresden the previous year. The conductor was by then widely regarded as the finest Strauss interpreter, and Ursuleac, who sang the title role, was the composer's own favourite soprano. Despite these credentials, the work, another Viennese romance, failed to generate much excitement or enthusiasm. '*Arabella*', Newman wrote for the *Sunday Times*, 'is poor Hofmannsthal and poorer Strauss; the music is merely the second or third infusion of the tired tea leaves that at first brewing yielded the 'Rosenkavalier' . . . The fluency is endless, the workmanship slick, the sounds quite pleasant in themselves, and the artistic result as near to zero as makes no matter.' Other critics, though not quite so brutal, expressed much the same opinion. The opera has gained in esteem since then. Beecham returned to the pit to give the end of the German repertory a lift with *Die Meistersinger*. 'Among the principals,' said the *Daily Telegraph*, 'the leading light and faultless hero was the Sachs, Rudolf Bockelmann' – who had earlier been praised for his Wotan.

The Italian repertory for that season brought back *Otello*, conducted by Beecham, with Melchior this time managing the title role in Italian, and the Australian baritone John Brownlee – a familiar face and voice at Covent Garden through much of the decade – as Iago. The London-born Joan Cross was Desdemona. She was already very well known to audiences at the newly reconstructed Sadler's Wells theatre on Rosebery Avenue, on the fringes of Islington, going on to direct the theatre's company during the Second World War and to become closely associated with the performance and production of the operas of Benjamin Britten in the postwar years. A guest conductor, the Italian Gino Marinuzzi – highly esteemed in his day – took over the revivals of *La Bohème* and *Turandot*, the latter including the Italian bass Ezio Pinza, later famous for his film appearances, in the relatively small part of Timur. The biggest star of this part of the season, though, was the Spanish mezzo-soprano Conchita Supervia, another of those now making her Covent Garden début. She was a consummate exponent of Rossini's own special style of coloratura singing, and it is not stretching the fancy too far to see something of Rossini's own mischievous cast of feature in the many charming pictures of her. She had come to the Royal Opera House to sing in *La Cenerentola* ('Cinderella'), the first London staging of the opera for over forty years. Indeed, Beecham and Toye had grave doubts about the piece, fearing it had fallen so far out of the repertory that it might flop. It created other problems. Supervia was also contracted to sing the role of Carmen, but for vocal reasons she did not want to perform the two operas in tandem. There was a row about that, involving an alleged breach of contract by the Royal Opera House. When that was sorted out, however, the vivacious Spanish lady brought an extra sparkle to the rehearsals of *Cenerentola*. Beecham, recalls the celebrated accompanist Ivor Newton in his memoirs *At the Piano*, had decided that she should arrive at the ball in the traditional fairytale coach, and had dug out some extra music by Rossini to accompany this spot of action. The next thing was to time it. Quick as a flash, Supervia had Toye and Beecham up on stage, high-stepping across it harnessed to the coach, while she gaily cracked a whip over their heads (a reminder of the fun Beecham had had years before, when he rode the carousel during the rehearsals for *A Village Romeo and Juliet*). Then the illness of the leading tenor, Dino Borgioli, forced a postponement of the first night. When the curtain did finally go up on *La Cenerentola* – with ballet sequences featuring Markova and Robert Helpmann and choreography by Ninette de Valois – the Spanish singer made it all worth waiting for. 'Mme Supervia's performance was amazingly fine,' wrote another distinguished critic of the time, Edwin Evans, in the *Daily Mail*. 'She made all those flourishes and runs sound as if, far from representing technical accomplishment, they were nothing more than the natural expression of an exuberant temperament. And her acting was the best seen on the Covent Garden stage this season.' She returned the following year.

Ballet followed opera. Colonel de Basil and the *Ballets Russes* brought with them to Covent Garden some interesting new productions: *Les Matelots* ('The Sailors'), with music by Georges Auric, a member of 'Les Six' (which had shared the bill with *The Gods Go A-Begging* in 1928); *Union Pacific*, about the construction of the American transcontinental railway, with music by the Russian-American composer Nicolai Nabokov; and *Choreartium*, to movements from Brahms's Fourth Symphony. Beecham opened this final part of the season by conducting Act II of *Swan Lake*, then bowed out to the Hungarian Antal Dorati, still under thirty years of age and just beginning his steady climb to international fame, and the Russian-born Efrem Kurtz, not quite so well known today.

In that very eventful year Beecham also found the time to conduct three performances of *A Village Romeo and Juliet* at the Royal College of Music, with a student orchestra and cast. 'The most heartbreaking music in the world,' Sir Hugh Allen, director of the College, said to Beecham. One of the student singers was Peter Pears, a few years before the start of his association with Benjamin Britten. According to Sir Neville Cardus, for many years the

celebrated music critic of the *Manchester Guardian*, Beecham recognised Britten's huge talent. 'The only English composer worth-
while,' to quote Cardus quoting Beecham, 'who has emanated from
our colleges of music.' Yet Beecham, the conductor and impresario
who did more than anyone else this century to promote opera in
Britain, was never really in sympathy with England's greatest opera
composer.

CHAPTER TWENTY-ONE

In 1934 both Elgar and Delius died. The account of these facts in Beecham's biography of Delius is of interest not just in itself, but for what it may reveal about Beecham himself. In public, as we have noted, he was sometimes rude about Elgar, as he was rude about so many people. In his biography, in the chapter leading up to Delius's death, he writes of the late friendship that sprang up between the two composers, with a most tender and touching sympathy towards both men. This, surely, is Beecham the private individual; the deeply sensitive and understanding artist, so often buried beneath the bluster of the public image and the hectic pace of his life.

It is, of course, the death of Delius – in Beecham's words 'the last great apostle in our time of romance, emotion and beauty in music' – that is more germane to this narrative. Since he had returned to Grez-sur-Loing from the festival of 1929, the composer's condition had deteriorated further, though he had still managed to dictate a few more pieces of music – the orchestral *A Song of Summer* and *Fantastic Dance*, the Third Violin Sonata – thanks to what Beecham calls his own 'iron resolution' and 'the almost angelic patience' of his musical secretary or amanuensis, the young Yorkshireman Eric Fenby. He finally expired at his home on 10 June 1934. He was first buried in the village churchyard at Grez, next door to his garden. But the following year his body was transported to England, and he was reinterred in the church cemetery at Limpsfield, a village near Oxted in Surrey. According to Beecham, this ceremony took place on 24 May 1935, though Lionel Carley, in his *Delius, A Life in Letters*, says 26 May. Whichever date is correct, it was, apparently, a perfect early summer's day, of the kind so beautifully evoked by a piece such as *On Hearing the First Cuckoo in Spring*. Vaughan Williams was among those present at the graveside, and Beecham arranged for a section of the London Philharmonic Orchestra to play some of Delius's smaller instrumental pieces during the accompanying service in the church.

He himself delivered what he called 'a short *oraison funèbre*', which he is too self-effacing to reproduce in his own book on the composer. Here are parts of it:

> It may have struck some of you as requiring a little explanation as to why Frederick Delius, who left these shores as a very young man, a wanderer and almost an exile, has returned to them finally only yesterday. You may like to know why it was he wished to lie here amid the countryside of the land which gave him birth. I think I am able to give you the explanation.
>
> The England that we live in today is not by any means that in which Delius was born, some seventy-five years ago. He was born in those days which excited and provoked the rage of the sages of the time. Carlyle, Matthew Arnold, Ruskin raged and preached against the brutality, inhumanity, and insensibility of that age.
>
> England at that time seemed to be a country given up to the worship of commercial prosperity and little else besides. It was a country that revolted the finer spirits of that time, and in certain cases drove them out of it elsewhere, where they hoped to find, and they did indeed find, a more sympathetic environment.
>
> Delius was born in a part of the world which was particularly odious to him and to the kind of critical intelligence I have mentioned. It was the arid, hard, business north.
>
> It was into this environment and these conditions that Delius was born, and among which he grew up – and he grew up a rebel and a dissentient. He strove to escape, and he did escape, and when he left this country as a young man he went to other countries and finally settled in the country which, in the opinion of everyone at that time, provided the outlet for his activities and the fitting soil for the reception of his great gifts, as well as circumstances in which he could work in peace and enjoy the sympathy of those about him.

Beecham went on, quite briefly, to relate (with no reference to himself) the changes in British social and cultural life which, in his opinion, had led to Delius's own final change of heart and his wish to be buried in an English churchyard. He concluded:

> I said we were here to bid farewell for ever to the mortal remains of Frederick Delius. I do so in no spirit of sorrow or regret. The most precious part of this man is the immortal part – his spirit as revealed in his work; and in whatever sphere that spirit is, I should like our greetings to pass beyond the confines of this

earthly sphere, and let him know that we are here not in a spirit of vain regret, but rather one of rejoicing that his music is with us and will remain with us for evermore.

The circumstances of the death of Delius's wife Jelka provide a moving footnote to this relatively private and personal interlude in Beecham's own life. 'Few women', he writes in his book, 'have been subjected to such a lengthy period of sustained distress and worry, and its consequences had become apparent to all her relatives and close friends . . . She paid for her devotion by a sudden decline in strength at the beginning of 1934 and the ominous signs of a cancerous growth.' He relates how her operation for this cancer coincided with her husband's final collapse and death, but how she left her own hospital bed to be with him at the end. Beecham then records how he helped her to set up a trust for the collective editing, publishing and recording of his major works. The Delius Society was a result of these efforts. Tragically she was not present at the subsequent ceremony at Limpsfield. On the way over from France she contracted pneumonia and was rushed to another hospital, this time in London. However, a recording was made of Beecham's graveside speech and a few hours later was played back to Jelka in hospital. A blackbird could be heard singing in the background. According to the young BBC recording engineer who was with her, she smiled and whispered, 'Dear Tommy'. Two days later she too was dead; she was buried beside her husband.

CHAPTER TWENTY-TWO

The hurly-burly of life at Covent Garden could hardly have been further removed from the quiet dignity of that day in an English country churchyard. It was these years at the Royal Opera House that inspired so many of the anecdotes and witticisms (about women giving their best performances lying down, and all the rest of it) that have clung to Beecham's name and reputation ever since. More to the point was his own punishing workload. As artistic director, he attended stage rehearsals, whether or not he was conducting, often with a whistle round his neck which he blew for attention to save his voice. He flogged the orchestra almost as hard as he flogged himself. He might rehearse with them all day, with a performance to follow. If there was no performance, rehearsals sometimes continued well into the night. There were compensations for the players: overtime pay, for a start. There was also the famous 'Nigger's Foot'. Beecham would call a break in rehearsal and send round to the Nag's Head pub at the corner of Floral Street (still going strong) for quantities of champagne and stout – dark with a kick to it. (There was, it should be said, nothing especially ugly or intentionally racist about the use of the word 'nigger' in those days. For many years it was attached to Dvořák's 'American' String Quartet.) All the same, not everybody had Beecham's superhuman energy. Paul Beard resigned as leader of the London Philharmonic Orchestra in 1936 for a less frantic life with Adrian Boult and the BBC Symphony Orchestra. 'Another season of Wagner at Covent Garden', he is reported as saying, 'would have killed me.'

In 1935, meanwhile, there was plenty of incident, with a few sparks flying for good measure. The Grand Opera Season opened smoothly enough on 29 April, with a new production of *Lohengrin* conducted by Beecham, except that Melchior had to step in at the last moment for the Swiss tenor Max Hirzel, who had gone down with a bad head-cold. Lehmann, Kipnis and the well-known German-American baritone Herbert Janssen were also in the cast.

'Glowing Production Opens Season', was the headline in the *Daily Telegraph*. The staging was traditional enough by today's standards, but the singing, Beecham's conducting and the playing of his orchestra augured well for the season. The press ritual of photographing the arrival of first-night celebrities caught Mr Neville Chamberlain, who was soon to succeed Stanley Baldwin as prime minister. For the second performance, a few nights later, the still indisposed Max Hirzel was this time replaced by the Swedish tenor Torsten Ralf, who arrived from Germany less than four hours before curtain time.

Beecham conducted two *Ring* cycles. By now these were such a regular feature of the Covent Garden seasons that it is easy to become a little blasé about them and to forget the enormous amount of organisation behind the staging of each one, not to mention the mental, emotional and physical demands made on the conductor and principal singers. During the first performance of *Das Rheingold*, the famous 'cyclorama' malfunctioned, blacking out the stage a little too effectively during the descent to Nibelheim. The house lights had to be turned on while emergency repairs were effected. The mishaps, said Richard Capell in the *Daily Telegraph*, 'were atoned for later in the piece by the production of the most impressive thunderstorm ever known at Covent Garden and a radiant rainbow cast by the new projectors.' Three nights later, *Die Walküre* was interrupted between Acts I and II by a relay of George V's Jubilee speech, marking his twenty-five years on the throne. This must have taken some of the force out of Fricka's embittered reproaches to Wotan in the second act. The first of these two cycles had Leider, Melchior and many of the other great names of previous seasons. For the second cycle, Leider was replaced by the Austrian soprano Anni Konetzni, not so well remembered today, but another fine Wagnerian and a regular performer at the Royal Opera House for years to come. Another member of the cast was the German soprano Rosalind von Schirach, sister of Baldur von Schirach, one of the Nazi elite and leader of the Hitler Youth movement. Her appearance as Gutrune was a portent of the way Beecham was soon to be drawn into the political arena.

Connoisseurs of Wagner were also treated during that season to two performances of *Tristan und Isolde* (Melchior and Leider) conducted by Beecham, and two more conducted by Wilhelm Furtwängler making his Covent Garden début. It must have been a fascinating experience to compare the two of them handling the same work: Beecham brisk and athletic, baton sharply prodding the air, other hand sometimes punching it, above all, eyes darting brightly among his players; Furtwängler tall and lanky, head wobbling about, eyes closed for much of the time, and seeming to be groping his way towards some metaphysical vision of the music. For all his apparently vague and uncertain gestures, the forty-nine-year-old conductor of both the Berlin and Vienna Philharmonic orchestras was already widely regarded as the greatest Wagnerian interpreter of his time. Neville Cardus said that his *Tristan* was 'one of the most sensitive and well-balanced performances that have been heard at Covent Garden for many years'. According to Cardus, Beecham took exception to this and promptly withdrew the critic's complimentary tickets. Beecham liked both Cardus and Furtwängler, but presumably he did not like being placed second, by implication at any rate, to the German maestro. He used to laugh at the way Sir Henry Wood sometimes behaved a little peevishly over the matter of his seniority among British conductors. But he could be just as quick to take offence.

That year saw the end of the traditional separation of the German and Italian repertories. Large helpings of Wagner were now interspersed with generally lighter dishes from Italy, mainly from the pen of Rossini. Indeed, this part of the season was billed – however unlikely it looked on paper – as a 'Wagner–Rossini Festival'. There was a revival of *La Cenerentola*, bringing a very welcome return of Conchita Supervia and of the popular Italian conductor Vincenzo Bellezza. The audience, however, was surprisingly subdued at the first performance of this revival, prompting Beecham to spread the word that it was quite all right to laugh and clap in a piece like *Cenerentola*. The customers had plenty more chances to do this with a new staging – also the first in England for a very long time – of *L'Italiana in Algeri* ('The Italian Girl in Algiers'), Rossini's youthful comic romp that he is said to have composed in a mere twenty-seven days. In this, Supervia stepped ashore at Algiers cuddling a tiny Chihuahua dog, which, says Ivor Newton, she had borrowed from some people she met in a restaurant and which was driven to the Royal Opera House for each performance. At the first of these, she was to be seen dextrously untangling its lead from around her legs while she went on singing with perfect charm and aplomb. 'Her command of this style of singing is beyond all praise,' said Edwin Evans in the *Daily Mail*. 'Her coloratura ripples along as if it were the most natural thing in the world. And all the time she is acting in a manner which places her in the front rank of the world's comediennes.'

The third Rossini offering was that perennial favourite *Il Barbiere di Siviglia*, for which Beecham and Toye brought the French-born Lily Pons, now settled in America, to Covent Garden for the one and only time. The press took to her as they had to Supervia. 'The pocket prima donna', they dubbed the petite Mlle Pons, who, if we are to read between the lines, turned on her accent for them a bit like Maurice Chevalier. Edwin Evans was equally captivated by her art. 'It is her sensational coloratura singing that kindles the enthusiasm of the audience into flame. It is unique, for she does not seem to study her approach to high notes. Her voice seems to reach out and pick them from some remote region.' Their tessitura apart (one mezzo, the other high soprano), Supervia and Pons excelled in the same repertory and generated much the same charm and sparkle.

The former was back for her *Carmen* performances, carried over from the previous season's plans. These were a source of some friction between her and Beecham, as she insisted on the original spoken dialogue of French-style *opéra-comique* in place of the more usual sung recitatives. An angry Beecham finally lost his temper during the dress rehearsal, complaining loudly about the boys' chorus in Act I, and stormed out of the theatre, declaring that nothing would induce him to conduct the production. Señorita Supervia was unperturbed. 'It's nothing,' she said. 'I've seen far worse in Italian opera houses.' She was right. Beecham was mollified and the performances, in a part she had already made famous, went smoothly ahead. She was, it seems, one of the few people who could challenge Beecham on his own ground, with her own combination of obstinacy and charm. It came as a terrible shock to everyone when she died the following year, aged only forty-one, as a result of complications in childbirth.

That season's staging of *La Bohème* did not have such an unruffled outcome. It was, at the time, the year's most publicised production, since it brought to Covent Garden the American soprano Grace Moore. Noël Coward, Sir Harry Lauder and the Irish prime minister Eamonn De Valera were just three of the many people from all walks of life who were entranced by the looks and charms of this singer. She had started out in night clubs and cafés, gone to Europe to study, learning the name part in the opera *Louise* with its composer, Gustave Charpentier, and then sang in Paris at the Opéra Comique and back home at the Metropolitan Opera. But what really made her name was her success as a film star, notably her musical screen hit *One Night Of Love*, so helping to create a fashion or craze for opera in the cinema that also lured the Polish tenor Jan Kiepura, Ezio Pinza, Richard Tauber, Lily Pons, even Kirsten Flagstad, to the silver screen. There were all-night queues in Floral Street for tickets, and police had to clear a way through the crowds every time she arrived at or left the theatre. Covent Garden seemed suddenly more like Hollywood. Of her actual appearances as Mimì, Richard Capell of the *Daily Telegraph* made the telling point that she had a real gift for preserving a convincing facial expression while singing – no mean feat. 'Technically,' he said, 'it was very clever, careful and clean singing, if not absolutely mature.' At any rate, she seems to have held her own vocally against a very strong male trio of the Italian tenor Dino Borgioli, John Brownlee and Ezio Pinza. Unfortunately, she upset Lady Cunard, who now had a place on the Covent Garden board. Miss Moore gave her candid opinion of the matter in her autobiography, *You're Only Human Once*. 'When the announcement was made of my contract to sing at Covent Garden, she [Lady Cunard] flew into a rage and said she didn't want a movie star there . . . My advance sale had taken Covent Garden out of the red for the first time in twenty-five years. She was infuriated that Geoffrey Toye was taking responsibility and getting the credit for launching me in London, where she was so accustomed to ruling the operatic roost. If I had been a failure, she would have been courteous and consoling, no doubt. The success was more than she could bear.' None of this was of any great import. Beecham's involvement, however, was. He sided with Lady Cunard, which brought into the open much wider areas of disagreement over questions of production and casting between him and Geoffrey Toye. Toye was in many ways an excellent chief executive for an opera house. He had worked in the City, thus gaining business experience. He was also a conductor, and composer of such attractive and popular pieces as the score to the ballet *The Haunted Ballroom*. But it was not long after the Grace Moore affair that he resigned as Covent Garden's managing director. Beecham, meanwhile, conducted a new production, by Otto Erhardt, of *Prince Igor*. Erhardt was a famous German producer of the time, recently forced out of Germany by the Nazis. The dancers in *Prince Igor* were from Colonel de Basil's *Ballets Russes*, which then took over the Royal Opera House for the summer months, with the London Philharmonic Orchestra still valiantly in attendance. One of their new productions was *The Beach*, with music by Jean Françaix and designs by the French painter Raoul Dufay.

Beecham followed the ballet with an autumn season of opera. 'It is curious', he wrote in the prospectus, 'that, while most persons insist that never before in London has the demand for music been so great, there is less opera to be heard today in this theatre than fifteen years ago, and far less than twenty-five years ago.' He hoped to correct this, and to make an autumn season an annual event. This one was to be financed largely from money held in trust by the old Imperial League of Opera, now resurrected as The London and Provincial Opera Society Ltd. True to its name, it was going to open at the Royal Opera House, then go on tour to the Midlands and the North of England. It saw the début of a mysterious new soprano who, to quote W. S. Gilbert's Mikado, was a source of innocent merriment for Beecham after all the unpleasantness surrounding Grace Moore. It began with his auditions for yet another Mimì. Among those to whom he listened was Dora Labbette. She was, of course, already a well-known and popular figure on the concert platform, often singing with Beecham. For this audition, however, she turned up disguised beneath a blonde wig. She got the part and, having started the deception, thought she had better carry on with it by assuming a new stage name. According to different accounts, the name Lisa Perli was either supplied by her agent Harold Holt, who dug it out of his files, or was inspired by her birthplace of Purley in Surrey. There was, of course, also the consideration that a foreign name, especially an Italian one, might help her new career. When Beecham learnt of this, he gleefully fell in with the whole prank. He told his friend Neville Cardus, who was also in on the 'secret', that he would unhair him, spifflicate him, break every bone in his body, belabour him with bludgeon and bastinado, if he breathed a word of it to anyone else. And when someone in the orchestra, seeing her on stage during rehearsals, cried 'Blimey, it's Dora!' Beecham roared back, 'Signora Perli, if you don't mind!' It was not a secret for very long. 'Dora Labbette a Superb Mimì', declared the *Daily Telegraph*. 'Stage Début Under Assumed Name.' Her Rodolfo, it should be added, was Heddle Nash, going from strength to strength, and the conductor was Clarence Raybould, another familiar figure in British music throughout the 1930s and 1940s.

During that same autumn season of 1935, Eva Turner – no foreign name for the lady who had been auditioned by Toscanini and made her début at La Scala, Milan – also made headline news, under very different circumstances. She was to sing Agathe in *Der Freischütz*. Just before the first performance started, Beecham was informed that her father, who had been in the audience, had died from a heart attack. It placed him on the horns of a nasty dilemma. If he went backstage and told her there and then, he would have to cancel the performance. On the spot he decided to keep the news from her until afterwards, though it must have taken a lot out of him emotionally, looking up at her on stage, knowing what he did. If it was any consolation to her, *The Times* considered her singing 'as good as anything that has been heard at Covent Garden for a long while' – which was saying something. She also sang in a revival of Verdi's *Un Ballo in Maschera* ('A Masked Ball'), with Clarence Raybould conducting this time, and Brünnhilde in an English-language *Siegfried*, conducted by Albert Coates.

The big novelty of that season was Beecham's staging of Delius's relatively early opera *Koanga*. This had been given its première in Germany by that almost forgotten champion of the composer, Fritz Cassirer, in 1904, but had languished in the thirty years since then. Musically, it was inspired by Delius's early days in Florida and his love for black folk song and dance. The story concerns an African chieftain, the eponymous Koanga, sold into slavery on a Louisiana plantation, and his love for Palmyra, a slave-girl. As a love story between a black man and woman it anticipated Gershwin's *Porgy and Bess*, which, as it happens, was receiving its première in Boston at almost exactly the same time as this Covent Garden production. John Brownlee, who had sung with Grace Moore, took the title role. He was partnered by Oda Slobodskaya, certainly a much less controversial figure in herself, but creating much interest in this instance as Palmyra. The production was eagerly awaited by musical London, including Constant Lambert, the highly gifted and still young English composer, conductor and critic, whose book on the contemporary musical scene, *Music, Ho!*, had just caused quite a stir. He wrote of it: '*Koanga* is a curiously transitional work, hence its unique interest for the student of Delius, and hence the reasons why it ultimately fails as an opera.' His opinion, that the opera was historically interesting but did not hang together very well, was shared by most people. So it came to Covent Garden, and after only three performances, it was shelved. But, as with other Delius operas, Beecham was able to pluck one orchestral passage from the score and lovingly endow it with a life of its own. This was the enchanting orchestral interlude 'La Calinda', based on an old Afro-American dance, a much-loved Beecham 'lollipop' in future years.

CHAPTER TWENTY-THREE

In January 1936 the London press carried the official news of Geoffrey Toye's resignation from the Royal Opera House, 'on questions affecting management and general policy'. Whatever the rights and wrongs of the affair, Beecham was now in charge. It was, for him and for Covent Garden, an even more remarkable year than those just gone by. Going back twenty-six years, the sensational London premières of *Elektra* and *Salome* may have generated more nervous energy and sheer animal excitement. But for the solid burden and scope of his work, 1936 at Covent Garden would take some beating. There were three full opera seasons and part of a fourth extending over the Christmas period and into the new year. He was not personally involved in two of these, but they were still his responsibility in one way or another. That was not the end of it. He also had a full diary of concert engagements: several important occasions with the Royal Philharmonic Society; a further series of fourteen Sunday symphony concerts given in the Royal Opera House, plus a charity concert with Richard Tauber (at which the London Philharmonic's new leader, David McCallum, made his début); and a major foreign tour. How Beecham managed it all may seem, to any ordinary mortal, little short of miraculous. No wonder some of the press photos of him, taken off guard at rehearsals, show signs of wear and tear.

The Grand Opera Season ran from towards the end of April into June. The German repertory, as in previous seasons, was by far the most substantial. Beecham's personal preferences may have been for French, Italian and Russian music, but, as he acknowledged, German opera was far and away the most popular with British audiences. So the season opened with *Die Meistersinger*, and such a traffic jam in Bow Street that society ladies and gentlemen were obliged to leave their cars or taxis and actually walk the last few yards to the brilliantly lit foyer, for fear of being late and once more incurring Sir Thomas's wrath. He was, as it happened, in conciliatory mood, waiting nearly ten minutes till everybody was settled before bringing down his baton on that first grand C major chord of the overture. 'In Sir Thomas Beecham's performances of Wagner,' observed *The Times*, 'it is generally the orchestra which claims first attention, but in this particular one there were many passages where the blending of orchestra and voices was particularly intimate, and the orchestra was most telling where it was most quiet.' Two newcomers to Covent Garden made their mark that night. The German soprano Tiana Lemnitz sang Eva, 'all gracefulness, sweetness and aplomb' for Richard Capell of the *Daily Telegraph*. She certainly looked very pretty and demure in the pages of the *Illustrated London News*. She was also a very versatile artist, taking in her stride almost everything from Mozart and Verdi to Janáček. The Austrian bass Ludwig Weber also made his successful début as Pogner, and went on singing at Covent Garden and Bayreuth until well after the Second World War.

Beecham's biggest signing of the season, in view of her enduring fame, was of the Norwegian soprano Kirsten Flagstad. She had been singing in Scandinavia for the best part of twenty years before she began to make any real impression elsewhere. Her breakthrough came in 1935 when, at the age of forty, she sang Sieglinde (in *Die Walküre*) and Isolde at the Metropolitan Opera. Perhaps the years of obscurity had served as a kind of long incubation period, allowing her voice to develop just that rich, full, sometimes doom-laden timbre that made her the most celebrated of all Wagnerian dramatic sopranos (though she was famous also for her performances of Gluck, Purcell, and the songs of her compatriot Grieg). At all events, news of her success in New York had preceded her across the Atlantic to Europe, and there were all-night queues in Floral Street once more for her Covent Garden début in *Tristan und Isolde* on 18 May. She was suffering from a heavy cold, and had a cut and a bruise, sustained while attending a performance a night or two earlier when somebody's powder compact dropped on her head from an upper part of the house. But Flagstad was known also for her stoicism (she could often be seen sitting placidly knitting in the wings while waiting to go on stage), and the night was another personal triumph. *The Times*: 'The first impression was of a simple and dignified presence, the second of a beautiful voice in which there is not one tone to be regretted.' The *Daily Telegraph*: 'She sang Isolde's music with a voice as beautiful as it was rich in power. Above all, it made an effect of youthfulness and easy resource, and the common sense of strain – the feeling that Wagner was merciless, not to say monstrous in his demands – was gratefully absent.' She took an almost unprecedented fifteen curtain calls. Interviewed afterwards, Flagstad was typically matter-of-fact. 'All the time I was afraid that I would cough or sneeze, my cold was so bad.' Her triumph overshadowed a little the début of her conductor, the Hungarian-born Fritz Reiner. With an impressive European track record already behind him, Reiner was by then settled in America, a teacher at the Curtis Institute in Philadelphia, where one of his pupils was Leonard Bernstein. In the years to come, this tough and irascible conductor built up the Pittsburgh Symphony and Chicago Symphony into two of the world's crack orchestras.

Reiner also conducted two performances of *Parsifal* (the title traditionally printed in the programmes in gothic script), with Leider, Ralf, Janssen, Weber (Gurnemanz) and Habich, with praise for all concerned. Beecham handled the season's two *Ring* cycles, Flagstad taking over from Leider for the second of these, exchanging the long golden plaits and the fateful goblet of Isolde for the winged helmet, spear and shield of Brünnhilde. Recovering from her cold, she made an equally strong impression on Ernest Newman in the *Sunday Times*. 'It was an unspeakable pleasure', he wrote of her singing in *Siegfried*, 'to hear this spacious music unfold its great lines so easily, so confidently. Singing seems to come so naturally to Mme Flagstad that she can give her whole mind not only to the psychology of her part but to the delicate modelling and nuancing of each phrase.' He reserved some praise for another new Scandinavian voice at Covent Garden, that of the Swedish mezzo-soprano Kerstin Thorborg, who also sang in those *Ring* performances.

One of the stars of the Italian part of the season was Giacomo Lauri-Volpi, a remarkable gentleman who was to sing 'Nessun dorma' at a gala concert in 1972, aged eighty. (Could he have inspired Luciano Pavarotti to do the same thing for the Italian World Cup football finals in 1991?) Still a sprightly forty-four in 1936, the Italian tenor was heard in *Rigoletto, Tosca* and *Aida*, all conducted by Vincenzo Bellezza. The last of these three works also featured the Swedish mezzo-soprano Gertrude Wettergen, who made her mark vocally and made her way into the picture magazines on account of her strikingly handsome looks. Malcolm Sargent made one of his rare appearances to conduct a revival of Charpentier's *Louise*, a French variant of the Italian *verismo* school of realism (which was also made into a film with Grace Moore). Beecham returned to the pit to conduct a new production of *Les Contes d'Hoffmann*. 'Signor Ezio Pinza', said *The Times*, 'was certainly sinister enough both as Coppelius and as Miracle. His fine voice took command of each situation.' It was, however, the staging of the production that made headline news. The sets and costumes by Gabriel Volkoff were striking enough. But Beecham had also brought in a well-known conjuror and illusionist, Noel Maskelyne, to provide some special effects: a ghostly image taking shape in the head of the huge wine barrel in Luther's tavern, another face appearing and disappearing in a picture frame, and, most extraordinary of all, a large harp seen to glide, apparently unaided, across the stage. Mr Maskelyne took a bow with Beecham at the end of the first night.

There were, in fact, one or two other surprises or shocks during the season, provided by the audience. One lady turned up with violet-coloured hair. Since her hair was going grey, she explained to a reporter, she saw no reason why she should not dye it any colour she chose. Another was the first to appear, in the best part of the house, in a trouser suit. Even allowing for the growing emancipation of the times, she was probably lucky not to be ejected.

The *Ballets Russes* took over for a long summer season, with Beecham's orchestra still in the pit. Their repertory this year included *Les Biches* ('The Does'), with Poulenc's entrancing score, and a new star dancer in David Lichine featured in a revival of *Prélude à l'Après-midi d'un Faune*. Then in early November, while Beecham and the London Philharmonic Orchestra were embarking on their own tour of Germany, the Dresden State Opera visited the Royal Opera House. This company was one of the most venerable and distinguished of all musical institutions, its name closely associated with those of Heinrich Schütz (going back to the seventeenth century), Weber, Wagner and, most recently, Richard Strauss – it had given the world premières of nearly all his operas. Fritz Reiner had been their principal conductor. Their musical director now was Karl Böhm, another of this century's biggest musical names. He, too, was making his Covent Garden début. They opened with *Der Rosenkavalier*, attended by the composer and the new German ambassador to Britain, Joachim von Ribbentrop. Strauss, of course, was no stranger to London, and during this visit he received the Royal Philharmonic Society's gold medal. No doubt Beecham, considering his close association with Strauss, would have bestowed this upon him if he had not been out of the country; in the event, it was presented by Sir Hugh Allen. The billing of other productions came as something of a surprise: *Die Hochzeit des Figaro* and *Don Juan*, being the company's German-language versions of *Le Nozze di Figaro* and *Don Giovanni*. Such novelties apart, it was the all-round excellence of the Dresden State Opera's productions that impressed the London critics. The company may not have boasted any of the big international stars that Covent Garden habitually 'skimmed from the cream of other opera houses', as *The Times* put it, but they made up for this with the kind of teamwork that came with a permanent personnel ranging from conductor to scene-shifters. Beecham must surely have agreed, remembering his own magical production of *Figaro* when he had his own band of singers and players, in 1917. Even in the grimmest year of the First World War, with all its deprivations and restrictions, the advantages of such a dispensation had come shining through.

The arrival of the British Music Drama Company at Covent Garden so soon after the departure of the Dresden State Opera was, in many ways, a piece of unhappy timing. The newly-founded British company could not hope to live up to the standards of the recently departed Germans. The two new operas it staged also emphasised the continuing poverty of British opera, compared with the riches from Germany, Italy, Russia and France. One of these was *Pickwick* by the company's chief conductor Albert Coates. It happened to make history. The BBC had just opened the world's first television service, and some scenes from it were transmitted a few days ahead of the Covent Garden première. At the Royal Opera House itself, the critics liked much of the music, while agreeing that the composer had not really succeeded in adapting such a rambling and episodic novel as *The Pickwick Papers* to the stage. The British Music Drama Company also presented Roger Quilter's light opera *Julia*. Quilter is remembered for his songs – some of the finest by any British composer – and his delightful *Children's Overture*. Alas, *Julia* soon joined *Pickwick* down that same sad road to near-oblivion. The company itself, despite its enterprise and the talent it contained, did not survive for very much longer.

Beecham's own winter season looked promising: *Die Fledermaus*, conducted by Stanford Robinson, a musical pillar of the BBC for over forty years; *Hänsel und Gretel*, with Maggie Teyte and the English baritone Dennis Noble; *Un Ballo in Maschera*, with Eva Turner; *Manon Lescaut*, conducted by Constant Lambert. Unfortunately, the season was hit by an influenza epidemic, which decimated audiences and casts. But it did bring to Covent Garden, for the one and only time, Hans Knappertsbusch, to conduct three performances of *Salome*. Knappertsbusch, a stolid and unflappable man, was famed for his equally broad, unhurried readings of

Wagner, especially of *Parsifal*. He also upset the Nazi authorities by ignoring them, and consequently had difficulty getting permission to come to London at all. Beecham, meanwhile, had been seeing something of Nazi Germany for himself.

CHAPTER TWENTY-FOUR

Beecham was no stranger to Germany. He had first gone there in 1897, during his student days, and two years later attended the Bayreuth Festival. In 1912, as we have read, he took his Beecham Symphony Orchestra with the Diaghilev Ballet to Berlin. During the early 1930s he returned several times, as guest conductor of the Berlin Philharmonic and Leipzig Gewandhaus orchestras, and to direct opera performances in Cologne, Wiesbaden and Munich. His two visits during 1936 were the most remarkable of his career.

This was the year of the Berlin Olympic Games. Adolf Hitler had been in power for a little over three years, and used the Games as an international shop window for Nazi achievements. On the face of it, Hitler's record so far was impressive. He had galvanised the German economy and dramatically reduced unemployment. Many people in Britain, France and America at that time rather admired his methods, and also saw in him and Nazi Germany a bastion against what they regarded as the far greater menace of Bolshevism. The more odious aspects of Nazi policy had not yet registered with the world at large. They were, however, apparent in the sphere of music. Mendelssohn's music was banned. Contemporary German-Jewish composers and other musicians – Arnold Schoenberg, Kurt Weill, Bruno Walter, Otto Klemperer – were hounded and forced out of the country. 'Aryan' musicians were not immune. Paul Hindemith was soon in hot water, on account of his irreverent early operas and some of his public utterances. Others, such as the Austrian-born Erich Kleiber, highly acclaimed musical director of the Berlin State Opera, voluntarily quit their posts and emigrated. One of those who, initially at least, found favour with the Nazis was Richard Strauss. He was appointed president of the newly created *Reichsmusikkammer* (a kind of Music Ministry), only to be removed because of his work with the Jewish writer Stefan Zweig on a new opera, *Die schweigsame Frau* ('The Silent Woman').

Beecham was certainly aware of all this through his work at Covent Garden. Various visiting German and Austrian artists, including the conductor Clemens Krauss and the Wagnerian bass Rudolf Bockelmann, were known for their Nazi sympathies. Strauss, of course, was tainted with his own Nazi associations. Then there was the case of Alban Berg's opera *Wozzeck*. Kleiber had given the world première of this in Berlin in 1925. Toye had wanted to buy in this production; but the opera was already proscribed by the Nazis (presumably because of its advanced musical idiom and 'decadent' anti-military sentiments) and everything to do with the production had been destroyed. British opera-lovers would have to wait until 1952 before they saw the work staged at the Royal Opera House. Closer to the realms of fiction was the case of the British-born contralto Margery Booth, who came over from Germany to sing in Beecham's 1936 performances of *Die Meistersinger* and later became a wartime British secret service agent operating from inside Germany.

Beecham became more personally involved with Nazi politics through his association with Wilhelm Furtwängler. As with Strauss, the Nazis wished to use the great German conductor as a kind of cultural ambassador, or shining example of the New Order. Furtwängler, for his part, tried to uphold the good name of German music and culture against Nazi excesses. In the process he often crossed swords with Hermann Goering (the big, bluff chief of the Luftwaffe who was also Prussian prime minister) and the propaganda minister, Dr Joseph Goebbels. At the time of the Berlin Philharmonic Orchestra's British tour during November and December of 1935, Beecham wrote to the newspapers, pointing out the freedom and independence the orchestra still enjoyed under Furtwängler's protection. It was also through Furtwängler that Beecham acquired one of his most valued assistants. This was Dr Berta Geissmar, a scholarly German-Jewish lady who had been Furtwängler's private secretary until the Nazis forced her from her job and out of the country. Beecham had already come across her once or twice, and met her again in April 1936 in New York, where she was doing research work for the Vienna Library archives (Austria at that time was still quite independent of Germany). He then signed her up as his own 'general secretary for all my musical affairs'. In that capacity she soon became indispensable to him. For his part he insisted that she should be allowed to accompany him to Germany, or travel about the country on his behalf, without fear or molestation.

The first of his two visits was to Bayreuth, to see the new productions and meet producers, designers and conductors as part of his preparations for the following year's projected 'Coronation

Season' at Covent Garden. Wagner, above all other composers, was extolled by Hitler, and the little town in Upper Bavaria, chosen by Wagner himself as the place for his Festival Theatre, had been turned by the Nazis into a kind of cultural shrine. The festival at that time was presided over by Winifred Wagner (née Williams), an Englishwoman who had gone to Germany as a child and had married the composer's son Siegfried. Her own two sons, Wieland and Wolfgang, were both brilliant opera producers and administrators, and continued the family dynasty right up to, and beyond, the time of the 1976 centenary production of the *Ring*. Beecham delayed his arrival until after the Führer's visit, no doubt wanting to avoid all the political ballyhoo. When he did arrive he was almost royally welcomed – it was Nazi policy to cultivate friendly relations with Britain – and installed, much to his delight, in a lovely old Baroque castle with an octagonal tower, built by one of the Margraves (Counts) of Bayreuth, just outside the town. According to Dr Geissmar, he went straight back to it after each day's work, to play the piano and follow the moves of a world chess championship (another glimpse into the more private and solitary side to his character).

The big talking point at the festival that year was a magnificent production of *Lohengrin* conducted by Furtwängler which, apparently, had moved Hitler to tears. There was talk of bringing this to London for 'Coronation Year', though the idea subsequently fell through. Beecham, however, did come away with plans for Furtwängler to conduct a *Ring* cycle at Covent Garden, and for the German stage designer Emil Preetorius to work on a new production of *Der fliegende Holländer*.

The second visit to Germany was in November, while the Dresden State Opera was giving its season at Covent Garden. The previous year, Beecham had taken his London Philharmonic Orchestra to Paris. Now, at the invitation of Joachim von Ribbentrop, he was going to take it on tour through the Fatherland. His programmes for the tour included a fair representation of British music: Elgar's *Enigma* Variations (a work of his which Beecham did like), some Delius, Lord Berners's suite from *The Triumphs of Neptune*, and the delightful overture which Vaughan Williams wrote for a production of Aristophanes' play *The Wasps*. There were other works by Berlioz, Dvořák, Handel (including Beecham's own Handelian *The Gods Go A-Begging*), Haydn, Mozart, Rimsky-Korsakov, Rossini and Sibelius; but no Beethoven, Brahms or Wagner, which Beecham said would be like taking coals to Newcastle. Surprisingly, perhaps, for a man who had not taken an order from anybody else for as long as he could remember, he agreed to drop the proscribed Mendelssohn's 'Scottish' Symphony. He shrugged it off, according to Dr Geissmar, with the comment that Queen Victoria, with her German blood, had loved the piece!

He was received in Berlin with even more honour than at Bayreuth. An official government car was placed at his disposal for the duration of the tour, with a swastika pennant plus the emblem of an eagle as a token of his special status. And before the first concert of the tour, in Berlin's Philharmonic Hall, he had an audience with Hitler in the Reichs Chancellery. It must have been an extraordinary confrontation: the one-time army corporal and half-starved drifter in Vienna, now risen by political cunning and brute force to a position of supreme power, and the lordly Englishman, born with a silver spoon in his mouth. Hitler is reported to have said that he would like to attend next year's Coronation in London, but felt that he could not put the English to so much inconvenience, to which Beecham replied, somewhat blandly it must be said, 'Not at all. There would be no inconvenience. In England we leave everybody to do exactly what he likes.'

The concert was attended by Hitler, Goebbels and other top members of the Nazi administration, also by the British ambassador, Sir Eric Phipps. Most accounts of it include the anecdote that after the opening item on the programme, one of Dvořák's Slavonic Rhapsodies, Beecham said to his players 'the old bloke seems to like it', referring to Hitler leading the applause in his box. But Leo Birnbaum, in the orchestra, has a spicier version of the story. According to him, Beecham and his players were standing, along with the audience, waiting for the Führer and his entourage to make their appearance before the concert could begin. 'The old bugger's late!' Beecham said to his leader. He had forgotten that the concert was being broadcast and that a microphone was close at hand. It was the second time his voice had been heard, none too discreetly, over the air. 'Old bloke' or 'old bugger', it was probably just as well that his colloquial English must have passed most of his listeners by. The orchestra and Beecham let their hair down afterwards, as guests of Furtwängler and the Berlin Philharmonic, fellow musicians united in comradeship by their art and good German beer, and, so it was said, treated to the spectacle of Sir Thomas dancing on a table. But politics soon reared its head again. The next day, as well as glowing reports about Beecham and his orchestra, the papers carried a picture of Beecham talking to Hitler in his box at the Philharmonic Hall. It was a fake, no doubt given the wink for publication by Dr Goebbels.

The tour proceeded, to Dresden, Leipzig, Munich, Stuttgart, Ludwigshafen, Frankfurt and Cologne, with an exhausting round of receptions and banquets, at which every local Gauleiter and other Party functionary wanted his moment of glory. In Leipzig, Beecham conducted Sibelius's Second Symphony before an audience that included Dr Karl Straube, then incumbent of the post Johann Sebastian Bach once held as Cantor of the Church and School of St Thomas. Alas, only a day or two before the concert, local Nazis had removed the city's statue to Mendelssohn, who had directed the famous Gewandhaus (Cloth Hall) Orchestra exactly a hundred years earlier. Beecham received several anonymous letters expressing a sense of outrage, sorrow or disgust at this act of political vandalism. 'May you, dear Sir', said one of them, 'be comforted by the fact that the thought of this act of racial hatred brings a blush of shame to the cheeks of millions of music-loving Germans.' In Munich, Hitler's deputy, Rudolf Hess, complimented the orchestra and said he had not expected to find such discipline among a group of Englishmen, to which Beecham replied that the English had their own brand of discipline. 'Instead of accepting it from others, we impose it on ourselves.' In Ludwigshafen, he was in at the beginning of a technological revolution. Ludwigshafen was the home of the great chemical company I. B. Farbenindustrie, who were experimenting with a new system of recording on magnetic tape. Beecham's concert in the company's acoustically excellent new concert hall was recorded by this process (and parts of it still exist). Perhaps the happiest moments of the tour for Beecham were when he managed to escape with Dr Geissmar for a private visit to Mainz Cathedral. In her book *The Baton and the Jackboot*, she recalls how astonished she was at his knowledge of the history of the building and its architecture. Afterwards they drove on for lunch to a village inn by the Rhine, where he displayed an equally impressive knowledge of the local wines.

Beecham had begun this year of 1936 – an *annus mirabilis* in terms of the sheer volume and scope of work he had got through – with several more Royal Philharmonic Society concerts. At one of them he conducted Walton's Viola Concerto with the Scotsman William Primrose taking the solo part. Beecham is not closely associated with Walton's music; but it was he who had prompted the composer to write the concerto for his old friend Lionel Tertis. As a matter of fact, Tertis at first declined to play the work as being too advanced for his taste, and the honour of giving the first performance of one of the most admired British concertos of this century went to Hindemith, another fine viola player. Tertis later regretted this.

Beecham ended the year in Liverpool, close to his birthplace, conducting the city's own Philharmonic Orchestra, for which he always felt a special affection. The principal trumpet at that time was Harry Mortimer, born into the tough and sturdy tradition of English brass band playing. At rehearsal, Beecham asked him to play up. Mortimer shouted back, via his leader, 'Tell him, if he doesn't shut up, I'll not play tonight.' It also told Beecham, after all his travels, that he was back home again.

CHAPTER TWENTY-FIVE

Nineteen-thirty-seven was a Coronation year, following Edward VIII's abdication in favour of his brother, who was duly crowned as George VI. The event was celebrated, along with all the souvenir mugs and plates and spoons, by the introduction of a new stream-lined train, the 'Coronation Scot', the last word in railway steam travel. Vivian Ellis, composer of *Bless the Bride* and other hit musical shows, wrote an orchestral piece about it, the sophisticated lilt of its melody evoking so much more besides: cocktails, soft lights, white tuxedos, monogrammed cigarette cases, the first television sets in glossy walnut cabinets – the high chic of the thirties. There was also a new magazine, *Night and Day*, featuring some of the best new writers, Evelyn Waugh, Christopher Isher-wood, Rose Macaulay, V. S. Pritchett, John Betjeman. Osbert Lancaster wrote about architecture; Constant Lambert had a music column, in which he reviewed Toscanini's visit to London to conduct the BBC Symphony Orchestra. Graham Greene's wickedly funny review of a Shirley Temple film helped to bring about the magazine's lamentably quick demise, when Twentieth Century Fox sued for libel.

In February at Covent Garden, Chaliapin, now sixty-four, gave one of his last recitals with Ivor Newton, whose fame as an accompanist is second only to that of his fellow Englishman Gerald Moore. The great Russian bass died in Paris the following year. In March the Russian-American Jascha Heifetz, perhaps the most fêted violinist of his time, gave his recital at the Royal Opera House with the pianist Emanuel Bay. Beecham, meanwhile, was gearing up for his Coronation Grand Opera Season. It boasted one of the largest cast lists ever assembled for a single season: nearly one hundred and thirty individual singers. There were also to be nine conductors, including himself. This situation had arisen partly because Beecham had entrusted the casting of some of the French and Italian operas to the veteran Italian baritone Cesare Formichi. This gentleman had made his Covent Garden début in 1924 and was famous for his Rigoletto and Scarpia, among other roles. Unfortunately, he now seems to have acted rather like the rascally kind of old-style impresario who must often have been the bane of Rossini and Verdi, signing up so many of his cronies (with a nice percentage on the side for himself) that in the end Beecham had almost more singers on his books than he knew what to do with. The season, for all its trumpeting, suffered accordingly.

It got off to a good enough start, though, with Beecham conducting *Otello*. In the title role was Giovanni Martinelli. He had not sung at Covent Garden for nearly twenty years, spending much of the intervening time at the Metropolitan Opera. He was now over fifty years old, and brought all his experience to bear on this most demanding of Verdian roles. Richard Capell of the *Daily Telegraph* was suitably impressed.

> Tradition and the score ask that when Otello utters his first words – 'Esultate! The Muslim is overthrown' – we should be at once dominated by a man of elemental force. Giovanni Martinelli has not this to give. But in compensation there was much – so much in the way of pure singing and sensitive art, and tone and phrasing equally beautiful, that his Otello earns a place in the history of the opera.

On that opening night Beecham also delivered another of his reprimands to the audience, this time because of premature applause at the end of Act I. 'Shush!' he hissed at them.

John Barbirolli, who had played the cello under Beecham's baton during the First World War, conducted *Tosca* and *Turandot*. His relations with Beecham had been blowing hot and cold. Beecham, or so it seemed, had been grooming Barbirolli for a career in opera. Barbirolli, for his part, felt that Beecham had made too many empty promises. Professional jealousy may have come into it. Just as Sir Henry Wood touchily defended his seniority against Beecham (there was one notorious slanging match between them on this subject, conducted through the correspondence columns of the press), so Beecham may have feared a challenge from the younger man. If that was the case, Barbirolli's recent appointment as chief conductor of the New York Philharmonic Symphony Orchestra, in succession to no less a person than Toscanini, must have put Beecham's nose badly out of joint. Nevertheless, there was Barbirolli in the pit with, as it happened, Toscanini in the audience for one of the performances. Barbirolli's Scarpia was the American baritone Lawrence Tibbett, one of the New York Metropolitan Opera's biggest stars, and another singer to enjoy a second career in films. Ernest Newman, writing in the *Sunday Times*, had some reservations about him.

> Lawrence Tibbett made his first appearance in London as Scarpia. I was present at his début, as Ford in 'Falstaff', in New York some twelve years ago, and still remember how full of promise his work was on that occasion. Whether that promise has been entirely fulfilled I should not like to say until I have heard him a few times more.

The critics had few, if any, doubts about Eva Turner's Princess Turandot. The Italian-born violinist-turned-critic Ferruccio Bonavia, writing for the *Daily Telegraph*, said of the production, 'Eva Turner's Turandot alone would have given it a distinction of its own.' *The Times* added: 'Few sopranos can sing at high tension as Miss Eva Turner does, without a screech or a whoop.'

The French part of the repertory for this Coronation season was especially interesting, thanks in large part to Dr Geissmar's negotiations, on behalf of her chief, with Jacques Rouché, director of the Paris Opéra and the Opéra-Comique. This brought to Covent Garden the Opéra's production of Paul Dukas's only opera, on the subject of the legendary Duke Bluebeard and his wives, *Ariane et Barbe-Bleue*. Dukas, a contemporary of Debussy and Ravel, is one of those unfortunate composers widely known by one work only, in his case the popular symphonic poem *L'Apprenti Sorcier* ('The Sorcerer's Apprentice'). Part of his problem was that he was extremely self-critical, destroying much of his own music, so that his surviving output is very small. Moreover, *Ariane et Barbe-Bleue*, a work he had every reason to be proud of, has itself been rather eclipsed by Bartók's *Duke Bluebeard's Castle*, composed a few years later. So M. Rouché, Beecham and Berta Geissmar between them were doing the composer a great service by having his opera staged in London. The part of Ariane was sung by Germaine Lubin, principal soprano at the Paris Opéra for thirty years, a striking-looking woman, as photographed in stylish black hat and veil, when the latter had ceased to be a mark of ladylike modesty for all but the elderly and was enjoying a brief spell of high fashion. She was a formidable singer as well, equally at home in Rameau and Gluck, or in any of the big Wagnerian roles. Indeed, her German sympathies and her fond associations with Bayreuth earned her three years in prison in the emotionally charged atmosphere following the Liberation of Paris in 1944. On the evening of the first Covent Garden performance of *Ariane et Barbe-Bleue*, Mlle Lubin had a more localised spot of bother. She had recently recovered from a bout of 'flu, and just before curtain-up she started a nose-bleed. 'If I had put down my back all the keys that Bluebeard gives me in the opera,' she said afterwards, 'I'm afraid the bleeding would not have stopped.' After about half an hour, though, it did, and her performance does not seem to have suffered too much as a consequence. 'Her clear tones, her dignified bearing, and her simple use of gesture,' reported *The Times*, 'showed how thoroughly had been her study of an exceedingly exacting role.' Her conductor was Philippe Gaubert, long-time principal conductor of the Opéra.

A happy piece of programme planning also brought *Pelléas et Mélisande* back to the Royal Opera House, this opera and *Ariane et Barbe-Bleue* sharing the same librettist, Maurice Maeterlinck, and the same symbolist-expressionist mood. Mélisande was sung by Lisa Perli (Dora Labbette), making splendid progress in her new career, to judge from the critics. The conductor this time was Albert Wolff. He was Paris-born and bred, despite his name, director of the famous Lamoureux Concerts, giving the first performances of works by Debussy, Ravel, Roussel, Milhaud and Poulenc, as well as composing, among other things, an opera of his own, *L'Oiseau bleu* ('The Bluebird'). The other notable French import was the Paris Opéra production of Gluck's *Alceste*, famous in operatic history as the vehicle of the composer's declaration on the reform of opera (1767). Lubin also sang in this, under Gaubert's baton. Surprisingly, in view of its historical interest, this opera was given only once during the season. Gluck, however, was also represented by three performances of *Orfeo* (*Orphée*). Originally Germaine Lubin was to have sung in this as well, but she returned to Paris, and Maggie Teyte took over as Eurydice.

Eugene Goossens, who had been pursuing his ambitions as a composer, presented his new opera, *Don Juan de Manara*. His first opera, *Judith*, had been produced in 1929. Both works had librettos by Arnold Bennett, the English novelist who had died a few years earlier. Bennett had based this new libretto on a fairly obscure play by Alexander Dumas the elder, much better known as the author of *The Three Musketeers* and *The Count of Monte Cristo*. Goossens himself conducted two performances, with Lawrence Tibbett in the title role. Ferruccio Bonavia said the opera was 'as full of thrills as a Hollywood production and as opulent as the most sumptuous of Russian ballets'. It proved, however, to be one more valiant but doomed attempt to launch British opera on the world stage, in the long years before Britten.

That left the German repertory, proportionately smaller than in previous years, but still including as much Wagner as any opera house in the world, not excepting Bayreuth. It was crowned by the two *Ring* cycles, conducted by Furtwängler, that Beecham had begun to negotiate during his visit of the previous year to Bayreuth. The casts for these were as strong as they could possibly be: Leider alternating with Flagstad, Melchior with the German Max Lorenz, another top *Heldentenor*, also Kerstin Thorborg, Rudolf Bockelmann, Ludwig Weber and Herbert Janssen; and praise was indeed heaped upon them. But it was Furtwängler whom the critics had really come to hear. 'Dr Furtwängler', said *The Times*, 'began his first cycle of *Der Ring des Nibelungen* at Covent Garden last night with a performance of *Das Rheingold* which was ideal as an introduction to the saga.' They waxed much more lyrical yet. 'Wagner,' wrote Richard Capell, 'who put his trust in posterity, has not been betrayed. Such a performance as was given last night of "Die Walküre" excels, and, in fact, leaves altogether out of the running, the present-day renderings at Covent Garden of all other kinds of opera of the past.' Surveying the first cycle as a whole, the *Observer* declared: 'Furtwängler's reading of "The Ring" may disappoint some Wagnerians because it does not force home the self-conscious pressure and size of the thing; yet how rich, complete, earnest, and sensitive it is, and how wonderfully everything on the stage comes into its own!'

While in London, Furtwängler also conducted his own Berlin Philharmonic Orchestra in a memorable performance of Beethoven's Ninth Symphony (always an event of great significance to him), after which he and his musicians were royally entertained by Beecham and the London Philharmonic Orchestra at the Savoy Hotel, in return for the hospitality they had received the previous year in the German capital. Dr Geissmar records that Furtwängler also agreed to be interviewed on television by Adrian Boult. The diffident and sober Furtwängler (he was teetotal) nearly backed out when he found he had to be made up before appearing in front of the cameras.

Flagstad headed the cast in three performances of the production of *Der fliegende Holländer*, with its splendid sets by Emil Preetorius, which Beecham had also negotiated the previous year during his time at Bayreuth. Fritz Reiner conducted these, and the three performances of *Parsifal*, in which Kerstin Thorborg made a very strong impression as Kundry. 'I would rank her as the greatest Wagnerian actress of the present day,' wrote Ernest Newman. There were, finally, four performances of *Tristan und Isolde*, again with changes of cast between Leider and Flagstad, and, this time, between Melchior and Walter Widdop. J. A. Westrup (better

known today as the celebrated author and scholar Sir Jack Westrup), writing in the *Daily Telegraph*, said: 'The real glory of this
performance lay in the orchestra. Sir Thomas Beecham maintained
the vivid, pulsing current of the score with extraordinary intensity,
and yet without any suggestion of forcing the pace.' Beecham was
not appeased by such high praise. Criticism of other productions –
not necessarily his own fault, or, at least, not directly so – had stuck
in his craw. 'Never before in the history of Covent Garden', he
sardonically told the last-night audience,

> has the Press attained to so high a state of excellence. We on our
> side have not been able to live up to it. We propose to devote the
> next six months to a careful reading of every word of abuse that
> has been written in the newspapers. We have become sadder and
> wiser people, for you know how seriously we take everything
> that is said about us.

Several more critics had their complimentary tickets withdrawn – a
sad little footnote to what was supposed to have been a very
special season.

Beecham's other engagements for the year might seem like an
appendage to all this, though they were enough to keep any normal
maestro pretty well stretched. During the opening and closing
months of the year he presided over more of his Sunday symphony
concerts at the Royal Opera House, sharing the workload with the
Czech conductor Fritz Zweig (who also took part in the next year's
Grand Opera Season), Sir Henry Wood (despite the rivalry between
them), Malcolm Sargent and Albert Coates. At these concerts Beecham was joined by his principal oboe, Leon Goossens, in a concerto
for oboe d'amore by J. S. Bach, by the pianist Edward Kilenyi in the
Delius Concerto, and by Elena Glazunov, the composer's adopted
daughter, playing his Piano Concerto No. 2. Beecham also took part
in more Royal Philharmonic Society concerts: an all-Mozart programme with the Hungarian-born Louis Kentner playing the C
minor Concerto (K491), a Beecham favourite to judge by the number of times it crops up in his programmes; the first London
performance of a concerto by the German composer Hans Pfitzner,
with the Swiss pianist Edwin Fischer; an all-British programme of
Bax, Delius, Vaughan Williams and Elgar; Beethoven's *Missa Solemnis*, with Isobel Baillie, Mary Jarred, Heddle Nash and the Leeds
Festival Chorus; a performance of Ernest Bloch's Hebrew Rhapsody
Schelmo, with Gregor Piatigorsky taking the solo cello part; the first
European performance of Rachmaninov's Third Symphony; and
three Sibelius symphonies in one evening, plus the *Karelia* suite.

That was still not all. During the year Beecham somehow found the time to go back to Germany, this time to conduct the Berlin State Opera – a singular honour – in their productions of Gluck's *Orfeo* and Mozart's *Die Entführung aus dem Serail*. He took the London Philharmonic Orchestra to Paris, where they gave a gala concert at the Opéra (the Palais Garnier) before President Lebrun and other members of the French government, during the interval of which he was invested with one of the orders of the Légion d'Honneur. And in the autumn of that year, all the frustrations of the Coronation season behind him, he was back in Berlin yet again, to make a famous recording of *Die Zauberflöte*, to which we shall refer in the appendix.

CHAPTER TWENTY-SIX

In March 1938 came the *Anschluss*, Hitler's annexation of Austria, and war seemed dangerously close. The prime minister, Neville Chamberlain, still hoped to avoid it by his policy of appeasement (this was also the year of the Munich Agreement), but the pace of British rearmament was stepped up. The first squadrons of the famous Spitfire fighter took to the air. People watched soldiers digging trenches and filling sandbags in Hyde Park. Beecham, meanwhile, was still firmly in the saddle at Covent Garden where, outwardly at any rate, life went on as usual. Dr Geissmar recalls the scene of those days, with the cream of society, market porters and vegetable sellers still forming a kind of cheerful scrum in and around Bow Street each night of the season, much as they had when Eliza Doolittle encountered Professor Higgins in Shaw's *Pygmalion*. She recalls, too, some of Beecham's backstage staff, like John Primrose, the elderly librarian (father of the viola player William Primrose), with his soft voice and dry Scots wit, whom Beecham dubbed 'Mr Daffodil'. As well as attracting 'characters', Beecham had a delightful way with nicknames.

Early in the year he welcomed Willem Mengelberg to London to conduct the London Philharmonic Orchestra at a Royal Philharmonic Society concert. (At the end of the war Mengelberg was to be banished by the Dutch government for his alleged Nazi sympathies.) Beecham appeared at these concerts as usual: with Louis Kentner in another Mozart concerto, and with Clifford Curzon in a performance of John Ireland's very attractive Piano Concerto, at which concert Arthur Bliss also directed the first performance of the suite from his recent ballet *Checkmate*. Beecham gave more concerts with the Hallé Orchestra. He resumed his winter series of Sunday symphony concerts at the Royal Opera House, where he was joined on stage at one concert by the Hungarian-born pianist Lili Kraus, a student of Bartók, Kodaly and Schnabel, and at another by his own principal cellist in the London Philharmonic, Anthony Pini, in the Dvořák Concerto. Sydney Beer, a wealthy amateur and patron of music who gave a lot of money to Covent Garden, also conducted at some of these concerts. The programmes for them now had charming covers of Pre-Raphaelite design, of Pan playing his pipes.

Beecham, of course, was mainly preoccupied with the forth-coming Grand Opera Season, for which new seating, new carpets and a new stage curtain (the first for nearly forty years) were being installed. He may have resented criticisms levelled at the Corona-tion Season – too ambitious, talent spread unevenly over too many productions – but he does seem to have taken them to heart. The new season was to be shorter by over a month, with the emphasis on quality rather than quantity, variety or novelty. A high standard was set by the opening night's production of *Die Zauberflöte*, conducted, it goes without saying, by Beecham himself. This was outstanding in several respects. Thanks once again to Dr Geiss-mar's intimate knowledge of the German musical scene, and of German opera houses in particular, Beecham secured from the Charlottenburg Opera the scenery based on prints and water-colours by the German architect and artist Karl Friedrich Schinkel for a Berlin staging of the opera in 1816. The most famous of these illustrations, cropping up time after time in books on opera and stage design, is of a great starry vault fringed with clouds, at the base of which the Queen of the Night makes her entrance. The rest of Schinkel's pictures, a fascinating blend of the classic and the romantic, are also of great historical interest, reflecting the cult of Egyptology that followed Napoleon's Egyptian campaign. The *Illus-trated London News* devoted a whole page to them. Such a visual feast was matched by the strength of the cast. This was headed, on the first night, by Richard Tauber as Pamino. The great Austrian-born tenor, whose real name was Ernest Seiffert, had made his professional début in the same role as long ago as 1913, but this was his first operatic appearance at the Royal Opera House. He had, in the intervening years, made a big name for himself in Viennese operetta, carrying this persona over into real life with his famous top hat and monocle. This may have predisposed some of the more high-minded of London's opera buffs against him. The critics, though, were soon won over. 'Better late than never, Tauber is welcome at Covent Garden,' Capell wrote in the *Daily Tele-graph*.

He had not been heard here in serious opera before, and his Tamino earned him new respect. A trace of mannerism in his singing detracted somewhat from the effect of youthful energy proper to the adventurous Prince. But the hero of the Flute is too often hard and wooden, and it was no unpleasant change to hear one who inclined to be luscious and what the Germans call 'weich'.

Such was the strength or depth of talent available to Beecham that for the closing performance he was able to call upon Julius Patzak in place of Tauber, a fellow Austrian also making his Covent Garden début, and a famous Florestan (in *Fidelio*) in years to come. There were also Tiana Lemnitz as Pamina (replaced at the second performance by yet another newcomer, Trude Eipperle) and the German baritone Gerhard Hüsch as Papageno.

Beecham shouldered a greater burden of the conducting this year. He stayed with his beloved Mozart for *Die Entführung aus dem Serail*, with Tauber as Belmonte, Heddle Nash as Pedrillo and Ludwig Weber as Osmin. Francis Toye, author and critic, and brother of Geoffrey, was enchanted with it. 'Never can a gayer interpretation of the opera have been given. Sir Thomas Beecham danced his way through the score with incomparable elegance ... Tauber's phrasing and diction were a delight.' The same critic was equally enthusiastic about Beecham's *Lohengrin*, with Lemnitz, Melchior and Thorborg in the cast. 'The orchestra under Sir Thomas Beecham was a model of sensitiveness, alertness and suppleness. Every detail of the score glowed with life.' Kerstin Thorborg as Ortrud was 'magnificent'. Beecham also conducted performances of *Die Meistersinger* (Lemnitz, Ralf, Janssen), *Fidelio* and *Elektra*. The last of these brought another top singer of her generation to Covent Garden for the first time, the Hungarian-born soprano Rosa Pauly (born Rose Pollack) in the title role. 'There is probably not another trio of "Elektra" singers in the world such as Pauly, Hilde Konetzni and Thorborg,' wrote Richard Capell, 'and there was no less clarity than gorgeousness in the orchestral playing.' This revival of *Elektra* brought two special tributes for Beecham. One was a letter to him from Stefan Zweig, whose collaboration with Richard Strauss on *Die schweigsame Frau* had, as we have noted, got the composer into trouble with the Nazis:

Allow me a sincere word of congratulation. I have heard many performances of *Elektra*, from the very first one. I have heard those of Mahler and Richard Strauss himself (with the unforgettable Bahr-Mildenburg) – but never in my life have I heard a more perfect than yesterday evening. I shall remain thankful to you for ever.

The other tribute was from the composer: the first and last pages of the autograph score, handsomely framed, together with a warm message of thanks – a treasured gift which went up in smoke when Beecham's London home was bombed in the war.

The German part of the season brought more highlights and some crises. Furtwängler conducted two more *Ring* cycles (with Frida Leider, Melchior, Thorborg, Bockelmann). We have already said how easy it is to become blasé about these *Ring* performances, which were such an outstanding feature at Covent Garden before the Second World War. The fact that there is little to add to what has already been recorded about Furtwängler's handling of this, the most huge, complex and controversial work in the whole history of the performing arts, is further comment upon the abundance of those Beecham years. Erich Kleiber conducted *Der fliegende Holländer* and *Der Rosenkavalier*. It was during a broadcast performance of the latter (such things always seemed to happen over the air) that Lotte Lehmann, as the Marschallin, suddenly stopped singing and said, '*Ich kann nicht mehr*' ('I can't go on'), and hurriedly left the stage. Officially, she was ill, having only just travelled back from America and not fully recovered from a bad bout of seasickness. Some commentators, though, suggest that her breakdown was compounded by politics. Backstage tension among pro- and anti-Nazi singers, and the worsening international scene, may well have contributed to her collapse. Happily for the audience, the Austrian soprano Hilde Konetzni, who was singing in *Elektra*, happened to be in the audience and bravely volunteered to take over. She was a larger lady than Lehmann and had to be sewn hastily into the Marschallin's gown. Berta Geissmar, hurrying backstage, remembers that this still left a portion of the singer's back exposed, which she covered with the black velvet cape from her own evening dress. Thus the evening was saved. Hilde Konetzni's sister Anni, incidentally, was also to be seen and heard at Covent Garden that season, in the *Ring* performances. There was a more familiar kind of crisis connected with one of the later performances of *Lohengrin*. At very short notice, a replacement had to be found for Herbert Janssen. The German baritone Carl Kronnenberg flew in on the same day. As we have read, this was not the first of such aeronautical dashes, but they were still a novelty and worth reporting, in this case by Richard Capell:

> Civilisation is making such progress that operatic artists think nothing of flying across from mid-Europe at a couple of hours' notice to make their début at Covent Garden. Summoned to

replace Herbert Janssen, who is not well, he [Kronnenberg] flew in from Germany, arriving in the afternoon, and by seven o'clock he was in Telramund's shoes, in the tenth century, amid battle axes, romanesque architecture and miracles.

After the unhappy experience of Cesare Formichi the previous year with his quixotic collection of singers and conductors, Beecham now had Vittorio Gui to conduct the Italian part of the season. The distinguished Italian maestro, who was also an opera composer, had served a long apprenticeship with Toscanini in Milan, and after the Second World War he was to do some of his best work with the Glyndebourne Opera. Beecham also brought back to the Royal Opera House Beniamino Gigli, surely the most celebrated name, after that of Caruso, in that corner of the Hall of Fame reserved for operatic tenors. His easy, warm, limpid tone certainly was glorious, though he was also sometimes criticised for certain vocal mannerisms. Gigli had first sung at Covent Garden in 1930. Now he was booked to sing in all three Italian operas of the 1938 season: *Rigoletto, Tosca* and *La Bohème*. Edwin Evans of the *Daily Mail* wrote of the first of these: 'Signor Beniamino Gigli's style has much improved during his absence from Covent Garden. He has also a better stage presence. His performance warranted his claim to be regarded as the greatest Italian tenor of the day.' His Gilda was the Italian soprano Lina Pagliughi, who was not very tall while at the same time very well upholstered. 'My dear boy,' Beecham said to Walter Legge, who was then his assistant artistic director, 'she looks like a tea-cosy.' Evans, though, readily praised her voice, 'of dazzling purity and brilliance.' There were all-night queues for the gallery (where many of the really dedicated opera-lovers were to be found) for the performance of *Tosca* three nights later. The papers also reported a severe gale that night, 'sweeping cabbage leaves and litter round Covent Garden', while the brave little band in the queue down Floral Street stuck it out with their camp stools and thermos flasks of coffee, plus cups of tea from kindly market porters. They were rewarded by the singing of Gigli, partnered this time by Iva Pacetti, who had sung Tosca to his Cavaradossi back in 1930. But Richard Capell had a few special words for Gui, 'surely the best Italian conductor known at Covent Garden since Serafin's season'. (Tullio Serafin had first appeared at the Royal Opera House in 1907, but his first big season had been that of 1931. He was to return again, in 1959 and 1960, when he was in his eighties, to prepare Joan Sutherland for her first *Lucia*.) In the first of two performances of *La Bohème* Gigli reminded everybody of days gone by, when theatres and opera houses were always going up in flames. As Rodolfo the poet, he accidentally set fire to the stove in Act I, dashed into the wings and came running back with a large red fire bucket to try to douse the smoke and flames. He and his colleagues resumed their singing while a real London fireman – an unusual visitor to that chilly Parisian garret – finished the job.

As usual, the summer months were given over to ballet, which included a revival of *The Gods Go A-Begging*. Antal Dorati was joined by his fellow Hungarian Georg Solti, just beginning to make a name for himself – he became musical director at Covent Garden in 1961, the year of Beecham's death. Then came an autumn opera season, this time given by the Covent Garden English Opera Society Limited, with Beecham as its artistic adviser and the Russian-American Vladimir Rosing as its director. The latter had earlier worked with Albert Coates in forming the short-lived British Music Drama Opera Company of 1936. Priority booking for this season, it is worth adding, went to surviving members of the old Imperial League of Opera, and to a lively new group, the Young People's Opera Circle, which also organised talks, visits backstage and attendance at rehearsals. Maggie Teyte sang in *Madama Butterfly*; Eva Turner and Walter Widdop were the stars of *Tristan und Isolde*. There was a new British opera, *The Serf*, by the Cornishman George Lloyd, which followed so many other native efforts down the path to oblivion.

CHAPTER TWENTY-SEVEN

In March 1939, as a timely mark of political solidarity, the French President Albert Lebrun paid a state visit to London. A gala evening at the Royal Opera House was a highlight. For the occasion the auditorium and main foyer were hung with French tapestries, including one celebrating the marriage of the English King Charles I to the French Princess Henrietta Maria. Rex Whistler produced a souvenir programme of baroque design, embossed with assorted national emblems and decorated with golden tassels. Among the celebrities photographed arriving at Covent Garden was the United States ambassador Joseph Kennedy, father of the future president. When war came, he believed Britain was doomed and resigned. The Sadler's Wells Ballet (later the Royal Ballet), featuring Margot Fonteyn and Frederick Ashton, was conducted by Constant Lambert. (They were on tour in Holland in May 1940 when the Germans invaded, and only just made it back to England, leaving behind much of their scenery, costumes and music.) Beecham conducted his London Philharmonic in a performance of Debussy's *Iberia* (from the orchestral *Images*), one of that composer's magnificent evocations of Spain so admired by the greatest Spanish composer, Manuel de Falla. Spain, as it happened, was just ending its Civil War: Generalissimo Francisco Franco was victorious, and another European nation fell under Fascist rule.

Throughout the autumn and winter of 1938–9, Beecham's diary had been as full as ever. His Sunday symphony concerts at Covent Garden featured an exceptionally strong contingent of guest artists. The veteran conductor Felix Weingartner, also scheduled to take part in the 1939 Grand Opera Season, gave a performance with the Polish violinist Bronislaw Huberman of the Beethoven Concerto. Huberman had recently founded the Palestine Symphony (now the Israel Philharmonic) Orchestra. Beecham appeared with two more equally distinguished Polish-born violinists, Samuel Dushkin (for whom Stravinsky wrote his Violin Concerto), playing the Mendelssohn Concerto, and the fourteen-year-old Ida Haendel, playing one of Mozart's concertos. He also appeared with the Russian-American cellist Raya Garbousova in one of Saint-Saëns's concertos, and with the Chilean pianist Claudio Arrau, playing Beethoven's 'Emperor' Concerto. During the same period he was busy with his Sibelius Festival. There were six concerts, the first of which opened the Royal Philharmonic Society's concert series for 1938–9. All seven symphonies were played, plus much of the composer's large output of incidental music and songs. The seventy-three-year-old Finnish master was not well enough to come to London, but listened to relays of the concerts on the radio at his home at Järvenpää. This event, incidentally, sparked off another round in the long-running feud between Beecham and Sir Henry Wood, based on the latter's easily injured pride *vis-à-vis* the younger man. In this case, Wood resented the publicity given to Beecham's festival, pointing out, in a letter to the composer himself, that he had already given what amounted to a Sibelius festival by including all the symphonies in his 1937 Proms season. But, he complained, because it was the Proms nobody had taken any notice. 'This', he added plaintively, 'has hurt your friend extremely.'

With the gala night for President Lebrun out of the way, Beecham could now concentrate on another Grand Opera season. For a little while the prospects for this looked distinctly gloomy. The previous Grand Opera season had shown a big loss, partly due to a drop in box-office receipts for Furtwängler's *Ring* performances – one unhappy sign of the political times. The same performances persuaded some of Covent Garden's Jewish financial backers to withdraw their support, so making the situation worse still. The Grand Opera Syndicate, after so many years of sterling service in the cause of opera at Covent Garden, had to wind up its affairs. For the last time Lady Cunard came to the rescue, drumming up fresh support among her friends in high places. Beecham himself wrote a typically defiant and pugnacious article in the *Daily Telegraph*.

> For something like two hundred years, Covent Garden has been the home of international opera. The renown of this ancient theatre is such that every foreign as well as native artist aspires to appear there some time during his or her career . . . And yet it is seriously proposed that because we are suffering from a temporary access of jitters and jumps that would bring discredit upon a community of elderly nuns we should discontinue an event that is as regular a feature of our yearly calendar as the Royal Academy, the Military Tattoo, or the Eton and Harrow cricket match. Even during the really grim days of 1914–18

London was never without an opera at some time or other of the year. I recall with special gratification certain performances at Drury Lane which I conducted myself to the sound of German bombs exploding within a few feet of the theatre, to say nothing of our own anti-aircraft guns . . . When the King and Queen visited Paris they attended a State performance at the Opéra – an institution, incidentally, which runs for ten months of the year. When the Prime Minister went to Rome, he was invited as a matter of course to the Opera, which paid him and his fellow countrymen the happy compliment of playing *Falstaff* . . . In Germany it is hardly necessary to inform the reader that in upwards of seventy towns, opera is being given practically all the year round. As for the rest of the world, I have yet to hear that at Stockholm or Prague, at Budapest or Brussels, or any other capital has it even been suggested that the opera houses should be closed. Only in London is such a proposition capable of utterance. And when it is remembered that our season lasts no more than seven or eight weeks, it will be realised how fantastic it is that such a sacrifice should be offered to the altars of prejudice or poltroonery . . . Let us on our part show that in matters of art and culture, and especially in music, which is the common property of the entire world, we can rise above the ephemeral conditions of purely political discord, and maintain our old reputation for national sanity and understanding. There must, and shall be, a season at Covent Garden.

There was. It opened on a somewhat controversial note – bearing in mind Hitler's latest moves against Czechoslovakia – with a new production of Smetana's *The Bartered Bride*, sung not in Czech but in German (*Die verkaufte Braut*). *The Times* made passing reference to this. 'Sir Thomas Beecham opened his summer season of opera at Covent Garden last night with every sign of festivity. His choice of Smetana's opera, which for the moment we must consent to call *Die verkaufte Braut*, helped to ensure this, for never was there a comedy so little clouded by hint of tragedy.' Tauber was back, and the same review made some interesting comments about his singing in such a work. 'It is not a voice of unlimited power, nor one which is most effective when exerted to the full. Nor did Smetana wish for such exertion; he did not intend to write for a Heldentenor.' Tauber also sang with Ezio Pinza in the performances of *Don Giovanni*. *The Times* had no doubts about his Don Ottavio. 'Herr Tauber added to the weight of male characterisation by filling out Don Ottavio into a man, so that he was no longer the mere stick that most tenors make him.' Beecham also conducted a *Ring* cycle, *Tristan und Isolde* and *Aida*.

He was admirably served by all his guest conductors. We have noted that Felix Weingartner was booked to take his part in the season. The Austrian maestro, now seventy-six years old, had studied with Liszt, succeeded Mahler as musical director of the Vienna Court Opera (State Opera), and conducted extensively in Europe and America. He had made his London concert début as long ago as 1898, but this was his first time at the Royal Opera House. He conducted Wagner. His *Parsifal* had Germaine Lubin as Kundry. 'By this performance', wrote J. A. Westrup, 'Miss Lubin established herself as a Wagner singer of the very first rank . . . The performance had the advantage of being conducted by Felix Weingartner, appearing for the first time at Covent Garden. It was an advantage since this veteran musician must have an unequalled experience of the work and its tradition.' Westrup spoke of the 'serenity and poise' of his interpretation. Westrup's *Daily Telegraph* colleague Richard Capell spoke of Weingartner's equally measured reading of *Tannhäuser* in a review headed 'Sober Minstrelsy'. 'It is unusual to hear this romantic opera treated so much like a classic; and the result was calculated rather to satisfy the faithful than to persuade unbelievers.'

Constant Lambert conducted *Turandot* with the incomparable Eva Turner again in the title role. 'Mr Constant Lambert', said *The Times*, 'established himself at one stroke as a conductor who can handle opera as surely as he regularly manages the sister art of the theatre, the ballet.' Vittorio Gui took care of the rest of the Italian repertory. There was Gigli in more performances of *Tosca*, partnered this time by the French-Italian soprano Gina Cigna; while *Il Trovatore* brought another exciting Covent Garden début, that of the twenty-eight-year-old Swedish tenor Jussi Björling. 'Covent Garden has gained a real tenor,' Capell wrote of him. 'A flowing line, bright clarity of tone, an easy production – all this belonged to him by second nature. It is a lyrical voice of ample power, the best of its kind that has come this way for a long while.' Björling was to be one of the biggest opera stars of the postwar years before his relatively early death in 1960.

One more conductor to appear in the Covent Garden pit that season was Basil Cameron, a pillar of the Promenade Concerts for many years to come, as assistant first to Sir Henry Wood and then to Malcolm Sargent. On this rare occasion at the Royal Opera House he took over a performance of *Tristan* when Beecham went down with a chill, a tough assignment for anyone, stepping in at short notice to handle such a stupendous score, with Lubin, Thorborg and Melchior up there on stage. He had studied in Berlin before the First World War, and on his return to England had called himself Basil Hindenburg, because at that time a German-sounding name was more likely to bring him work. He probably hoped nobody remembered in 1939.

Beecham recovered from his chill and, 'silver-haired, flush-faced', in the words of a *Daily Mail* reporter, 'he strutted onto the stage, blew his nose and threw back his head', to deliver his customary end-of-the-season speech. A certain weariness seems to have overtaken his earlier mood of defiance. He would, he told the audience, do his best to present a season next year, but in view of diminishing support he wondered if London deserved one. In any case he would not be conducting, partly on medical advice, partly for the sake of his sanity. Privately, he said that the public must be getting tired of him after all that time. Despite such world-weariness, his plans for the future were exciting enough: Berlioz's *Les Troyens*, Puccini's *La Fanciulla del West*, Gluck's *Iphigénie en Tauride* – all comparative rarities – and *Boris Godunov*. Weingartner was to return. These plans came to nothing. War was declared on 3 September 1939, following Hitler's invasion of Poland, and there was to be no more opera at Covent Garden for six long years. Beecham's reign was over.

CHAPTER TWENTY-EIGHT

At the end of the 1939 season at Covent Garden, Beecham, as we have noted, planned to take a year's rest from conducting. He was now sixty years old, feeling very tired, and suffering again from gout, among other aches and pains. Then came the war and, as he said, 'I heard there was a national emergency, so I emerged.' He started giving concerts with the London Philharmonic Orchestra up and down the country. This time, however, he was not destined to spend the war years upholding British musical life, as he had done twenty-five years before. Other musical institutions, above all his old enemy the BBC, were now better placed to do that. At the same time the members of his own orchestra, deprived of their work at Covent Garden and of their recording contracts, felt compelled to follow the example of the London Symphony Orchestra and formed themselves into a self-governing limited company. Beecham accepted the inevitability of such a move and gave the orchestra his blessing, appealing, with all his usual wit and persuasion, for funds on their behalf. In April 1940 he gave his last wartime concert with the London Philharmonic Orchestra, an all-Sibelius affair in aid of the Finnish people, whose war against their giant Soviet Russian neighbour had largely been ignored by the rest of the world. Afterwards the orchestra gave him a farewell dinner at Pagani's, the London restaurant long famous as the haunt of musicians, before he departed from his homeland for four long years.

The following month he arrived in New York on board the Italian liner *Rex* (just a week or two before Mussolini brought Italy into the war on Hitler's side). The city must then have presented an extraordinary sight to people like Beecham, arriving from blacked-out Europe: Manhattan Island, the Chrysler and Empire State buildings, ablaze with light. Broadway, the Great White Way, was still pulsating with the songs and dances of George and Ira Gershwin, Rodgers and Hart, Jerome Kern, Irving Berlin, Cole Porter; Benny Goodman, the 'King of Swing', had recently raised the roof of Carnegie Hall with his band; the blind jazz pianist Art Tatum was attracting the likes of Horowitz and Rachmaninov to marvel at his fabulous technique. The United States, of course, was still a neutral country. President Franklin D. Roosevelt may personally have favoured the Allied cause, and his country had given refuge to some famous musical victims of Fascism: Paul Hindemith, now teaching at Yale University; Béla Bartók, already ill with leukaemia, in New York; Arnold Schoenberg in Los Angeles, where he once had a meeting with the film tycoon Sam Goldwyn to discuss, of all outrageously improbable things, ideas for a musical. But the American Congress, and American public opinion as a whole, were still strongly isolationist.

Beecham, in fact, did not stay in New York very long. He proceeded to Australia, arriving in Sydney early in June. He was interviewed almost at once on the radio by his old friend Neville Cardus, whom the *Melbourne Herald* had engaged to cover the visit. According to Cardus, Beecham gave him a tough time, responding curtly to his questions, so that the critic was soon thrown off balance, and the interview was a disaster. Next day, Cardus recalls, people asked him if both of them had been drunk. This seems to have set the unfortunate tone for the rest of the tour. Beecham abruptly cancelled further rehearsals with one orchestra. 'Does that mean the orchestra's on top form?' someone innocently asked him. 'No,' he snapped back, 'it's getting worse.' He was rude about his audiences, whom he described as 'a coughing chorus'. He added insult to injury by saying he didn't like Sydney Harbour Bridge, the nation's proudest landmark before the building of the Opera House. And, according to Alan Jefferson, in his book *Sir Thomas Beecham: A Centenary Tribute*, when asked by a reporter why he had come to Australia he replied, 'Why do you go to a zoo?'

America was a different story. He was back there in November 1940, at the start of four busy and on the whole extremely successful years. He was often rude about Americans as well. He despised their jazz, though its spontaneity and vitality should have appealed to one side of his own nature, and he might have had great fun conducting such jazz-inspired pieces as Gershwin's *Rhapsody in Blue* and *An American in Paris*. He also attacked American films and radio, American food and the crime rate. But, in general, he liked the American way of life. His association with the United States, in fact, went right back to 1893 when, aged fourteen, he first accompanied his father on one of his business trips, to New York and to the World's Fair in Chicago. He made his musical début there in 1928, conducting the New York Philharmonic Orchestra in Carnegie Hall, on which occasion he was joined by Vladimir Horowitz, also making his American début, in Tchaikovsky's Piano Concerto No. 1 (a performance they repeated, as we have noted, at a Royal Philharmonic Society concert in 1932). During this visit Beecham also conducted two other top American orchestras, the Boston Symphony and the Philadelphia. Through the 1930s – notwithstanding his work at Covent Garden, and all his other concert engagements in Britain and on the European continent – he returned several times, on occasions conducting in New York the Musicians' Symphony Orchestra, an ensemble of out-of-work orchestral players (this was during the worst years of the Depression), just as Leopold Stokowski did in the film *One Hundred Men and a Girl*. At one of these concerts, incidentally, he accompanied the Spaniard José Iturbi in a Haydn harpsichord concerto, in spite of the rude things he said about the instrument ('the sound of two skeletons copulating on a tin roof', was one description of it ascribed to him).

Beecham's American diary for the years 1940 to 1944 was full from the start. He spent much time speaking at ladies' luncheons, lecturing at colleges and universities, traversing the continent on the tracks of the Baltimore and Ohio Railroad, the Pennsylvania, the New York Central, the Union Pacific, the Atchison, Topeka and Santa Fe, dining, sleeping, reading, to the hypnotic wail of their locomotives, the clang of their bell sounding each town and station on the line. 'One spends one's life in trains and hotels,' he said. 'It's a sort of moto perpetuo.' He treated his listeners to old and cherished themes; the paramountcy of Mozart in Western music, the debasing effects of radio and film, the pros and cons of opera sung in its original language or in translation. He gave many press interviews. 'An orchestra represents the most exact epitome of what a well-ordered social system should be. One hundred men are on an equality, though they are not all of equal gifts. All are subordinate to one purpose and there is variety within unity.' On the problems of the translation of opera libretti: 'French is almost impossible to render adequately in English; the accents fall in the opposite manner. German and Italian can be very well done into English, and Russian best of all.' He broached the subject of politics and war. 'Our system of government, the democratic, represents the slow evolution of man's freedom and permits us to make fools of ourselves in our own way. The opposing philosophy forces us to make fools of ourselves in someone else's way . . . Incidentally, *Die Meistersinger* is not Hitler's favourite opera, in spite of what Nazi propaganda states. His favourite opera is *The*

Merry Widow. I know because he told me so.' Asked if he had really invested and lost five million dollars of his own money staging opera in London, he replied, 'It wasn't quite that much. But someone added up the total for me and when I heard it I fainted and had to be revived with brandy.' He was a gift to the press, as suave and diffident in manner as any titled Englishman was supposed to be, but as willing to talk and as outspoken as any American.

   One of Beecham's first musical assignments was conducting the Seattle Symphony Orchestra on the Pacific coast for their 1941–2 concert season, in succession to the Russian-American conductor Nikolai Sokoloff. Most of his other engagements took him back to the Atlantic seaboard. He again conducted the Philadelphia Orchestra, in Baltimore and Washington DC. In New York he frequently conducted the city's WPA Orchestra. (The Works Progress Administration had been initiated by President Roosevelt in 1935, as part of his New Deal programme for bringing America out of the Depression. Funded by the federal government, it gave employment to millions through road-building and other public works programmes, and, on a smaller scale, through sponsorship of the arts.) Beecham also conducted another publicly funded orchestra of that time, the New York City Symphony Orchestra. And across the East River he was a guest of the Brooklyn Academy of Music, with their own orchestra. He travelled up to Canada, to conduct in Toronto and Montreal. He went to Chicago, to take part in the Ravinia Park summer music festival. Among the soloists he teamed up with during these years were the distinguished American harpsichordist and scholar Ralph Kirkpatrick (who catalogued the works of Domenico Scarlatti), playing Bach's D minor Harpsichord Concerto and Falla's lesser known Chamber Concerto for the same instrument (quite outside the usual Beecham repertory); William Primrose, principal viola of the NBC Symphony Orchestra (the ensemble specially formed for Toscanini) in Berlioz's Symphony *Harold en Italie*; the young English composer and pianist Stanley Bate, who had studied with Vaughan Williams and took the solo part in his own concerto; and the American composer Courtland Palmer, playing his Piano Concerto in another concert sponsored by the WPA and the dynamic and social-minded mayor of New York, Fiorello La Guardia. Beecham conducted works by much more established American composers including Aaron Copland, William Schuman and Virgil Thomson. He struck up a warm friendship with the last of these. 'Virgil', he is reported as saying, 'is the only man in the world who can keep me up until four in the morning.'

Virgil Thomson was also music critic of the *New York Herald Tribune*. Another eminent critic of the day (and author of an important book on Sibelius's symphonies) was Olin Downes of the rival *New York Times*. He was clearly fascinated by Beecham, and has left us some vivid pen portraits of his rostrum manner.

> Judged by the conventions of conducting, his technique, if such it can be called, and his style are precise examples, at least to the casual glance, of what a conductor should not do. The more conclusively does he demonstrate the fact that it is one thing to conduct for an audience and another to conduct for the players, and also that it is what a conductor thinks and not what he does that counts. He may run all around the conductor's stand, or lean over, his toes perilously near its edge, in favouring a group or a player of a solo passage with his exclusive attention. He may crouch or most ungracefully crook a knee, or stoop far down and rise like a large and ungraceful bird flapping its wings in the air. He may indicate a sforzando in the manner of a man hurtling a brick or a bomb at a foe, or beat the measure freely with one arm while holding the baton in a clenched fist, invisible to the orchestra, at his back. It remains that the orchestra understands him, and that singularly inspired music floods torrentially and with precision from him and the instrumentalists . . . Of all the guest leaders who have appeared with New York's WPA Orchestra only one other conductor – namely, Otto Klemperer – has achieved results commensurate with Beecham's.

(Klemperer, another refugee from Hitler's Germany, had been conducting the Los Angeles Philharmonic Orchestra. He was taken seriously ill in 1939, but resumed his career after the war, first in Hungary and then, with spectacular success, in Britain.)

In January 1942 – with the United States now in the war, following the Japanese air attack on the Pearl Harbor naval base – Beecham made his début at the New York Metropolitan Opera, joining Bruno Walter as principal conductor for the forthcoming season. His opening programme was a real curiosity: his affectionate staging of Bach's cantata *Phoebus und Pan*, followed by Rimsky-Korsakov's *The Golden Cockerel*, sung in French. The Australian baritone John Brownlee in the Bach piece, and Ezio Pinza as King Dodon in *The Golden Cockerel*, were both old friends from Covent Garden days. A few nights later he conducted *Carmen*, with the celebrated Russian-American baritone Leonard Warren as Escamillo and the French soprano Lily Djanel making her Metropolitan début in the title role. 'Vocally', wrote Downes, 'the part lies low for her, and this was not for the best good of her singing . . . But here is a Carmen, praise be, who refused to over-act.' Of Beecham he said,

> There was a general impression of a conductor straining every nerve to put life into the show on the stage and also to communicate something like life to an orchestra which, as a rule, played villainously without precision, and frequently with poor balance. Sir Thomas, one could say, was pulling and hauling. He accomplished a good deal.

If Olin Downes's comments are to be believed, then Beecham must also have been yearning for the Covent Garden days with his own orchestra down there with him in the pit.

During the next two years, in fact, Beecham was almost as frequently seen a figure at the Metropolitan Opera as he had been at Covent Garden, working with some familiar voices and faces, becoming acquainted with some new ones. He conducted revivals of *Carmen* with the American mezzo-soprano Gladys Swarthout. Howard Taubman, a colleague of Downes on the music staff of the *New York Times* (and biographer of Toscanini), has given us this operatic memory of one of the Metropolitan's leading singers throughout the 1930s and 1940s, as she sang with Beecham:

> Hers is an agreeable, if not electrical, Carmen. One cannot forget that Miss Swarthout is a lady. Her performance is still the result of reflection rather than inner compulsion. She is handsome. Now she must make her Carmen irresistible. Vocally, she is fortunate. Her voice has the color for the music, and her top tones have the proper force and volume . . . Sir Thomas Beecham's conducting gave the performance impulse and unity.

The cast also included Leonard Warren, retained as Escamillo, the French-Canadian tenor Raoul Jobin as Don José, and Licia Albanese as Micaëla. The Italian-American Albanese had broadcast and recorded with Toscanini, and was a well-loved figure at the Met for over twenty years. Beecham's performances of *Faust* (the opera which had originally opened the Metropolitan in 1883) also had Albanese as Marguerite. He conducted the American tenor Charles Kullman as the Chevalier Des Grieux in several performances of Massenet's *Manon*. Kullman was familiar to European opera-lovers through his numerous appearances at the Berlin State Opera, at Covent Garden, the Salzburg Festival, and elsewhere.

Two other Metropolitan Opera performances that Beecham conducted during the war years are of special interest. One was a charity performance, sponsored by Mrs William Randolph Hearst, wife of the newspaper and publishing magnate, of Charpentier's *Louise*. The star of this was Grace Moore, whom Beecham and Lady Cunard had cold-shouldered at the time of her Covent Garden appearances in 1935. 'At the first rehearsal,' she says in her autobiography, 'Sir Thomas kept the whole cast waiting for thirty minutes and then walked in blissfully unconcerned. However, when we had our dress rehearsal there was no question about his brilliant musical abilities. Much to my chagrin the actual performance next day was slow in tempo and fatigued.' Olin Downes, on the other hand, wrote well of her performance with Beecham. 'Her voice has gained in sensuous quality and warmth. It really expresses emotion, which seems to come from her and not from a pipe in her throat.' The cast also included, once again, Ezio Pinza (whom Downes considered 'today the best singer at the Metropolitan') and Raoul Jobin. Beecham took over a performance of *Tristan und Isolde* from Bruno Walter (now settled in the United States), who was ill. Isolde was sung by the American soprano Helen Traubel, regarded, after Flagstad, as the Metropolitan's leading Wagnerian soprano of that period. She was supported by Lauritz Melchior, Herbert Janssen and Kerstin Thorborg. For Beecham, Miss Traubel apart, this production must have seemed like old times. For Olin Downes it was a great occasion, and one on which the orchestra must have played a good deal better than in the earlier performances of *Carmen*.

> The performance of *Tristan und Isolde* last night was on the whole the most poetic and romantic interpretation of this particular opera that we have heard for many years in the Metropolitan Opera House. This was of course consequent upon Sir Thomas Beecham's treatment of the score. One need not agree with every detail of it to have profited greatly by its lyrical beauty and intensity, its remarkable sensitiveness and tonal proportions, such that the singers never had to bawl and every tone and word of the text, when properly enunciated, came over the footlights, and light and shade, immense power of climax were achieved by means of contrast and an exquisite elasticity of tempo and dynamics. We have waited long for such a sincere and imaginative performance.

Beecham's operatic work took him south of the border to Mexico City in the summer of 1944, to direct what was billed as a Mozart Festival, with productions of *Le Nozze di Figaro*, *Don Giovanni* and *Die Zauberflöte*. He took with him members of an opera company from Cincinnati which he had earlier conducted, including the excellent John Brownlee. There was, however, a vacancy for the small but important part of the Commendatore in *Don Giovanni*. A local bass, Ignacio Rufino, was found who had just the right voice for the part, but there were personal problems of a distinctly Latin American nature. Various versions of the story exist, but Ivor Newton's is probably the most reliable. The singer was out on parole from a local jail, awaiting trial for having shot dead his wife's lover. Now he feared the dead man's father, who had sworn vengeance. He insisted, therefore, on being carried off into the wings immediately after his mortal sword-fight with the Don, instead of waiting on stage to be discovered by Donna Anna. As he explained, he did not wish to present himself as a sitting, or rather recumbent target for this avenging father. Beecham had to agree. It was brave enough of him and the rest of the cast to go on with the show.

Beecham pursued his lifelong involvement in litigation of one sort or another throughout his American years. He filed a costly lawsuit against the Columbia Recording Corporation, and, though he was not directly involved, joined in a famous dispute between the American Federation of Musicians and the broadcasting companies over the vexed question of the broadcasting of recorded music. These topics are referred to again in the final chapter of this book. There was also a matter of divorce. In March 1942, the *New York Times* carried a review of one of Beecham's concerts with the New York City Symphony Orchestra in Carnegie Hall. The programme included a new work by Richard Arnell, another English composer then living in the United States, and a Mozart piano concerto played by Betty Humby. This thirty-four-year-old English pianist was not a big name in the world of concert music, but she had won a scholarship to the Royal Academy of Music in London at the tender age of ten, studying under the Academy's celebrated teacher Tobias Matthay, and with Myra Hess. Beecham had first appeared publicly with her in London in 1937, when he gave his services, and lent his name as president, to a society giving a series of Mozart concerts at the Cambridge Theatre. Now, five years later, their association had blossomed into romance. Both were married already (Margaret Betty Thomas, to give her married name, had a growing son), and both now sought a divorce. Beecham's was the one that naturally captured the headlines. He had been estranged from Utica for over thirty years, from about the time of his entanglement with Mrs Maud Foster and that other divorce action of 1911. His two sons by her, Adrian and Thomas, had grown up and gone their own way in life. And there the matter, a sad little well of loneliness at the heart of his otherwise full and sometimes frantic life, had rested until now, in the middle of the Second World War. Filing his divorce action, Beecham, so it was reported in the American press, claimed that Utica, during all those years, had taken no interest in his life and work. Indeed, he had received from her 'only carping criticism in my chosen work'. She had 'belittled the success which I continually attained'. Nevertheless, he stated that he had, over the years, made over to her huge sums of money, both to support her and to bring up their two sons. Beecham secured his divorce from a judge in Boise, Idaho, on the grounds of 'extreme cruelty', in January 1943. The following month he married Betty Humby. He had arrived in New York in 1940, with the ever-faithful Lady Cunard still in attendance. He returned with his new Lady Beecham, on an Atlantic convoy battering its way through a hurricane to war-torn England in September 1944. They docked in Liverpool. 'I always', he said, relaxing at last in a barber's chair, 'come to Liverpool for a shave.'

CHAPTER TWENTY-NINE

In the autumn of 1944, as the Soviet Red Army and British and American forces closed in on Germany from east and west, Beecham was waging his own private war with the Hallé Concerts Society. It was over the matter of his honorary presidency, which the Society had bestowed on him in succession to Elgar in 1934. They had written to him in America, informing him that they now wished to make the Lord Mayor of Manchester their president, as this might help them to secure a municipal subsidy, and hoped he would understand. They were, perhaps, a trifle tactless in their approach. Back in England Beecham penned a long letter to the *Manchester Guardian*. He would not, he declared, resign as president. Indeed, he was going to have 'President of the Hallé Concerts Society' blazoned across the top of all his stationery. If the Society also appointed the Lord Mayor to the position, so be it. There were, he reminded everybody, precedents for such a state of affairs. 'For one hundred years, during the Middle Ages, Christendom beheld the edifying spectacle of rival Popes, one in Rome and the other in Avignon, each periodically addressing the whole body of the faithful as if he alone were the true vice-regent of heaven upon earth.' Some readers must have wondered what on earth was going on. The Hallé Society secretary, Ernest Bean, described his meeting with Beecham. Failing to pacify Sir Thomas, he decided to sit back and enjoy the great man sounding off. He summed up Beecham in such a mood as 'Puck, Ariel, Beau Brummel, Count Almaviva, the Spanish Inquisitor, Louis XIV, Judge Jeffreys, Till Eulenspiegel and Captain Hook all rolled into one.' Bean went on, 'I had the exhilarating feeling of one watching a gusty Restoration comedy not only being acted but improvised on the spot.' The affair blew over soon enough when it was found that no real provision for a president existed in the first place.

It was all probably a smokescreen for a much deeper sense of unease that Beecham now felt about his own future. His anxieties seemed borne out by events. The Second World War ended in

Europe in May 1945. It had been called, in Britain, 'The People's War', and it had produced the Beveridge Report, with its proposals for a Welfare State. At the ensuing general election, Britain's wartime leader, Winston Churchill, was dismissed, and the new Labour government under its prime minister Clement Attlee set about the task of creating a more equitable society through planning and controls. None of this was much to Beecham's liking, even public funding of the arts, which he had seemed to favour in the past. For him it must all have smacked too much of regimentation and conformity. More worrying still for him was his personal situation. There was no place for him with the BBC, except as an occasional conductor. The other big orchestras were all going their own way, notably the Hallé, now rejuvenated by John Barbirolli. He did give some concerts with the London Philharmonic Orchestra, whose leader at that time was Jean Pougnet. At a Royal Philharmonic Society concert in late 1945 he and the orchestra were joined by the exciting young English pianist Denis Matthews, who later turned to teaching and broadcasting. At another concert, in Leicester, Beecham showed some of his old sparkle by demanding a home-made Melton Mowbray pie in exchange for an encore. But, of course, that orchestra was now its own boss. They engaged him, not the other way round. 'I'm not going to be wagged by any orchestra,' he said.

The postwar world of British opera upset him most of all. In 1945 the Sadler's Wells Company, conducted by Reginald Goodall, gave the première of Britten's *Peter Grimes*, which everybody hailed as the true renaissance of British opera. It brought Beecham no cheer. The Royal Opera House, which had been used as a dance hall through the war years, reopened in 1946 with *The Sleeping Beauty* under an entirely new dispensation. Its supremo, with the very businesslike title of general administrator, was David Webster, who had worked for the Ministry of Supply during the war. His musical director was the Austrian conductor Karl Rankl, whose name must certainly have grated on Beecham's ears. He would surely not have wanted to work with them. What hurt him deeply was that they did not even consult him about the running of the opera house. He lashed out a few years later, in a speech to the Incorporated Society of Musicians in Brighton, calling the Covent Garden management a 'set of hapless ignoramuses and nitwits'. Privately he muttered sarcastically about 'the Twilight of the Sods'.

In a restless frame of mind, meanwhile, Beecham made two more fairly brief visits to the United States (one to San Francisco, where the Charter of the United Nations was just then being drafted), to conduct various orchestras. Then he made up his mind. He was going to create another orchestra that he could call his own. The situation here was complicated by Walter Legge who, we may recall, had worked with Beecham at Covent Garden just before the war, and during the war had directed the musical side of ENSA, the forces entertainments organisation (Every Night Something Awful, as servicemen jokingly called it). Legge was now forming the Philharmonia Orchestra, primarily for recording purposes. Beecham conducted the still fledgling Philharmonia at their first public concert – an all-Mozart affair – at the Kingsway Hall in October 1945, and was suitably impressed. According to Legge he then proposed, over what turned out to be a rather stormy lunch at Boodle's club in London, taking over the orchestra and reshaping it to his own ends. He also said he would rename it Royal Philharmonic, since it was going to work closely with the Royal Philharmonic Society, as the London Philharmonic had done in pre-war days. ('The name Philharmonia is ridiculous anyway. No one will ever remember it.') Legge rejected this idea; but he did suggest that he and Beecham might share the orchestra in some way, adding that in his opinion there was no room in London for two major new orchestras. Beecham, in his turn, dismissed all this and went straight ahead with his own plans for a Royal Philharmonic Orchestra.

Once again his method was to engage as many of the best available players as possible, and, in the words of the well-known scholar and music broadcaster Bernard Keeffe, 'play them like a superb piano'. He worked very fast. In not much over three weeks he had assembled a new squad of players. It was a fascinating blend of age, experience and brilliant new talent. As with all his previous orchestras, it remained an all-male ensemble, excepting the soloist on the harp, with its traditionally ladylike qualities. ('If they're pretty,' Beecham said of female players, 'they distract the rest, if they're not well-favoured in looks, they'll distract me!') There was Archie Camden, whose career stretched back to 1906, as principal bassoon. Reginald Kell and Gerald Jackson, founder members of the London Philharmonic, returned as first clarinet and first flute. James Bradshaw, another London Philharmonic founder member, was on timpani. Others were only just out of uniform. Most of them came from the RAF. Dennis Brain, principal horn, had played with the Central Band of the RAF. His father Aubrey, it will be recalled, was the BBC Symphony Orchestra's first horn. Dennis achieved even greater fame, inspiring new works from Hindemith, Britten and Malcolm Arnold among others, and his death in a car crash in 1957 shocked the whole musical world. He was joined in the horn section by another old friend from the RAF Band, Norman Del Mar, who had also been directing the enterprising Chelsea Symphony Orchestra. The latter vividly recalls his first encounter with Beecham, 'in a cloud of cigar smoke'. He was soon under the Beecham spell. 'Whereas other conductors just conducted, with Tommy it was always an event.' A third RAF recruit, though not actually a founder member of the orchestra, was the clarinettist Jack Brymer who, like Dennis Brain, was soon to win laurels as a world-class player. He, too, spoke of the special joy of playing with Beecham. 'There was no such thing as a definitive performance with Tommy. The music was recreated every time. He really loved and enjoyed it. Not like some of them.' Dennis Brain's brother Leonard sat with Brymer among the woodwind, playing cor anglais. The orchestra's first leader was John Pennington, former first violin of the pre-war London String Quartet, one of whose founder members was Albert Sammons.

Beecham's title for his new orchestra, as he had already revealed to Walter Legge, was 'Royal Philharmonic'. After his death, when the connection with the Royal Philharmonic Society was no longer so close, the orchestra had to fight hard to retain its royal and commercially valuable prefix. That, however, was still far into the future. The first full rehearsal was held in St Pancras Town Hall, only four days before the opening concert – a very different state of affairs, in the difficult days of 1946, from the rehearsal time Beecham had been able to lavish on the London Philharmonic Orchestra before launching it in 1932. They all moved right across London for the concert itself, given on Sunday afternoon, 15 September 1946, in the very large Davis Theatre in Croydon (long since demolished). This time Rossini's *William Tell* overture opened the proceedings. It was – no pun intended – a relatively low-key affair compared with the London Philharmonic's much heralded début in the fine old Queen's Hall of fourteen years before. 'Sir Thomas Beecham's newly enlisted orchestra made its first appearance yesterday afternoon in the enormous Davis Theatre,' *The Times* reported next day.

The programme, containing Mozart's 'Linz' Symphony and tone poems by Tchaikovsky and Delius ('Over the Hills and Far Away'), had been well rehearsed and was played with alert responsiveness to Sir Thomas Beecham's spirited command. Characteristic *brio* and musicianship were not wanting, but the chief impression was of vitality, as yet, rather than virtuosity. Many details were finely turned and the balance in the main was excellent. Though the standard was not exceptional, there is evidently the making of a fine instrument here.

The same review also noted that a full list of the orchestra's personnel was not printed in the programme. This was because Beecham had still not decided on his final line-up of players. He had some of the best in the land; but over the next few weeks, others were given their marching orders and new ones brought in, until he was satisfied that, for the moment at any rate, he had the finest available team.

With its teething troubles sorted out, the Royal Philharmonic Orchestra moved swiftly into the mainstream of British musical life. As planned, it became the principal new orchestra of the Royal Philharmonic Society seasons. The programmes for these events, from the end of the 1940s and throughout the 1950s, are like a window upon postwar British concert life. Among guest conductors were Sergiu Celibidache, Paul Hindemith, Jascha Horenstein, Rudolf Kempe, Otto Klemperer, Josef Krips, Rafael Kubelík, Nicolai Malko, Jean Martinon, Pierre Monteux, John Pritchard, Igor Stravinsky, the Swiss conductor Paul Sacher (a celebrated patron of contemporary composers), Hans Schmidt-Isserstedt and William Walton. Soloists included Ginette Neveu, the much talked-of young French violinist who was to be killed in an air crash in 1949, the pianists Gina Bachauer, Clifford Curzon, Julius Katchen, Moura Lympany, and the husband-and-wife team of Cyril Smith and Phyllis Sellick, who continued as a three-handed duo after he had lost the use of one hand following a stroke.

Beecham himself, along with many of his favourite works, continued to support British composers, even if it may sometimes have gone against the grain. He exhumed Holbrooke's early orchestral piece *Ulalume*. He conducted the ballet suite *Punch and the Child* and the symphonic portrait *Lord Byron* by Richard Arnell; Britten's Violin Concerto (soloist Bronislav Gimpel); Alan Rawsthorne's piano concertos Nos. 1 and 2 (soloists Phyllis Sellick and Colin Horsley, respectively); Vaughan Williams's *Pastoral* Symphony (solo soprano Margaret Field-Hyde); and Walton's Viola Concerto (soloist Frederick Riddle, who had made the first recording of the work in 1937). He also presented the symphonic suite *From Sea to Sea* by the Canadian composer Alexander Brott. Another notable performance, during the 1951–52 season, was of *A Mass of Life*, marking the British début of the German baritone Dietrich Fischer-Dieskau (spelt 'Dieskow' in the programme).

Beecham had given the same work in his new orchestra's first major engagement, the 1946 Delius Festival. This was not on quite the same comprehensive scale as the Festival of 1929, but it did include at least one interesting and little-known item, serving as a reminder of the composer's strong Scandinavian connections. This was of extracts from the incidental music he wrote for *Folkeraadet* ('The People's Council'), a play by his close contemporary Gunnar Heiberg, Norway's best-known and most provocative dramatist next to Ibsen. Both the play and Delius's music for it, which includes a parody of the Norwegian national anthem, had been loudly booed when first performed. The next year Beecham and the Royal Philharmonic Orchestra took part in a London Music Festival, promoted by the British dance-band leader and impresario Jack Hylton, who had backed Beecham's old orchestra, the London Philharmonic, through the war years. The venue for this was the Harringay Arena near Finsbury Park, for want of a more suitable locale in the still bomb-scarred capital. It turned out to be a London Festival in more ways than one, with the sounds of local trains and buses and the cries of bookies and punters from the neighbouring greyhound-racing track all echoing round the draughty arena, with its makeshift corrugated iron roof.

The Richard Strauss Festival in the autumn of that same year, 1947, was much more important for the orchestra, in terms of publicity and prestige. This was one of Beecham's most generous-hearted acts on behalf of a fellow artist and a long-standing friend. Through the war years Strauss and his family had lived in Germany, then Austria, and finally in Switzerland, their situation, politically and financially, going from bad to worse. At the end of the war Strauss composed his *Metamorphosen* for strings, with its dirge-like quotation of the Funeral March from Beethoven's *Eroica* Symphony, conveying grief at the destruction of his country – one of his rare expressions of personal feeling. Beecham's aim, in staging the festival, was to rehabilitate the name of the composer, who many people assumed must already be dead, and earn for him some much-needed cash. Generosity apart, he was taking a big gamble bringing a German composer, especially one with his former Nazi associations, back to London so soon after the war. The gamble paid off handsomely. The eighty-three-year-old composer was marvellously sprightly for someone of his age, patiently and cheerfully correcting press reporters who kept asking him if he was really the composer of the 'Blue Danube' Waltz!

The opening concert, on a Sunday, was given at the Theatre Royal, Drury Lane, the scene of so many of Beecham's triumphs of days gone by, where Rodgers and Hammerstein's smash hit musical *Oklahoma!* was now lifting the spirits of a still drab and austerity-ridden Britain. Neville Cardus was there:

> Richard Strauss was warmly welcomed back to London by the audience at Drury Lane Theatre on Sunday the moment they saw him entering his box. At eighty-three he is, as ever, pink and upright; his white hair merely emphasizes the immaculate way he wears his dinner jacket . . . Sir Thomas Beecham conducted *Don Quixote* with subtlety of nuance, not a point was missed.

The Frenchman Paul Tortelier, just embarking on his career, played the important solo cello part. The BBC promoted two studio performances of *Elektra*, with Beecham, the Royal Philharmonic and a cast that included the German mezzo-soprano Elisabeth Hoengen and the Bulgarian soprano Ljuba Welitsch, who were both appearing at Covent Garden at that time. At the final concert, in a packed Albert Hall, Strauss himself conducted the Philharmonia Orchestra this time, in a taxing programme that included his *Sinfonia Domestica*, that massive celebration of married strife and bliss.

The festival was important also for one of Beecham's latest protégés. This was Norman Del Mar, who stepped up from his place in the orchestra to conduct the suite or 'Symphonic Fantasia' from the opera *Die Frau ohne Schatten*. 'The tone and abandon and certainty and clearness', wrote Cardus of his conducting, 'stirred Strauss to long and untiring hand clapping.' In his definitive three-volume work on the composer's life and music, Del Mar records his own memories of the festival. He recalls Strauss embracing Beecham after the second of those studio performances of *Elektra*. 'I had not realised', he observes, 'that Beecham was so small or that Strauss was so large.' He is speaking here of height, not weight. Beecham, at sixty-eight, despite his back trouble and his gout, still carried himself extremely well, with something of a military bearing, so that, alone on the rostrum, he always looked much taller than he was. It took a really tall man like Strauss to correct this impression. The octogenarian composer – the last great German romantic – died two years later.

CHAPTER THIRTY

In 1948 Beecham visited South Africa, still a part of the British Commonwealth, to conduct local orchestras in Cape Town, Johannesburg and Durban. He arrived in a wheelchair, suffering from a bad attack of sciatica. Despite this, he seems to have been in a better humour than when he had visited Australia eight years earlier, cheerfully playing encores in exchange for cases of bananas and oranges for British children, for whom such 'luxuries' were only just coming back into the shops. During 1949, his seventieth year, he visited North America, attending the Montreal Festival, then heading south for Dallas. Once home he returned close to his birthplace, to celebrate this important birthday year with a concert by the Liverpool Philharmonic Society, an institution for which he always had the warmest affection. And he began his association with the Glyndebourne Opera.

The story of this remarkable enterprise began in 1934, when the old Etonian John Christie realised his dream of staging opera in a specially built theatre in the grounds of his stately home, Glyndebourne, situated at the foot of the South Downs near Lewes in Sussex. In a roundabout way he was helped by the Nazis, since he was able to acquire the services of three of the most talented and experienced men already in the business of opera, each of whom was glad to get out of Germany: the conductor Fritz Busch (formerly chief conductor at the Dresden Opera), the producer Carl Ebert (who had worked at the Berlin State Opera), and the manager Rudolf Bing (concert and opera impresario). It was they who really ran Glyndebourne, establishing it as something quite unique: an opera festival with the atmosphere of an exclusive country house party. There was even croquet on the lawn.

Up to the war, relations between Beecham and Christie had been distant and frosty. Christie was rude about Beecham's management of Covent Garden. Beecham spoke dismissively of 'Christie's Minstrels'. After the war things were different. Both men now found themselves on the same side in their dislike of the new Covent

Garden regime, though there was no sudden reconciliation. Beecham turned down an offer to conduct a 1946 production of
Carmen with Kathleen Ferrier in the leading role, on the grounds
that it was 'to be made the subject of experiments with comparatively raw and under-developed material'. Apart from such objec-
tions, the much-loved contralto was probably not best suited to
portray such a *femme fatale*. She did go on to sing at Glyndebourne
in other productions – the name part in Britten's *The Rape of
Lucretia*, conducted by Ernest Ansermet, and in Gluck's *Orfeo*
with the lesser-known but distinguished Austro-American conductor Fritz Stiedry – before her tragically early death from cancer in
1953. As far as Beecham and Christie were concerned, nothing
happened until the summer of 1948, when Beecham and the Royal
Philharmonic Orchestra gave a short season of Mozart concerts at
the Glyndebourne theatre. This was the prelude to a close association between the orchestra, the Glyndebourne Opera and, by
extension, the Edinburgh Festival, which Rudolf Bing had inaugurated the previous year primarily as a new opening for the company
away from Glyndebourne itself. Bing directed the first three annual
Edinburgh festivals before departing for New York to manage the
Metropolitan Opera for the next twenty-two years. So it was that
in the late summer of 1948 the Royal Philharmonic Orchestra
first accompanied the Glyndebourne company to the Scottish
capital, and for many years thereafter served as its resident orchestra, as the London Philharmonic had served at Covent Garden in
pre-war days.

Beecham himself conducted the Glyndebourne company only
once. This was at the 1950 Edinburgh Festival. He did not conduct
a Mozart opera, as everyone might have expected, but the chosen
work had strong personal associations for him. It was *Ariadne auf
Naxos*, again in the original version that he had first staged in
London at His Majesty's Theatre in 1913 (see page 62). One
striking aspect of this new production was the design: the sets and
costumes were by Oliver Messel, a very successful British stage
designer of the postwar years. It was interesting in several other
respects. Miles Malleson, a fine old character actor known to
millions of British cinemagoers who was also a scholarly man,
made his own adaptation of Molière's *Le Bourgeois Gentilhomme*
and played the part of M. Jourdain which had been taken by
Beerbohm Tree in 1913. The production also brought to the fore
two rising stars of the postwar generation of British singers: April
Cantelo, who went on to sing regularly at Glyndebourne and with
the English Opera Group, and the tenor Alexander Young, who

some years later was chosen by Stravinsky to sing the title role in the composer's own recording of *The Rake's Progress*. *The Times* devoted nearly a whole column to *Ariadne*.

> In last night's performance, five female voices without a wobble between them explained to a sceptical twentieth century one of the mysteries of the eighteenth – that, as Byrd said two centuries before that, there is no music to compare with singing if it be well ordered; you can listen for ever to supremely good singing . . . The orchestra under Sir Thomas Beecham phrased some of Strauss's most delicious strains exquisitely. And the thread on which all these jewels were strung was the personality of M. Jourdain as portrayed in its full ripe egregiousness by Mr Miles Malleson.

As well as a favourable mention of April Cantelo, there was also special praise for one of Germany's newest opera stars, Ilse Holl-weg, who took the part of Zerbinetta. This, as *Kobbé's Complete Opera Book* says, is one of the most taxing ever written for coloratura soprano. Beecham maintained a high profile at that year's festival, conducting also performances of Haydn's oratorio *The Seasons*; his old American friend Virgil Thomson's Cello Concerto, with Anthony Pini; and, on the closing night, directing an orchestra of over one hundred and fifty players in an open-air performance of Handel's *Music for the Royal Fireworks*. At the press of a button, he also fired off some cannons mounted high up on the floodlit castle – something to carry him back in spirit to the days of long ago with his 'Fireworks Orchestra'.

With barely time to recover from the festival, Beecham then got ready for his tour of the United States with the Royal Philharmonic Orchestra. It was the fulfilment of a wish going back forty years to take a British orchestra on such a tour. They all sailed on the *Queen Mary*, arriving in New York on 12 October 1950. Conductor and orchestra were scheduled to give over fifty concerts during a two-month tour that began in Hartford, Connecticut (the day after they arrived), proceeded through New Jersey and Pennsylvania to Washington DC, swung back through Baltimore to New York and Boston, cut a broad swathe through the southern states to New Orleans, came north again through Tennessee and Kentucky to Chicago, and finally returned to the east coast through Detroit, Pittsburgh and Philadelphia, and so back to New York. They took with them a repertory of nearly sixty works. There were no real novelties or surprises, just solid Beecham fare, with good helpings of Berlioz, Delius, Handel, Haydn, Mozart, Sibelius,

Richard Strauss, plus two Beethoven symphonies and a variety of shorter pieces – more than enough to ring the changes from one concert to the next. Lady Beecham (Betty Humby) played two piano concertos (by Mozart and Delius); other soloists were drawn from among the orchestra's own principals.

No orchestra and conductor can have faced a tougher test of stamina and mettle, quite apart from specific questions of musicianship. They had to fight against fatigue of body and mind, brought on by constant travel, hurried or irregular meals, and one hotel after another. Every other night there was a new hall to be faced, each with its own acoustics, platform arrangements, temperature and humidity. At Pittsburgh and Richmond, Virginia, they played in a mosque, at Buffalo in a music hall. Added to this frantic pace, there must have been many other aspects of that tour to distract, bewilder or unsettle the men of Beecham's Royal Philharmonic: refrigerators, washing machines, central heating (an unexpected problem for many of their instruments), aspects of a life-style still rare or virtually unknown in postwar austerity Britain.

In a letter to the *New York Times* Beecham introduced his orchestra and expressed his hopes for the tour. The Royal Philharmonic, he proudly told readers, was independent of any state or municipal support, and was not acting on behalf of any government or other official body. It did not seek to educate or enlighten, only to please. They certainly did that. The adjectives and phrases 'magnificent', 'superb', 'brilliant', 'noble tone', 'clarity', 'flawless articulation' followed them down to the Gulf of Mexico and back to Niagara Falls. Just a few people were a shade less than ecstatic. 'The Royal Philharmonic Orchestra is a good orchestra,' wrote the critic of the *Toledo Blade*, 'but we have two or three of our own that are better. If anybody tries to tell you differently, point a finger at him and say the mystic word "Anglophile". That'll shut him up.'

Beecham himself received plenty of coverage. 'Sir Thomas Beecham, a little more gray and portly than on his last visit with the Metropolitan Opera, walks slowly nowadays,' reported the *Boston Daily Globe*, 'but the moment he has begun to conduct, the passion and the swiftness of his gestures are those of a young man.' According to the *Chicago Daily News*, 'At seventy-one Sir Thomas is a figure of strength and nobility whether you speak personally or musically. And those qualities, which must include grace (in every sense) and honesty, sound in his orchestra as surely as he leads it.' Olin Downes of the *New York Times* was still on hand to cover the last of the three concerts at Carnegie Hall:

This concert demonstrated anew how terribly the composer is at the mercy of the interpreter. For if one judged the 28-year-old Wagner who composed 'The Flying Dutchman' by the way the overture to that opera has been repeatedly played on recent occasions in the city, he would put down Wagner as a decidedly second-rate artist. But when Sir Thomas took up his baton last night and let loose the elements in the orchestra one was simply swept away by the power and inspiration of the music and the grandeur of the conception.

The final work was Berlioz's *Te Deum*, which Downes believed had not been heard in Carnegie Hall since the inaugural concert in 1891. 'The audience, which applauded and cheered afterwards, made such a demonstration that Sir Thomas and his men, in a manner quite contrary to the tradition here at an orchestral concert, played two encores at the end of the program.' By a remarkable coincidence, the very last concert of the tour was given in Bethlehem, Pennsylvania. They were home again just in time for Christmas.

The tour had its share of unrehearsed high points, both funny and quite moving. Jack Brymer remembers that it was snowing hard at Rockford, Illinois, delaying Beecham's arrival at the hall. When he did get there he hurriedly peeled off coat and scarf before stepping straight onto the podium. He and his leader, David McCallum, then exchanged swift glances. He still had on his bedroom slippers. Beecham smiled, the audience laughed, and they all carried on. At the railroad depot in New Orleans, a little black girl took his hand and said she wanted to go on the train with him to Jackson, Mississippi. They had their picture taken. New Orleans, the birthplace of jazz, with its old French connections, was a relatively free and easy place. But in 1950, throughout the American South, racial segregation was almost everywhere still in force, and the ghastly spectre of the Ku Klux Klan still stalked the land. That picture, of the septuagenarian English knight and baronet holding hands with the little black child, spoke volumes for his own humanity, heedless of law, convention or prejudice.

CHAPTER THIRTY-ONE

The Festival of Britain of 1951, staged one hundred years after the
Great Exhibition organised by Prince Albert in 1851, was intended
to mark the nation's postwar recovery. It was celebrated all over
the country, but its centrepiece was the South Bank in London,
where a large area of derelict land on the Thames opposite Charing
Cross and the Embankment became the site for an exhibition of
British art and technology, past and present. There was the Dome
of Discovery, the futuristic Skylon, the old Shot Tower (once used
for making lead shot) bouncing radio signals off the moon, the
Pleasure Gardens, and the Emett Railway, a fun ride based on the
drawings of the cartoonist Roland Emett, whose quaint and fanciful
trains, cars and other contraptions enlivened the pages of *Punch*
and *Lilliput*. In its midst was the exhibition's one permanent feature, the Royal Festival Hall, the first major concert hall to be built
in London since the Queen's Hall, which, as we have noted, had
been destroyed during the war. Its ultra-modern design and novel
acoustics attracted interest and controversy all over the world. The
whole festival was something else for Beecham to shake his fist at.
For a country so deeply in debt, it seemed to him a feckless
indulgence, 'a monumental piece of imbecility and iniquity'. The
Festival Hall itself he was variously reported as calling 'a repellent,
unattractive and monstrous structure' and 'a giant chicken coop',
opinions founded on its original exterior, since he swore he would
never set foot inside it. Ironically, the hall's first general manager
was Ernest Bean, who had had that famous encounter with Beecham at the time of the row over the presidency of the Hallé Society
in 1944. It was officially opened by the King on 3 May 1951; there
followed a brief service of dedication by the Archbishop of Canter-
bury and then a concert of British choral music, from Handel to
Vaughan Williams, given by a special orchestra and choir drawn
from other London orchestras and choral societies, directed by Sir
Adrian Boult and Sir Malcolm Sargent. A special correspondent for
The Times was full of praise for the building. 'From every seat,' he

reported, 'one can see and hear everything.' The acoustics, which others had criticised during tests as being too dry and confined, delighted him. 'The clarity continues to astonish, since the words of the choir were actually intelligible.'

Beecham celebrated the year in his own way. He had met Leopold Stokowski during his war years in America, and now invited him to conduct the Royal Philharmonic Orchestra during a series of concerts up and down the country. Stokowski was three years younger than Beecham and every bit as flamboyant and controversial in his own way. He had been born in London, and began his career as organist at St James's Church, Piccadilly, before settling in the United States, where he built up the Philadelphia Orchestra into one of the world's best, founded several other orchestras, including an All-American Youth Orchestra, and, as we have noted, appeared in several films. His appearances as Beecham's guest conductor during the summer of 1951 were his first in Europe for nearly forty years. Beecham himself gave the opening concert at the rebuilt Colston Hall in Bristol (twice burnt down within a hundred years), reckoned at the time to be one of the best new British concert halls outside London.

This was also the year that Beecham and the new Covent Garden management buried the hatchet, and he returned, after an absence of twelve years, to conduct two productions. The first of these was *Die Meistersinger von Nürnberg*, during a season that also presented *Parsifal* with Kirsten Flagstad and the Czech-born baritone Otakar Kraus, *Madama Butterfly* with Victoria de Los Angeles, and the première of Vaughan Williams's opera *The Pilgrim's Progress*, with such rising British stars as Monica Sinclair and Michael Langdon. In the small, austerity-format programmes Beecham was billed as 'guest conductor', but acted as though he was still running the show. He would not accept any cuts in Wagner's score, which meant that performances, taking intervals into account, would have to start extra early in order to end before midnight. He also demanded, and got, over twice as many extras as the Royal Opera House had provided for. Among these were Colin Davis, a future musical director of Covent Garden, the music scholar and critic David Cairns, and Bernard Keeffe, all still in their twenties. Keeffe recalls 'those gimlet eyes as we rushed on stage disguised as tailors or bakers'. The cast included the German soprano Elisabeth Grümmer, making her Covent Garden début, Ludwig Weber, an old friend of pre-war days, the English mezzo-soprano Constance Shacklock (remembered in years to come as the indefatigable lady who turned up season after season, on the last

night of the Proms, to sing 'Rule, Britannia') and the Welsh baritone Geraint Evans, with his foot on the first rung of the ladder to
fame, as the Nightwatchman. The producer was Heinz Tietjen,
conductor and formerly artistic director of the Bayreuth Festival,
whom Beecham had known before the war. At the first performance on 29 June, he was greeted like a hero returned from exile.
'The cheering that greeted Sir Thomas Beecham on his return to
Covent Garden last night must easily have been heard out in Bow
Street,' wrote the critic of the *Daily Mail*. 'He proceeded fully to
justify all our esteem and affection. Many in the audience must
have had memories of past performances of "Die Meistersinger"
conducted by Beecham, but last night's seemed to be as mellow as
any I have heard.' The *Daily Telegraph* reported: 'Sir Thomas
Beecham's return, after 12 years, to the conductor's desk at Covent
Garden made a splendidly festive occasion of last night's full-length
revival of "The Mastersingers". The wondrous score has always
been supremely congenial to him, and once again there was something like magic in his evocation of all the charm and beguiling
lyricism it contains.' 'Brilliant, tender, incandescent by turns,' said
The Times, 'it was never turgid in the Teutonic vein yet never less
than majestic.' In a later performance the great Austrian bass-
baritone Hans Hotter, approaching the peak of his career, sang
Hans Sachs in place of Karl Kamann.

The second opera that Beecham conducted at Covent Garden in
1951 was a more quixotic choice. This was the Irish composer
Michael Balfe's *The Bohemian Girl*, composed in 1843, first performed at Covent Garden in 1862, and now mainly remembered
for its aria 'I dreamt that I dwelt in marble halls', a great favourite
with Victorian balladeers. Beecham prepared a new edition of the
score, while Dennis Arundell, a top English producer, supplied a
new and less dated version of the libretto. Beecham arranged for it
to be produced and rehearsed in Liverpool under the aegis of the
Arts Council as a part of that city's contribution to the Festival of
Britain; it was then staged at Covent Garden for a short season,
from mid-August to the beginning of September. The heroine was
sung by the twenty-one-year-old American soprano Roberta Pe-
ters, who went on to sing regularly at the Metropolitan Opera.
Picture Post, Britain's top-selling illustrated magazine, called her
'The Girl from the Bronx' and carried photos of her prettily made
up for the part. Also in Beecham's cast was the well-known English
mezzo-soprano Edith Coates, then a member of the Covent Garden
Company. Critical reaction was mixed. 'Sir Thomas Beecham',
commented the *Daily Mail* critic Stanley Bayliss, 'has done many

surprising things in the past, but in spite of the great applause last night, I doubt very much whether he will be able to persuade the critical that "The Bohemian Girl" is really worthy of production at Covent Garden. It is not even a very interesting period piece.' *The Times* was a little more charitable:

Last night *The Bohemian Girl* was revived in style at Covent Garden as a period piece with a special appropriateness for minds temporarily attuned to the Victorianism of 1851, when it was eight years old . . . The cavatinas, in their long succession, when played with the refinements Sir Thomas Beecham brings to them and sung in proper lyrical style, exert still the charm that they have always done.

Their critic, however, had to admit that 'some of the tunes are banal and one gets sick of the eternal arpeggio accompaniments to them'.

Beecham's *rapprochement* with Covent Garden incidentally sparked off a new row with the BBC. As reported in the press, he had rejected as 'preposterously inadequate, thoughtlessly impudent and magnificently inept' the Corporation's first offer for a broadcast performance, on their new Third Programme network, of *The Bohemian Girl*. After taking his curtain calls at the end of the Covent Garden run, he could not resist having another go at them. 'I have', he told a delighted audience, 'made a profound discovery, so world-shaking that I feel I must pass it on to you. If anyone wants a job doing nothing at all, and to be remunerated on the grandest possible scale, apply to the BBC!'

He had, in the meantime, come to terms with the Royal Festival Hall. Amid news of the Korean War, the Cold War, the atomic bomb, and the general election that brought Winston Churchill back as prime minister, *The Times* carried the announcement that Sir Thomas Beecham and his Royal Philharmonic Orchestra were to make their first appearance in the new auditorium. The occasion was the opening, on 17 October 1951, of the 140th concert season of the Royal Philharmonic Society, and all seats were sold weeks in advance. The evening's programme included a Haydn symphony, Debussy's *Iberia*, Delius's *In a Summer Garden*, and the suite from Rimsky-Korsakov's *The Golden Cockerel*. Such a programme, reported *The Times*,

was calculated to show off the beauties, the refinements, the enchantments of sheer sonority that can be extracted from an orchestra of virtuoso players like the Royal Philharmonic. Every note was in place, every phrase shaped to the finest curve, every shade of tone balanced with the utmost nicety. And it all flowed in Sir Thomas Beecham's most ingratiating, most compelling manner.

He had opened that concert with the Prelude to *Die Meistersinger*. In December he was back at Covent Garden to direct two more performances of the opera. The second of these, on 17 December, turned out to be his last in the Royal Opera House.

That fact, sad in itself, in no way indicated any general falling away of Beecham's energy or activity as he entered the final decade of his life. In 1952 and again in 1956 he appeared at the Edinburgh Festival. On the former occasion he conducted, among other works, a moving performance of Berlioz's tender and touching oratorio *L'Enfance du Christ* ('The Childhood of Christ'), far removed in style and spirit from the massive pomp of the *Grand' Messe des morts* or the wild romantic abandon of the *Symphonie fantastique*. In 1955, the year of Sibelius's ninetieth birthday, he gave an all-Sibelius concert that was specially beamed to Finland, and broadcast a tribute to the composer on the BBC's long-running *Music Magazine*. He also made the trip to Finland to visit Sibelius at Ainola, his home among the tall birches and pines just outside the village of Järvenpää, about an hour's drive from Helsinki. Sibelius had drunk and smoked quite heavily for much of his life. Beecham loved his cigars as much as ever. But the wine and the brandy probably did not flow quite so copiously any more. In 1957 Beecham took the Royal Philharmonic Orchestra on tour again, this time to Paris, Switzerland and Vienna. That was also the year he was made a Companion of Honour. He made several more North American visits, travelling from coast to coast to conduct in San Francisco, Seattle, Vancouver, Toronto, Chicago, Pittsburgh; he appeared with his friend Stokowski's old orchestra in Philadelphia, and, in Carnegie Hall, with New York's Symphony of the Air (the NBC Symphony Orchestra, reconstituted after Toscanini had left them in 1954).

He was also involved with more opera, though of a quite different kind from either Wagner or Balfe. In 1953 he rescued from obscurity Delius's early opera *Irmelin*. The producer was Dennis Arundell, and it was staged at the New Theatre, Oxford, with help from the Arts Council and the Delius Trust. *The Times* was full of praise for Beecham. 'It is astonishing that he can, merely by taking a train to Oxford, shake out of his suitcase an unknown and exquisite opera all of a piece and without apparent effort.' Sad to say, only the opera's Prelude, which was, in any case, composed at a later date, is known to most people today. Two years later, at the beautiful old Theatre Royal in Bath, as part of that city's Festival Beecham revived a work by one of the lesser-known eighteenth-century composers he had loved since his youth. This was André Grétry's comedy-ballet *Zémire et Azor*, with a scenario by the famous French librettist Jean-François Marmontel, based on Charles Perrault's fairy tale *Beauty and the Beast*. It proved to be a very happy collaboration between Beecham, conducting the Bournemouth Symphony Orchestra, the producer Anthony Besch, who had worked with Carl Ebert at Glyndebourne, the designer Oliver Messel, and a cast that included the French tenor Michel Sénéchal, a specialist in Baroque and Classical opera as well as a fine character actor.

Throughout the 1950s Beecham was also recording as much as ever. And he was as outspoken as ever. He told the people of Edinburgh that festivals were bunk. 'They are for the purpose of attracting trade to the town. What that has to do with music I don't know.' He excoriated contemporary music, now reaching out through the postwar experimentations of Pierre Boulez, Karlheinz Stockhausen and Luciano Berio into the strange and for many people forbidding realms of *musique concrète*, electronics and aleatory concepts (leaving options open to the performers). 'In old music you stand alone, alone and naked, and every note you play has got to be perfect. No one notices in modern music how many wrong notes you play.' Nor, according to Charles Reid, did he have any time for the new breed of 'purists', the new disciples of 'authentic performance', with their 'parsimonious handfuls of strings and oboes'.

In 1954 Beecham had conducted two of his last concerts with provincial British orchestras, the City of Birmingham Orchestra, and his old friends of the Liverpool Philharmonic, when he cracked jokes with his audience about having to go to Merseyside for decent potted shrimps and good old Eccles cake. That year he also conducted two concerts during the Diamond Jubilee Season of the Proms. He had conducted at a Promenade Concert in 1915; but this was the first time he had figured in the Proms ever since the BBC had taken them over in 1927. The event was widely seen as another peace move, this time towards the Corporation. He was, it hardly needs saying, rapturously welcomed by the Promenaders. By then he was what David Webster at Covent Garden had already called him, an institution. He had indeed become a unique father-figure to the British music-loving public, and especially to the young, most of whom can have had only the haziest idea of his astonishing career. His concerts were like family gatherings. Even in the vast spaces of the Royal Albert Hall he could draw the audience around him in an almost magical way. This was the era of his famous 'lollipops', his encores. The general idea was to calm his audience after some rousing conclusion to the official programme, and send them home peaceful and contented. Massenet's 'Last Sleep of the Virgin' or the hushed, perfumed enchantment of the Intermezzo from Delius's incidental music to James Elroy Flecker's *Hassan* fitted this role perfectly. But there were other much more rumbustious 'lollipops', such as Chabrier's *Joyeuse Marche* or Delius's merry *Sleigh Ride* (with more than a touch of the Naughty Nineties about it), into which Beecham would launch with a shout or a wink, as though life, when all was said and done, was a great and joyous romp.

The term 'lollipop' had, it seems, come from Lady (Betty) Beecham. The two of them were now, like Noël Coward, tax exiles from Britain. They lived for much of the time in the South of France, returning to England for periods of only a month or two at a stretch before the Inland Revenue could grab Beecham and start to unravel his finances. Far more worrying to him, though he hardly ever mentioned it, was Betty's health, which had been deteriorating for some years. In the late summer of 1958 they journeyed to Buenos Aires, where he was to conduct a short season of opera, including *Carmen*, *Fidelio* and *La Flauta magica* ('The Magic Flute'), at the opulent Teatro Colón, Latin America's premier opera house. It was there that she died. Their relationship seems to have been marked by some forbearance on his part. She liked to play at politics behind the scenes, for which he occasionally reprimanded her in the gentlest terms. As a pianist she suffered lapses of memory which Beecham usually managed to cover up. After one such unhappy performance, he was heard to say – out of her hearing – that there was no need to wheel the piano off the stage. 'It will slink off by itself.' But of all the women in his life, she was probably the one he loved the most. He spoke of her afterwards simply as a 'wonderful comrade'. When it came to matters close to the heart, the man who was so voluble on practically any other subject under the sun was surprisingly reticent. Indeed, in the opinion of Bernard Keeffe, who was able to observe him closely during these years, 'the public bravado and wit were defence mechanisms – he was a rather shy and vulnerable, childlike personality'. On his return to London, somebody, still ignorant of the facts, asked after Lady Beecham. He hid his feelings again, behind a touch of sardonic wit. 'On tour,' he replied, 'with Vaughan Williams.' That composer had died in August. Sibelius had died the year before. Beecham's own health was letting him down. His gout, his sciatica and other ailments plagued him more and more. He needed surgery on one of his feet. He often had to conduct sitting down. Hopes that he might do *Les Troyens* at Covent Garden (one of his most cherished ambitions) and *Die Zauberflöte* at Glyndebourne were dashed because of sickness. One of his last American tours was curtailed.

On Saturday 7 May 1960 he and the Royal Philharmonic Orchestra travelled to Portsmouth to give a concert in the Guildhall. He treated his players to lunch, rehearsed them briefly, then invited them back to his hotel room 'for the serious business of the day', to watch the televised football Cup Final (Wolverhampton Wanderers 3, Blackburn Rovers 0). In the evening he conducted Mozart, Haydn, Schubert, Delius, Saint-Saëns, and his own Handelian Suite, *Love in Bath*. Ivor Newton was there, and recalls that after a lesser-known 'lollipop' he told the audience that the sender of the first postcard giving the correct name and composer of the piece would receive a photograph of the orchestra and lunch at the Queen's Hotel. Laughter, cheers and applause followed him as he made his slow, painful way back to his dressing room. It was his last public appearance.

In 1959, in Switzerland, he had married yet again. His new bride, the third Lady Beecham, was Shirley Hudson, his secretary and orchestral assistant. He was eighty years old, she was twenty-seven. Two years later in London on 8 March 1961, after a second coronary thrombosis, he died. *The Times* carried a three-column obituary. 'As an interpreter of a wide range of music he counts as one of the comparatively few executant geniuses this country has ever produced. Continental Europe and America alike recognized him as such. In the last two decades of his life his stature was recognized as second to none among the great conductors of the world.' Surveying his whole career, from 1899 up to a matter of weeks before he died, *The Times* also reminded its readers of his colossal achievements as a founder of orchestras, and his years of tireless endeavour in the realm of opera. Across the Atlantic, Harold Schonberg delivered a more individual portrait in the *New York Times*. Orchestral players the world over, he wrote, called him 'Tommy', but never to his face. Nobody could take liberties with that short, courtly, Edwardian conductor with the Shavian tongue. 'Like the king in *Princess Ida*, he was a peppery potentate, and his acid opinions ranged impartially over music, musicians, audiences, socialism, literature, wine and food. And now,' said Schonberg, 'the 81-year-old master is dead. It is hard to accept the fact. For Sir Thomas, jaunty and apparently indestructible, full of spirit, indomitable, testy and choleric, strong-minded, sometimes unexpectedly gentle, seemed to have been around as long as the Tower of London.' The composer Malcolm Arnold, who had been principal trumpet in the London Philharmonic Orchestra, spoke for nearly everyone who had ever known Beecham when he said simply, on the BBC's *Music Magazine*, that with his death, humour and life had gone out of music. Beecham was first buried at Brookwood cemetery, near Woking, in Surrey. In 1991 his remains were removed to the graveyard of Limpsfield parish church and placed close to those of Frederick and Jelka Delius. The Australian-born pianist Eileen Joyce and the cellist Beatrice Harrison repose in the same quiet English churchyard.

APPENDIX: BEECHAM ON RECORD

In his early days Beecham was as scathing about the gramophone as he was about radio. 'Improvement', he said, 'is so imperceptible that it will take quite five thousand years to make it any good.' Words, with Beecham, were not always at one with actions. His recordings are a testimony to every period and aspect of his life and times. Some have fallen by the wayside. Many more are constantly being brushed up and re-issued, to keep his art and his memory green.

Beecham was born just two years after Thomas Alva Edison in America produced his original phonograph in 1877. Edison named it after a system of shorthand called phonography, and conceived it as an office dictating machine. The British prime minister William Ewart Gladstone and the poet laureate Alfred Lord Tennyson duly spoke into it. Brahms tried to record one of his piano pieces on a phonograph. His voice can be made out at the start of the recording, but the music is a hopeless jangle. The real future of recording, in fact, lay with the German-American Emile Berliner's gramophone, which used discs instead of cylinders – much easier to replicate and to store. (It is interesting to note that in an earlier age musical boxes and polyphons also progressed from cylinders to discs.) Berliner produced his first, manually-operated gramophone in 1889. His classic model, with a spring motor, came out in 1898. Soon afterwards this featured in the London artist Francis Barraud's picture of his dog Nipper cocking his head towards the horn – none other than the world-famous picture of 'His Master's Voice'.

Early recordings were mostly of vocalists or instrumentalists, because it was easier for them to sing or play into the large acoustic horn. Precious recordings from around the turn of the century have preserved for us the voices of Enrico Caruso, Nellie Melba, Emma Calvé, Pol Plançon, Emma Albani, Victor Maurel, and such stars of music hall as Harry Champion, George Robey and Vesta Tilley; also, among instrumentalists, Edvard Grieg, Joseph Joachim and Pablo Sarasate. The American Columbia Company, however, did manage some very early recordings of John Philip Sousa and his United States Marine Band. And by 1913 recording techniques were sufficiently advanced to allow the Gramophone Company to issue, on eight single-sided discs, Artur Nikisch and the Berlin Philharmonic Orchestra playing Beethoven's Fifth Symphony. The Gramophone Company, incidentally, registered that 'His Master's Voice' picture as their trademark in 1900, though they did not technically change their name to His Master's Voice (HMV). Later, in 1931, they were to merge with the Columbia Gramophone Company to become Electrical and Musical Industries (EMI).

Beecham made his recording début in 1910, with the Gramophone Company. His studio manager was the American Will Gaisberg, whose brother Fred had worked closely with Emile Berliner. Beecham recorded excerpts from the productions of *Les Contes d'Hoffmann* and *Die Fledermaus* which he was currently staging as part of his season of 'opéra-comique' at His Majesty's Theatre. His singers included Walter Hyde, Frederick Ranalow and the soprano Caroline Hatchard, whose rendering of 'The Doll's Song' from *Les Contes d'Hoffmann* included the sound of the doll's clockwork being wound up – a pioneering piece of recorded sound effects. Very soon afterwards he recorded a suite or 'selection' of music from Eugène d'Albert's opera *Tiefland*, which he was staging at Covent Garden, coupled with similar selections from Verdi's early opera *Nabucco* (billed as *Nabucodnosor*). Some obscurity surrounds these latter items. They are generally credited to the Beecham Symphony Orchestra; but they were probably recorded by a wind band which Beecham had assembled at about this time to take on tour. In 1912 he recorded, almost certainly with his full orchestra this time, several operatic overtures and other orchestral excerpts, including the Entr'acte from Edmond de Missa's *Muguette*, which he had also presented during his 1910 season at His Majesty's Theatre – probably the only piece of that composer's music on record.

The First World War hardly curtailed Beecham's recording activities. Indeed, during those war years his recording work with the Beecham Symphony Orchestra kept him extremely busy, though some of their recordings were never released. They include: the overtures to *Le Nozze di Figaro*, *Die Zauberflöte*, *Oberon*, *Il Barbiere di Siviglia* and *The Bartered Bride*; the 'Polovtsian Dances' from *Prince Igor*; the Scherzo from Mendelssohn's incidental music to *A Midsummer Night's Dream*; Sibelius's *Valse*

Triste; the 'Hungarian March' from *La Damnation de Faust*; parts of Tchaikovsky's Sixth ('Pathétique') and Dvořák's Ninth ('From the New World') symphonies; and – by way of another real rarity – a minuet from Lully's ballet *Les Amants magnifiques*. Moving into the field of what was then still contemporary music, Beecham cut discs of some of the Waltzes from *Der Rosenkavalier*, and several dances from *L'Oiseau de Feu* – probably the very first recordings of Stravinsky's music. He also made a wartime recording with Clara Butt of a patriotic song specially written for a Royal Philharmonic Society concert in February 1917, 'Have you news of my boy Jack?', with words by Rudyard Kipling and music by Edward German – a remarkable period gem that has been reissued in recent years.

Soon after the war – while Beecham was involved with the problems of his father's Covent Garden Estate – experimental work began on electrical recording, using microphones instead of the old acoustic horns, with marked improvements in sound quality. The first commercial electric recordings were released in 1925. Beecham made some of his last acoustic recordings with the London Symphony Orchestra, of pieces by Fauré, Mozart and Rimsky-Korsakov. One of his first electric recordings, made in 1927, was connected with the Columbia Graphophone (the British branch of the organisation) Company's plans for marking the centenary of Beethoven's death with an issue of all the symphonies, performed by different orchestras and conductors. The veteran German-born Sir George Henschel conducted the First Symphony. Henry Wood was entrusted with the *Eroica*. Beecham stepped chronologically between them with his recorded account of the bright and buoyant Second Symphony. Next year came Columbia's tribute to the centenary of Schubert's death. This was a composer much closer to Beecham's heart; but it was the rather curious prize-winning symphony by Kurt Atterberg described on page 108 that Beecham recorded at the time. Also in 1928, Columbia issued Beecham's near-complete version of *Messiah*, which, says Roland Gelatt in his book *The Fabulous Phonograph*, 'remained a touchstone of imaginative Handelian performance for two decades'. ('Phonograph', it should be noted, was for a long time the word generally used in America for both the phonograph proper and the gramophone.)

Through the 1930s, during his years as artistic director at Covent Garden, Beecham also recorded a large part of his orchestral repertory with the London Philharmonic Orchestra. Much of it was done under the auspices of Walter Legge, who was fast becoming the world's most dynamic and successful recording impresario. The following list, by no means exhaustive, gives some idea of how much music Beecham and the London Philharmonic recorded together, on top of all their other commitments: Beethoven, Symphony No. 2 (again); Berlioz, *La Damnation de Faust* (extracts); Lord Berners, *The Triumph of Neptune*; Brahms, Symphony No. 2, *Tragic* overture; Bizet, suites, *La jolie Fille de Perth, L'Arlésienne* (Nos. 1 and 2), *Carmen*; Chabrier, *Rhapsodie, España*; Debussy, *Prélude à l'Après-midi d'un Faune*; Dvořák, Slavonic Rhapsodies; Handel, Beecham's own suites, *The Gods Go A-Begging, The Origin of Design*; Haydn, Symphonies Nos. 93, 99, 104; Mendelssohn, incidental music to *A Midsummer Night's Dream* (extracts), overtures *The Hebrides, Ruy Blas*; Mozart, Symphonies Nos. 29, 31 ('Paris'), 36 ('Linz'), 40, overtures *Le Nozze di Figaro, Don Giovanni*; Nicolai, overture *Die lustigen Weiber von Windsor* ('The Merry Wives of Windsor'); Offenbach, *Les Contes d'Hoffmann* (extracts); Puccini, *La Bohème*, Act IV (Perli, Brownlee, Easton, Nash); Rossini, overtures *La Gazza ladra* ('The Thieving Magpie'), *Semiramide, Guillaume Tell*; Schubert, Symphonies Nos. 5 and 8 ('Unfinished'); Sibelius, Symphony No. 4, *Finlandia*, incidental music to *The Tempest*, tone poems *En Saga, The Return of Lemminkainen*; Suppé, overture *Morning, Noon and Night*; Tchaikovsky, Symphony No. 5, symphonic fantasy *Francesca da Rimini*; Wagner, overtures *Tannhäuser, Die Meistersinger*, Prelude to Act III of *Lohengrin*; Weber, overtures *Der Freischütz, Oberon*.

The background to that classic recording of Sibelius's brooding and enigmatic Fourth Symphony had its lighter side, according to Walter Legge, who was in charge of it. He sent a test pressing of the original recording to the composer, who replied with a long list of criticisms relating to such matters as tempo and expression marks. Beecham, meanwhile, had rather sneakily telephoned Sibelius and extracted from him a congratulatory telegram. When, however, Legge confronted him with the composer's earlier list of criticisms he cheerfully capitulated, saying, 'You win this round, my boy! We'll do the whole damned piece all over again and I'll pay the orchestra.' So he recorded the work twice within a matter of weeks, during 1937, the commercial recording being made largely from the second of the two performances.

Beecham was not usually a sympathetic partner in concerto work, but when he did venture into this part of the concert repertory he seems generally to have preferred violinists to pianists. From the 1930s come his recordings with Joseph Szigeti of the

Mendelssohn Concerto, Mozart's Violin Concerto No. 4 and Prokofiev's Violin Concerto No. 1 – one of his increasingly rare forays
into the music of his contemporaries. With Jascha Heifetz he recorded the Sibelius Concerto, alternately warm, romantic, tough
and brilliant. There were yet other classic Beecham recordings
dating from this time. During the 1934 Leeds Triennial Festival he
recorded live, with the London Philharmonic Orchestra and the
Leeds Festival Chorus: Borodin, 'Polovtsian Dances' from *Prince
Igor*; Handel, *Israel in Egypt* (extracts); Mozart, Mass in C minor
(extracts, with Dora Labbette); Sibelius, incidental music to *The
Tempest*. And there was his famous 1936 account of Berlioz's *Le
Carnaval Romain*. Said the *Musical Times*,

> The London Philharmonic Orchestra began its career under Sir
> Thomas Beecham with a performance of Berlioz's *Carnaval Ro-
> main*. This recording catches all the verve and wealth of tone
> that the orchestra throws into the work and enables us to ob-
> serve more closely than was possible amid the fire and smoke
> (the emotional excitement of that opening concert) how watch-
> ful and precise a performance it was.

During the same decade Beecham also found himself in the vanguard of technological research and development. In 1934 he recorded with the London Philharmonic parts of the first two
movements of Mozart's 'Jupiter' Symphony for Alan Blumlein,
a young Columbia recording engineer who was experimenting
with 'Binaural Sound', or what later became known as stereo-
phonic sound. Blumlein was killed in the Second World War,
working on a radar-controlled bombing device, before he could
resume his pioneering recording work. But Beecham's two recorded extracts for him have since been reissued. Two years later,
during their tour of Germany, Beecham and the London Philharmonic gave the concert described on page 157 at the I. B. Farbenindustrie Works at Ludwigshafen, part of which was recorded on
experimental magnetic tape. The minuet and trio from Mozart's
Symphony No. 39 have also been reissued as a testimony to that
historic event.

Beecham's wartime recording work in America drew him more
into litigation and politics than technology. He took the Columbia
Corporation to the Supreme Court in an attempt to stop them
issuing his recordings with the New York Philharmonic-Symphony
Orchestra of Sibelius's Seventh Symphony, Mendelssohn's 'Italian'
Symphony, the Suite from *The Golden Cockerel* and Tchaikovsky's
Capriccio Italien, on the grounds that they were sub-standard. He

also sued them for damages. He subsequently withdrew his action, learning a salutary and costly lesson about the risky business, no matter who you might be, of taking on a big American corporation in the courts. Beecham also tried to act as arbiter in a famous nationwide dispute between the American Federation of Musicians (AFM), the recording companies, and the hundreds of radio stations, big and small. The AFM's tough president, James C. Petrillo, was claiming, with some justice, that unlicensed use by the radio stations of so much recorded music (not to mention hundreds of thousands of juke-boxes) was putting his members out of work. He therefore ordered a ban on any further recording work by them, and the recording industry slowly ground to a halt. Beecham wrote a long letter – an article, really – to the *New York Times*. Taking a very different line from the one quoted at the beginning of this chapter, he wrote, 'Those of us who, since the beginning of this century, have been occupied with the making of music realize, perhaps more than others, what a revolutionary invention the gramophone was and how we should have been eternally grateful had it appeared on the scene two hundred years earlier.' He went on, 'We could have appraised the art of the man whom Saint-Saëns once declared to me to have been the greatest virtuoso of all time, Franz Liszt.' What a tragedy, therefore, that it should now be seen, in America at any rate, as a threat to music and musicians instead of a blessing. Getting down to business, he proposed that the radio stations should follow the example of the BBC (for once presenting that institution in a favourable light) and pay a small fee or royalty on the performance of recorded music, the proceeds to be channelled back to the AFM and its members. An Act of Congress along these lines might settle the matter. He attracted much support for his views. Eventually the major American recording companies, Decca, Columbia and RCA Victor, reached their own agreements with the AFM, paying them a royalty on the sale of their records; these, however, were not so comprehensive or legally binding as the ones Beecham had proposed, and there was more industrial trouble in the years ahead.

In June 1948, meanwhile, the American Columbia Corporation held a press conference in New York to launch a sensational new type of recording. This was the long-playing (LP) record, which not only revolved at less than half the speed of the existing standard 78 rpm disc, but had more grooves (microgrooves). The new LP records, after one or two initial hiccups, also offered new strength and clarity of recorded sound. Within a year or two, treasured collections of 78 rpms, filling whole cabinets,

even whole rooms in people's homes – and with every break
between sides embedded in their listeners' minds – were made
sadly redundant.

From the last days of the 78 rpm era and on into the age of the
LP record, Beecham kept the Royal Philharmonic Orchestra as
busily employed in the recording studio as he had kept the London
Philharmonic Orchestra before the war. One of their earliest recordings, made soon after the Strauss Festival of 1947, was of *Ein
Heldenleben*, that Beecham warhorse, with a fine rendering of the
solo violin part by Oscar Lampe, the orchestra's leader at the time.
The next year they recorded *Don Quixote* with Paul Tortelier, who
had played the work with them during the Festival. Another 1947
recording was of Beethoven's Fourth Piano Concerto, with Artur
Rubinstein. Beecham appeared several times in the concert hall
with this ebullient and charismatic artist, but this was their only
recording together. Their choice of Beethoven, rather than of Mozart or Chopin, in which they individually excelled, adds to the
recording's interest, as does Rubinstein's choice of rarely-heard
cadenzas by Saint-Saëns. Beecham and the Royal Philharmonic
re-recorded such favourites as the Mendelssohn Violin Concerto,
this time with Heifetz, Schubert's 'Unfinished' Symphony, and
Debussy's *Prélude à l'Après-midi d'un Faune*. Other recordings
include: Balakirev, Symphony No. 1, symphonic poem *Tamara*;
Bantock, *Fifine at the Fair*; Bax, *The Garden of Fand*; Beethoven,
Mass in C (Beecham Choral Society, Jennifer Vyvyan, Monica
Sinclair, Richard Lewis), and overture *Die Ruinen von Athen*;
Debussy, symphonic suite *Printemps* (Beecham had given the first
London performance of this in 1913); Dvořák, Symphony No. 8,
symphonic poem *The Golden Spinning Wheel*; Franck, symphonic
poem *Le Chasseur Maudit*; Grétry, ballet music from *Zémire et
Azor*; Haydn, the complete 'London' symphonies, Nos. 93–104;
Liszt, *A Faust Symphony* (Beecham Choral Society, Alexander
Young); Rimsky-Korsakov, symphonic suite *Shéhérazade* – one of
Beecham's most ravishing performances on record; Schumann, in-
cidental music to *Manfred*; Sibelius, Symphonies Nos. 6 and 7,
incidental music to *Pelléas et Mélisande*, symphonic poems *The
Oceanides* and *Tapiola*; Tchaikovsky, Symphonies Nos. 3 and 4,
fantasy-overture *Romeo and Juliet*, suite from *The Nutcracker*.
Beecham also recorded Mozart's Bassoon and Clarinet concertos
with two of the orchestra's principals, Gwydion Brooke and Jack
Brymer. 'Tommy's recordings were certainly different from his
concerts,' says Brymer, 'calmer and more studied, but none the less
original in style and dynamics.' Brymer also recalls that sometimes

his recording sessions for a particular work were separated by weeks or even months, and that they sometimes also moved from one studio to another. 'Yet tempi and acoustics always matched.'

Beecham recorded with other orchestras. His famous account of Sibelius's Second Symphony, for example, was recorded live at a concert he gave with the BBC Symphony Orchestra at the Royal Festival Hall in December 1954, marking the composer's eighty-ninth birthday – no separate recording sessions on that occasion. And with the French Radio National Orchestra he recorded Berlioz's *Symphonie fantastique*; Bizet's youthful and effervescent Symphony in C, also the *Carmen Suite* No. 1; Fauré's *Dolly Suite* and *Pavane*; Franck's Symphony in D minor; Lalo's Symphony in G minor.

Delius, it need hardly be said, occupies the centre ground in Beecham's catalogue of recorded music. 'That's how I want my music played,' the composer said, after hearing an early Beecham performance of *Brigg Fair*. This is not quite such exclusive praise as it may sound. Delius handed out similar compliments to others; and, as we have already made clear, Beecham has had no monopoly of his music. Sir Henry Wood, Sir John Barbirolli, Sir Malcolm Sargent, Meredith Davies, Eric Fenby, Sir Charles Groves, Vernon Handley, Sir John Pritchard and Geoffrey Toye among Beecham's compatriots, Rudolf Kempe, his successor as chief conductor of the Royal Philharmonic Orchestra, and, in America, Eugene Ormandy, have all given loving and sensitive performances, in concert or on record. But Beecham's own legacy of Delius recordings is never likely to be equalled. As Charles Groves said, 'We're always up against the ghost of Beecham.' He recorded many pieces twice, with the London Philharmonic Orchestra before the Second World War, and again with the Royal Philharmonic after it. Heading the list, as Delius's largest and most ambitious concert work, must come *A Mass of Life*, which Beecham recorded in 1952 with the Royal Philharmonic Orchestra, the London Philharmonic Choir and soloists Rosina Raisbeck, Monica Sinclair, Charles Craig and Bruce Boyce. He recorded these other Delius works, listed in their approximate order of composition: *Florida Suite*; *Marche Caprice* and *Sleigh Ride*; *Paa Vidderne* ('On the Heights'); 'La Calinda' from *Koanga*; *Paris, the Song of a Great City*; *Over the Hills and Far Away*; *Sea Drift* (Royal Philharmonic Orchestra, BBC Chorus and, again, the Canadian baritone Bruce Boyce); 'The Walk to the Paradise Garden' from *A Village Romeo and Juliet*; *Brigg Fair: An English Rhapsody*; *Fennimore and Gerda* (extracts); *In a Summer Garden*; *On Hearing the First Cuckoo in Spring* (the piece, as conducted by Beecham, that sent 'tingles down the spine' of the young David Willcocks, future musical director of the Bach Choir); *Summer Night on the River*; *Song of the High Hills* (Royal Philharmonic Orchestra and Chorus, the Norwegian baritone Einar Nørby); *Dance Rhapsodies* Nos. 1 and 2; Violin Concerto (soloist Jean Pougnet); *Eventyr* ('Once Upon a Time'); *A Song Before Sunrise*; incidental music to *Hassan* (extracts); Prelude to *Irmelin*. Beecham recorded the Piano Concerto with Betty Humby (Lady Beecham) and the London Philharmonic Orchestra in the autumn of 1945, though this seems not to have been issued commercially. Beecham himself can be heard playing the piano, accompanying Dora Labbette in the song *Twilight Fancies*, a rare recording made at the time of the Delius Festival of 1929. The one Delius work he did not record was the *Requiem*, composed in 1914, which he did not like.

Finally there are the opera recordings. Considering how much of his life was devoted to opera, this category of Beecham's recorded work is a sadly fragmented one. Quite a number of his opera performances, at Covent Garden, at the Metropolitan Opera and for the BBC, were recorded at the time. Some, such as a wartime performance of *Louise* at the Metropolitan Opera, and one of his postwar BBC *Elektra* performances, have been circulated as pirated recordings. Much more recorded material of this nature is probably lost forever, or of such poor technical quality that it is never likely to excite the air waves again. There is also the case of *Tristan und Isolde*. For a long time this was believed to have been recorded in its entirety at a live Covent Garden performance conducted by Beecham during his Coronation Season of 1937, with Melchior and Flagstad in the title roles. It now transpires that a good part of this, including the Prelude and much of Act I, comes from a recording made at the Royal Opera House the previous year, with Fritz Reiner conducting. We are therefore left with just a handful of complete and *bona fide* Beecham opera recordings. They are all the more interesting and precious for that.

In 1929 Beecham recorded Gounod's *Faust*, with a BBC orchestra and chorus and a cast headed by those British stalwarts Miriam Licette, Heddle Nash and Robert Easton. He made a second recording of the same opera with a largely French cast after the Second World War, but this was very soon eclipsed technically and commercially by the advent of the LP record. His first really important opera recording, meanwhile, was made in 1937 (the same year as the hybrid *Tristan und Isolde* mentioned above). This was of *Die Zauberflöte*, recorded in Berlin with the Berlin Philharmonic

Orchestra and a most interesting cast of singers. His invaluable assistant for the recording, Walter Legge, would have liked Richard Tauber and Alexander Kipnis in the roles of Tamino and Sarastro, but these two singers were ruled out on account of their Jewish connections. The two parts were sung by the Danish-born tenor Helge Roswänge (Rosenving-Hansen) and Wilhelm Strienz, a singer passed over by most of today's musical encyclopedias and dictionaries but a fine German bass of his generation. Tiana Lemnitz was Pamina, Gerhard Hüsch was Papageno, and Erna Berger sang the Queen of the Night, a role for which she was already famous. Tucked away in the chorus was the twenty-two-year-old German soprano Elisabeth Schwarzkopf, whom Walter Legge married after the war, guiding her to fame as an almost flawless singer of Strauss and Mozart opera and of German *Lieder*. The recording is notable for the absence of spoken dialogue, which Beecham considered an encumbrance, especially for non-German listeners. (He had previously replaced the dialogue with sung recitatives in stage productions.) The main recording sessions were crammed into seven hectic but exhilarating days during November 1937. Beecham hurried back to Berlin in March of the following year for another, even briefer session, but one last side still had to be committed to disc without him. Despite all the haste, Legge always considered it as musically the best recorded performance of *Die Zauberflöte*. In 1938, as we have read, Beecham brought him in as assistant artistic director at Covent Garden, a working partnership of marvellous promise that was soon broken up again by the war.

In April 1948, for the BBC's new Third Programme, Beecham gave two studio performances of *A Village Romeo and Juliet*, the Delius opera he had first performed at Covent Garden in 1910. After some acrimonious exchanges between Beecham and the Corporation, who complained about the extra cost of it all, a commercial recording followed. The orchestra was his own Royal Philharmonic, plus Chorus. The British cast included the soprano Lorely Dyer, married to the conductor Stanford Robinson, then in charge of opera within the BBC's music department, and the baritone Gordon Clinton, a Beecham 'discovery', who sang regularly with him in the postwar years. Clinton, it is worth noting, also recorded with Beecham a performance of *Sea Drift*, in addition to the recording of the work already mentioned on page 214.

In 1956 came two undisputed triumphs. Beecham recorded *Die Entführung aus dem Serail*, again with his Royal Philharmonic Orchestra plus the Beecham Choral Society and another interesting cast: the Canadian soprano Lois Marshall (also chosen by Toscanini for a famous recording of the *Missa Solemnis*), the French-Canadian tenor Léopold Simoneau, an outstanding postwar Mozartian, plus three top Germans, the soprano Ilse Hollweg, who had sung in Beecham's 1950 Edinburgh Festival performances of *Ariadne auf Naxos*, the tenor Gerhard Unger, and the bass Gottlob Frick, putting in a splendid performance as Osmin. So Beecham had recorded the two great Mozart *Singspiel* operas, but none of the Italian-language masterpieces. Plans were afoot early in 1961 for a recording of *Don Giovanni*, just before he died.

Also in 1956, Beecham made his most celebrated opera recording, of *La Bohème*. He claimed a special knowledge of the work, going back to 1920, when Puccini had been at Covent Garden to oversee the production of *Il Trittico*, and Beecham had taken the opportunity to go through the score of *Bohème* with him. The recording owes its existence to the happy coincidence that found Beecham and two of the greatest star singers of the postwar years, Victoria de Los Angeles and Jussi Björling (who had made his Covent Garden début under Beecham's auspices just before the war), all in New York during the same two or three weeks in the early spring. The American baritone Robert Merrill was also in the cast. The recording sessions, with the RCA Victor Symphony Orchestra and Chorus, were therefore crowded into that brief period of time. America's top music critic, Harold Schonberg, was not entirely happy with Björling's age (forty-five) for the part of Rodolfo, or with what he considered to be Victoria de Los Angeles's rather cool, dispassionate singing of Mimì. Beecham himself seems not to have been entirely satisfied with her on this account. These minor reservations apart, the result was almost instantly and universally hailed as a triumph for all concerned. The well-known British critic and broadcaster Edward Greenfield, in his notes accompanying the recording's reissue on compact disc, accepts that technically it has long since been surpassed by other recordings. But, he goes on,

> What is never likely to be improved on is the magic of the performance. Plainly, the need to work against the clock provided an extra challenge to everyone, not least to Sir Thomas himself . . . The inspiration of the occasion brought a concentrated intensity, whether in comic, dramatic or poetic moments, such as is hard to achieve in the usually cold atmosphere of the recording studio.

Two years later came the recording of *Carmen*, which Beecham this time made with the French Radio National Orchestra and Choir, with the *Petits Chanteurs de Versailles*. Through Walter Legge, Beecham approached Maria Callas for the title role, the Greek-American soprano whose phenomenal fame and adulation dated from her 1950 début at La Scala, Milan. She declined, on the grounds that her French was not good enough, and so the chance of a unique musical collaboration was missed. The part went to Victoria de Los Angeles, so bringing about her second recording with Beecham, though Russell Miller and Roger Boar, in their entertaining book *The Incredible Music Machine*, recount that this time things did not go smoothly at first. The Spanish soprano phoned David Bicknell, one of EMI's top producers in London, to say that she could stand no more of Beecham's tantrums and was going home. Bicknell rushed over to Paris and cornered the seventy-six-year-old maestro in his Ritz Hotel apartment, 'wearing baggy blue trousers, red braces and a silk shirt'. At that moment, like a scene from a Marx Brothers film, a waiter backed through the doors with a meal no one had ordered, and, said Bicknell, 'all Tommy's wrath burst on this poor fellow's head'. Eventually everything was smoothed over, the recording was completed and was another huge success. De Los Angeles was joined by the Russian-Swedish tenor Nicolai Gedda, just reaching his peak, and two lesser-known but excellent French singers of the day, the baritone Ernest Blanc and the soprano Janine Micheau, star of the Paris Opéra and Opéra-Comique.

Beecham's occasional work in films makes an interesting appendage to his recording career. In 1936, the year of his tour of Germany with the London Philharmonic, he and his orchestra also provided the music for a British film biography of Mozart, *Whom The Gods Love*. This included staged excerpts from *Le Nozze di Figaro* and *Die Zauberflöte*. In 1951 he conducted a filmed version of *Les Contes d'Hoffmann*, appearing very briefly at the beginning and end of the performance. The orchestra this time was the Royal Philharmonic, and the cast included the voices of the British bass Owen Brannigan and the mezzo-soprano Monica Sinclair, both just beginning to make a name for themselves. Three years earlier, in 1948, Beecham had participated in a real classic of British cinema. This was *The Red Shoes*, a cinematic celebration of the ballet, featuring the Australian-born Robert Helpmann, the young Scottish ballerina Moira Shearer, and the Russian choreographer and dancer Léonide Massine, veteran of the Diaghilev days. Brian Easdale, a composer at that time much in demand by the British film industry, wrote the score. Beecham and the Royal Philharmonic Orchestra performed it. The ballet itself – 'The Red Shoes' of the title, based on a story by Hans Christian Andersen – and the part of a tyrannical impresario, Boris Lermontov, played by the German-born film star Anton Walbrook, must all have carried Beecham back in spirit to those golden days of thirty years before, with Diaghilev, Nijinsky, Karsavina, and the whole glittering world of the *Ballets Russes*.

ACKNOWLEDGEMENTS

I would like to thank the following institutions and organisations for their willing and often very friendly help in the writing of this book: British Broadcasting Corporation; British Film Institute; The British Library; EMI Records, UK, especially Suzanne Lewis of the Archive; Glyndebourne Festival Opera; *The Gramophone*; Hallé Concerts Society and Orchestra; London Philharmonic Orchestra; London Symphony Orchestra; Royal College of Music; Royal Opera House, Covent Garden, especially Jane Jackson of the Archive Department; Royal Philharmonic Orchestra; Royal Philharmonic Society; Theatre Museum, Covent Garden; Theatre Royal, Drury Lane.

Many more individuals have been of great help to me, especially the following: John Amis; Sir Malcolm Arnold, CBE; Leo Birnbaum; Jack Brymer, OBE; the late Norman Del Mar, CBE; Lyndon Jenkins; Bernard Keeffe; Sir Yehudi Menuhin, OM; Norman Morrison; Sir David Willcocks, CBE, MC. Gordon Martin of Wandsworth Libraries Music Department also came to my aid on many occasions.

The photographs come from the Hulton Deutsch Collection Limited, London, except for nos. 3, 4, 8, 10, 11, which are from the Royal Opera House Archives. Photograph no. 6 © Fox Photos Ltd, no. 15 © Erich Auerbach.

Finally, a special word of thanks to my two editors, Elisabeth Ingles and Julian Shuckburgh, for their strong support.

Alan Blackwood

BIBLIOGRAPHY

Beecham, Sir Thomas: *Frederick Delius* (Hutchinson, 1959).

Beecham, Sir Thomas: *A Mingled Chime: Leaves from an Autobiography* (Hutchinson, 1944, reprinted 1976 as *The Lyric Stage*).

Borovsky, Victor: *Chaliapin, A Critical Biography* (Hamish Hamilton, 1988).

Cardus, Neville: *Sir Thomas Beecham: A Memoir* (Collins, 1961).

Carley, Lionel: *Delius, A Life in Letters, 1909–1934* (Scolar Press, 1988).

Chisholm, Anne: *Nancy Cunard* (Sidgwick and Jackson, 1979).

Del Mar, Norman: *Richard Strauss: A Critical Commentary on his Life and Works*, 3 volumes (Barrie and Jenkins, 1962).

Elkin, Robert: *Royal Philharmonic* (Rider, 1945).

Foreman, Lewis: *Bax, A Composer and his Times* (Scolar Press, 1983).

Foreman, Lewis: *From Parry to Britten, British Music in Letters 1900–1945* (Batsford, 1987).

Gammond, Peter and Horricks, Raymond: *The Music Goes Round and Round* (Quartet Books, 1980).

Garafola, Lynn: *Diaghilev's Ballets Russes* (Oxford University Press, 1989).

Geissmar, Berta: *The Baton and the Jackboot* (Hamish Hamilton, 1944).

Gelatt, Roland: *The Fabulous Phonograph*, 2nd revised edition (Cassell, 1977).

Gilmour, J. D. (editor): *Sir Thomas Beecham: Fifty Years in the 'New York Times'* (Thames Publishing, 1988).

Gilmour, J. D.: *Sir Thomas Beecham: The North American Tour 1950* (North Beach Printing Co., Inc., Washington).

Goossens, Eugene: *Overture and Beginners: A Musical Autobiography* (Methuen, 1951).

Gray, Michael: *Beecham, a Centenary Discography* (Duckworth, 1979).

Hall, Barrie: *The Proms and the Men who made Them* (Allen and Unwin, 1981).

Haskell, Arnold: *Diaghileff, His Artistic and Private Life (Gollancz,* 1935).

Hughes, Spike: *Glyndebourne: A History of the Festival Opera* (Methuen, 1965).

Jefferson, Alan: *Sir Thomas Beecham, A Centenary Tribute* (Macdonald & Janes, 1979).

Kennedy, Michael: *The Concise Oxford Dictionary of Music* (Oxford University Press, 1980).

Kennedy, Michael: *The Hallé Tradition: A Century of Music* (Manchester, 1960).

Lifar, Serge: *Serge Diaghilev, His Life, His Work, His Legend* (Putnam, 1940).

Melba, Nellie: *Melodies and Memories*, introduced and annotated by John Cargher (Hamish Hamilton, 1980).

Moore, Grace: *You're Only Human Once* (Latimer House, London, 1947).

Mosley, Diana: *Loved Ones, Pen Portraits* (Sidgwick & Jackson, 1985).

Newton, Ivor: *At The Piano: The World of an Accompanist* (Hamish Hamilton, 1966).

Pearson, John: *Façades: Edith, Osbert and Sacheverell Sitwell* (Macmillan, 1978).

Prieberg, Fred K.: *Trial of Strength: Wilhelm Furtwängler and the Third Reich* (Quartet Books, 1991).

Procter-Gregg, Humphrey (editor): *Beecham Remembered* (George Duckworth, 1977).

Reid, Charles: *Thomas Beecham, An Independent Biography* (Gollancz, 1961).

Rosenthal, Harold: *Two Centuries of Opera at Covent Garden* (Putnam, 1958).

Sadie, Stanley (editor): *The New Grove Dictionary of Music and Musicians*, 20 volumes (Macmillan, 1980).

Schwarzkopf, Elisabeth: *On and Off the Record: A Memoir of Walter Legge* (Faber & Faber, 1982).

Smyth, Ethel: *Beecham and Pharaoh* (Chapman and Hall, 1935).

Smyth, Ethel: *Memoirs*, abridged by Ronald Crichton (Viking, 1987).

Teyte, Maggie: *Star on the Door* (London, 1958).

White, Eric Walter: *Stravinsky, The Composer and His Works* (Faber & Faber, 1966).

Wilhelm, Kurt: *Richard Strauss: An Intimate Biography* (Thames and Hudson, 1989).
Woolf, Leonard: *Beginning Again* (Harcourt Brace, New York, 1963).

INDEX